T0373303

LUTZ WINDHÖFEL

ARCHITECTURAL GUIDE
BASEL

**NEW BUILDINGS
IN THE TRINATIONAL CITY SINCE 1980**

Birkhäuser
Basel

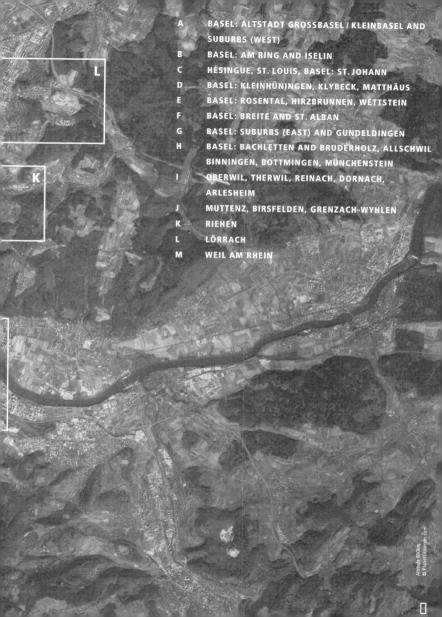

A   BASEL: ALTSTADT GROSSBASEL / KLEINBASEL AND
     SUBURBS (WEST)
B   BASEL: AM RING AND ISELIN
C   HÉSINGUE, ST. LOUIS, BASEL: ST. JOHANN
D   BASEL: KLEINHÜNINGEN, KLYBECK, MATTHÄUS
E   BASEL: ROSENTAL, HIRZBRUNNEN, WETTSTEIN
F   BASEL: BREITE AND ST. ALBAN
G   BASEL: SUBURBS (EAST) AND GUNDELDINGEN
H   BASEL: BACHLETTEN AND BRUDERHOLZ, ALLSCHWIL
     BINNINGEN, BOTTMINGEN, MÜNCHENSTEIN
I   OBERWIL, THERWIL, REINACH, DORNACH,
     ARLESHEIM
J   MUTTENZ, BIRSFELDEN, GRENZACH-WYHLEN
K   RIEHEN
L   LÖRRACH
M   WEIL AM RHEIN

Altitude 80 km.
© PlanetObserver.com

CONTENTS

Organization and Use
The Star Is the City
This Book's Foundations, Boundaries, Criteria, and Selection

A   **Basel: Altstadt Grossbasel / Kleinbasel and suburbs (West)**

1   Morger & Degelo: Museum of Music, 1997–1999, Im Lohnhof 9

2   Gmür / Vacchini: Retail Building Conversion (Papyrus), 1999, Freie Strasse 43

3   Mathias E. Frey Architekten: Taxidermy Facilities and Workshops of the Natural History Museum 2009–2012, Stapfelberg 2/4, Schlüsselberg 3+5

4   Rüdisühli Ibach Architekten in collaboration with Stauffenegger, "Parapluie" Tram Shelter at "Kunstmuseum", 2005–2009, St. Alban-Graben

5   Silvia Gmür and Vischer AG: University Institute in the Engelhof, 1986–1990, Nadelberg 4

6   Fierz Architekten: University Administration Building, 2001–2003, Petersplatz 1

7   Naef, Studer & Studer: University Institute in the Rosshof (Economy Sciences Centre), 1984–1988, Petersgraben 49/51

8   Herzog & de Meuron: Courtyard Residential Building, 1987–1988, Hebelstrasse 11

9   Gmür / Vacchini: Klinikum 1, Cantonal Hospital Renovation, 1989–2003, Spitalstrasse 21

10   Gmür / Vacchini: Women's Clinic with Operating Theatres, 2000–2003, Spitalstrasse 21

11   Herzog & de Meuron: Rossetti Building, Cantonal Hospital, 1997–1999, Spitalstrasse 26

12   LOST Architekten, Remodelling and Renovation of the "Ackermannshof" 2009–2011, St. Johanns-Vorstadt 19–21

13   Nussbaumer Trüssel: Designing the Rhine Promenade underneath the Mittlere Brücke, 2001–2004, Unterer Rheinweg / Oberer Rheinweg

B   **Basel: Am Ring and Iselin**

14   Diener & Diener Architekten: Vogesen School, 1992–1996, St. Johanns-Ring 17 / Spitalstrasse

15   Fierz & Baader: Institute of Anatomy, University of Basel, 1993–1996, Pestalozzistrasse 20

16   Andrea Roost Architekten: Bio-Pharmazentrum of the University, 1996–2000, Klingelbergstrasse 50–70

17   Stump & Schibli Architekten, University Paediatric Hospital of Basel (UKBB), 2004–2010, Spitalstrasse 33

18   Urs Gramelsbacher: Residential Building with Meeting Hall, 1993–1995, Missionsstrasse 37

19   Atelier-Gemeinschaft (Michael Alder, Hanspeter Müller, Roland Naegelin): Home for the Mentally Handicapped, 1997, Birmannsgasse 37

20   Brogli & Müller Architekten: Lindenhof Nursing Home, 1988–1991, Socinstrasse 30 / Eulerstrasse

21   Alioth Langlotz Stalder Buol with Diener & Diener: "Holbeinhof" Seniors Residence and Nursing Home, 2000–2002, Leimenstrasse 67

22   Vischer AG Architekten, Vera Oeri Library / Basel Music Academy, 2006–2009, Leonhardsgraben 40

23   Wilfrid and Katharina Steib: Public Prosecutor's Office and Municipal Jail, 1991–1995, Binningerstrasse 21 / Innere Margarethenstrasse 18

24   Richard Meier & Partners: Euregio Office Building, 1995–1998, Viaduktstrasse 40–44

CONTENTS

25   Blaser Architekten, Market Hall Restoration
and Remodelling, 2005–2012, Steinentorberg /
Innere Margarethenstrasse

26   Diener & Diener Architekten, Tower Block at the
Market Hall, 2007–2012, Steinentorberg 18

27   Herzog & de Meuron: Residential and Office Building
(formerly Schwitter), 1987–1988, Allschwilerstrasse 90 / Sierenzerstrasse / Colmarerstrasse

28   Zinkernagel Architekten: Wasgenring Schoolhouse
Expansion, 1994–1995, Blotzheimerstrasse 82

C   **Hésingue, St. Louis, Basel: St. Johann**

29   Daniel Stefani & Bernard Wendling: Kindergarten
and Club House, St. Louis, 1992–1993, rue Anne de
Gohr / rue de A. Baerenfels

30   Herzog & de Meuron: Pfaffenholz Sports Complex,
St. Louis, 1992–1993, 5, rue de St. Exupéry

31   Herzog & de Meuron: REHAB – Swiss Centre for
Paraplegics, 1999–2002, Im Burgfelderhof 40

32   Michael Alder: Luzernerring Housing Development,
1991–1993, Bungestrasse 10–28

33   Voellmy Schmidlin Architektur, Conversion of an
Auto Shop into an Art Gallery, 2008–2009,
Kannenfeldplatz 6 / Entenweidstrasse 8+10

34   Erny, Gramelsbacher, Schneider: Im Davidsboden
Housing Development, 1989–1991, Gasstrasse /
Vogesenstrasse

35   Urs Gramelsbacher, Wooden Town House,
2006–2011, Lothringerstrasse 98a

36   Miller & Maranta: Volta School, 1999–2000,
Wasserstrasse 40 / Mülhauserstrasse

37
38   Vittorio Magnago Lampugnani Studio di
Architettura: Novartis Campus Master Plan and
Peter Walker: Plan for Parks, Gardens and
plants / the example: inner courtyard "Forum 1"
and "Forum", since 2003 between Voltastrasse,
Elsässerstrasse, Schiffmühlestrasse and the Rhine

39   Vogt Landschaftsarchitekten: The Campus Park
and the Green, Novartis Campus, 2004/2009,
Fabrikstrasse

40   Marco Serra, Reception Pavilion and Underground Car Park, Novartis Campus, 2002–2007,
Fabrikstrasse 2

41   Diener, Federle, Wiederin: Novartis Campus Forum 3,
2002–2005, Forum 3

42   SANAA / Kazuyo Sejima + Ryue Nishizawa: Novartis
Campus Fabrikstrasse 4, 2005–2006, Fabrikstrasse 4

43   Märkli Architekten: Novartis Campus Fabrikstrasse 6
(Visitor Centre), 2002–2006, Fabrikstrasse 6

44   Yoshio Taniguchi: Laboratory Building with Shop
and Pharmacy, Novartis Campus, 2005–2010,
Fabrikstrasse 10

45   Vittorio Magnago Lampugnani, Studio di Architettura:
Administrative Building with Dodici Restaurant,
Novartis Campus, 2005–2008, Fabrikstrasse 12

46   Frank O' Gehry: Administrative Building with
Auditorium WSJ-242 / WSJ-243, Novartis Campus,
2003–2009, Fabrikstrasse 15

47   Adolf Krischanitz, Laboratory Building WSJ-152
with Auditorium and Knowledge Centre, Novartis
Campus, 2003–2008, Fabrikstrasse 16

48   David Chipperfield: Laboratory Building with
Cha Cha Restaurant, Novartis Campus, 2006–2010,
Fabrikstrasse 22

49   Fumihiko Maki + Maki and Associates, Office
Building, Novartis Campus, 2006–2009, Square 3

50   Eduardo Souto de Moura, Laboratory Building /
Technical Research and Development (TRD),
Novartis Campus, 2005–2011, Physic Garden 3

51   Álvaro Siza da Vieira, Laboratory Building, Novartis
Campus, 2005–2010, Virchow 6

CONTENTS

D   Basel: Kleinhüningen, Klybeck, Matthäus

52   Luca Selva Architekten: Densa Park Housing
       Development, 2007–2012, Neuhausstrasse 28–36,
       Salmenweg 12–16

53   Diener & Diener: Stücki Shopping Centre with Hotel,
       1999–2009, Hochbergerstrasse 68 and 70

54   Wilfrid and Katharina Steib: Wiesengarten
       Housing Development, 1983–1986, Wiesendamm /
       Altrheinweg / Giessliweg 37

55   Ackermann & Friedli: Ackermätteli School,
       1995–1996, Rastatterstrasse 32

56   Barcelo Baumann Architekten: Bollag Studio
       Complex, 2007–2009, Gärtnerstrasse 50

57   Morger & Degelo: Dreirosen School Expansion,
       1990–1996, Breisacherstrasse 134 / Klybeck-
       strasse 111–115

58   Morger & Degelo: Housing Co-op, 1990–1993,
       Müllheimerstrasse 138/140

59   Degelo Architekten: Bonifacius residential building,
       2006–2010, Amerbachstrasse 37

60   Diener & Diener Architekten: Hammer 1
       Housing Development, 1978–1981, Hammerstrasse /
       Bläsiring / Efringerstrasse

61   Diener & Diener Architekten: Hammer 2 Housing
       Development, 1980–1985, Efringerstrasse /
       Amerbachstrasse / Riehenring

62   Trinkler + Engler / Trinkler Engler Ferrara: Residential
       and Multi-family Building with Kindergarten,
       Daycare and Semi-public Park, 1997–2004, Efringer-
       strasse 96 and Riehenring 199/201

63   Wilfrid and Katharina Steib: Residential Building on the
       Water's Edge, 1994–1996, Unterer Rheinweg 48–52

E   Basel: Rosental, Hirzbrunnen, Wettstein

64   Morger Degelo Marques: High-rise for Basel Fair,
       2000–2003, Messeplatz

65   Theo Hotz: New Fair Hall, 1998–1999, Messeplatz 1 /
       Riehenring / Isteinerstrasse

66   Diener & Diener Architekten: Studio Homes,
       Apartment Building and Hotel, 2000–2002, Isteiner-
       strasse 90–96, Schönaustrasse 10 and 31–35

67   Proplaning Architekten: Housing Development,
       1997–1999, Schönaustrasse / Erlenstrasse

68   Fierz Architekten: Conversion and Renovation of the
       Badischer Bahnhof (Railway Station), 2001–2008,
       Schwarzwaldallee 200

69   Christian Dill: Housing and Therapy Facility,
       1992–1997, Riehenstrasse 300

70   Diener & Diener Architekten: Eglisee Supermarket
       (Migros), 1996–1997, Riehenstrasse 315

71   Michael Alder: Rankhof Stadium, 1993–1995,
       Grenzacherstrasse 351

72   Mario Botta: Jean Tinguely Museum, 1994–1996,
       Grenzacherstrasse 210

73   Herzog & de Meuron: Roche Building 97, 2006–2011 /
74   Herzog & de Meuron the Roche complex
       (1991–2015), Wettsteinallee / Grenzacherstrasse

75   Diener & Diener Architekten: Warteckhof
       Development (former Warteck Brewery), 1994–1996,
       Grenzacherstrasse 62 / 64 / Fischerweg 6–10 /
       Alemannengasse 33–37

F   Basel: Breite and St. Alban

76   sabarchitekten: Breitezentrum Basel, (Urban Meeting
       Place, Hotel, Library, Kindergarten, Resource Center
       for the Visually Impaired, Commerce), 2000–2005,
       Zürcherstrasse 149

77   Koechlin Schmidt Architekten: "Wildensteineregg"
       Residential Development, 2008–2011, Wilden-
       steinerstrasse 10 + 12 / Baldeggerstrasse 30 /
       Bechburgerstrasse 9

78 Miller & Maranta: Schwarzpark Apartment Building, 2001–2004, Gellertstrasse 135/137

79 Zwimpfer Partner: The Office Building As Residential Building, 2007–2009, Adlerstrasse 35

80 WWG Schnetzer Puskas Ingenieure with Steinmann & Schmid Architekten: Urban Rail Transit Station Basel-Dreispitz, 2003–2006, Walkeweg/Walkewegbrücke

81 Herzog & de Meuron: Central Switch-Yard, 1998–1999, Münchensteinerstrasse 115

82 Bürgin & Nissen in collaboration with Zwimpfer Partner: Swisscom (former Communications Centre), 1984–1989, Grosspeterstrasse 18

83 Burckhardt + Partner: Office Building, 1998–2000, Lange Gasse 15

84 Herzog & de Meuron: SUVA House (Swiss Accident Insurance), 1991–1993, St. Jakobs-Strasse 24/Gartenstrasse 53/55

85 Mario Botta: BIS Administration Building (Bank for International Settlements, formerly UBS), 1990–1995, Aeschenplatz 1

G   Basel: Suburbs (East) and Gundeldingen

86 Bürgin Nissen Wentzlaff: PAX Insurance Administration Building, 1992–1994 and 1995–1997, Aeschenplatz 13

87 Diener & Diener Architekten: Picassoplatz Businesscenter (former office building for Basel Life), 1990–1994, Lautengartenstrasse 6/Dufourstrasse

88 Märkli: Picasso House, 2002–2008, Brunngässlein 12

89 Gigon/Guyer Architekten: Conversion of Museum of Fine Arts and Laurenz Building, 2001–2007, St. Alban-Graben 10 and 16

90 Michael Alder: Conversion of Industrial Architecture, 1986, St. Alban-Tal 42

91 Urs Gramelsbacher: Residential Building, 1997–1999, St. Alban-Tal 38a

69 Diener & Diener Architekten: Residential Building with Craft Studios, 1984–1986, St. Alban-Rheinweg 94/96

93 Wilfrid and Katharina Steib: Museum of Contemporary Art, 1977–1980, St. Alban-Rheinweg 60

94 Diener & Diener Architekten: Residential Building with Office and Retail Space, 1994–1995, Steinenvorstadt 2/Kohlenberg 1

95 Burckhardt + Partner: Leonhard High School, 1995–1998, Leonhardsstrasse 15

96 Diener & Diener Architekten: Training and Conference Centre, 1990–1994, Viaduktstrasse 33

97 Herzog & de Meuron: Office and Retail Building "Elsässertor II", 2000–2005, Centralbahnstrasse 4

98 Cruz y Ortiz with Giraudi & Wettstein: Pedestrian Overpass at SBB Train Station, 2001–2003, Centralbahnplatz/Güterstrasse

99 Silvia Gmür Reto Gmür: Apartment and Studio Building, 2005–2006, Frobenstrasse 4

100 Burckhardt + Partner: Office and Housing Complex, Thiersteinerallee, 2001–2003, Thiersteinerallee 14–30, Tellstrasse 48–52, 60–66

H   Bachletten and Bruderholz, Allschwil, Binningen, Bottmingen, Münchenstein

101
102 Herzog & de Meuron: Actelion Business Centre, Allschwil, 2005–2010, Hegenheimermattweg 95

103 Burckhardt + Partner: Elco-Park Housing Development, 2006–2012, Baslerstrasse 270, 272, 274/Merkurstrasse/Spitzwaldstrasse

104 Wymann & Selva: Kaltbrunnen Schoolhouse, 1995–1996, Kaltbrunnenpromenade 95

105 Luca Selva Architekten: Piranesiesque Generational Building, 2010–2013, Höhenweg 53

CONTENTS

106 Hanspeter Müller: Youth Centre, Binningen, 1995, In den Schutzmatten 10

107 TrinklerStulaPartner Architekten: Residential Building, Binningen, 2008–2010, Schlüsselgasse 4

108 Peter Stiner and August Künzel: Etoscha House in the Zoological Gardens, 1998–2003, Binningerstrasse 40

109 Silvia Gmür: One-Room House, 1990, Sonnenbergstrasse 92

110 Dolenc Scheiwiller Parli Architekten: Villa and Apartment House

111 Herzog & de Meuron: Exhibition Warehouse of the Laurenz Foundation, Münchenstein, 2000–2003, Ruchfeldstrasse 19

112 Berrel Architekten with Zwimpfer Partner Krarup Furrer: St. JakobArena, Münchenstein, 2001–2002, Brüglingen 33

113 Herzog & de Meuron: Plywood House, Bottmingen, 1985, Rappenbodenweg 6

114 Michael Alder: Single-Family House, Bottmingen, 1988, Kirschbaumweg 27

115 Ackermann & Friedli: Am Birsig Community Centre and Housing, Bottmingen, 1998–1999, Löchlimattstrasse 6

I   Oberwil, Therwil, Reinach, Dornach, Arlesheim

116 Proplaning Architekten: Bus and Streetcar Depot for Baselland Transport AG (BLT), Oberwil, 2001–2007, Grenzweg 1

117 Nissen & Wentzlaff Architekten: Therwil: Bahnhofstrasse Süd, 2004–2009, Bahnhofstrasse 28

118 Herzog & de Meuron: House for an Art Collector, Therwil, 1986, Lerchenrainstrasse 5

119 Morger & Degelo: Community Centre Reinach, 1998–2002, Hauptstrasse 10

120 Morger & Degelo: Single-Family House, Dornach, 1995–1996, Lehmenweg 2 / Schlossweg

121 Otto + Partner: Bus Terminus at Dornach-Arlesheim Railway Station, 2006–2009, Bahnhofstrasse

122 Proplaning: Obere Widen Residential Development, Arlesheim, 1997–1999, Birseckstrasse / Talstrasse

123 Klaus Schuldt and Andreas Scheiwiller: Zum wisse Segel, Villas, Arlesheim, 1997–2000, Zum wisse Segel 5, 7, 10, 11, 12

J   Muttenz, Birsfelden, Grenzach-Wyhlen

124 Bürgin Nissen Wentzlaff: Hotel, Supermarket (Coop), Apartments, Muttenz, 1996–1998, St. Jakobs-Strasse 1 / Hauptstrasse

125 Rosenmund + Rieder Architekten: Apartment Building, Muttenz, 2005–2007, Langmattstrasse 6

126 Rosenmund + Rieder Architekten: Expansion of „Freidorf" Housing Estate with an Apartment Building, Muttenz, 2000–2006, St. Jakobs-Strasse 143–153

127 Frank O. Gehry: Vitra-Center, Birsfelden, 1992–1994, Klünenfeldstrasse 22

128 Bürgin Nissen Wentzlaff: Bank and Office Building (Baselland Cantonal Bank), Birsfelden, 1994–1996, Hauptstrasse 75/77

129 Nissen Wentzlaff Architekten: Office Building for Roche Pharma AG, Grenzach-Wyhlen, 2005–2007, Emil-Barell-Strasse 1

K   Riehen

130 Kunz und Mösch Architekten: Five Units in a Long House, 2007–2009, Hörnliweg 1–9

131 Ueli Zbinden Architekt: Riehen-Niederholz S-Bahn Station, 2004-2008, Rauracherstrasse

132 Rolf Brüderlin: Hebel School Expansion, 1993–1994, Langenlängeweg 14

CONTENTS

133 Metron Architekten: Im Niederholzboden Housing Development, 1992–1994, Im Niederholzboden / Arnikastrasse 12–26

134 Rolf Furrer and François Fasnacht: Riehen Dorf Tram Shelter, 1995, Baselstrasse, and Lachenweg Bus Shelter, 1992, Lachenweg / Grenzacherweg

135 Stump & Schibli Architekten: "Zur Hoffnung" – Residential School for Children, 1995–2005, Wenkenstrasse 33

136 Renzo Piano: Beyeler Foundation Museum, 1994–1997 and 2000, Baselstrasse 101

137 Wilfrid and Katharina Steib: Haus zum Wendelin Nursing Home, 1986–1988, Inzlingerstrasse 50

138 Stump & Schibli: Retirement Home in the Oberdorf, 2004–2007, Inzlingerstrasse 46

139 Michael Alder: Vogelbach Housing Development, 1991–1992, Friedhofweg 30–80

L   Lörrach

140 Wilhelm und Hovenbitzer und Partner: Extension and Renovation of a Single-Family Dwelling, 2010, Steinenweg 22

141 Thoma.Lay.Buchler.Architekten: Niederfeldplatz Neighbourhood, 2010–2013; Brühlstrasse 18–26 / Kreuzstrasse 50–56

142 Günter Pfeifer: Department Store Conversion into Library, 1992–1993, Baslerstrasse 128

143 Schaudt Architekten: Alt Stazione Cinema Café (house Zum Storchen), 1993–1996, Baslerstrasse 164/166

144 Wilfrid and Katharina Steib: Auf dem Burghof Theatre and Convention Complex, 1996–1998, Herrenstrasse 5

145 Würkert & Partner Architekten: Peja Restaurant, New Building and Remodelling with a Passageway to Chesterplatz, 2008–2010, Chesterplatz 5

146 Detlef Würkert and Hans Ueli Felchlin: Nansen-park Housing Development, 1994–1997, Nansen-strasse 5/7 / Gretherstrasse / Haagenerstrasse

147 Wilhelm + Partner: Stadion Housing Development, 1990–1994, Haagenerstrasse / Winterbuckstrasse

148 Lederer Ragnarsdóttir Oei: Baden-Württemberg Cooperative State University (DHBW) / New Building for the Lörrach Vocational Academy, 2005–2008, Hangstrasse 48

M   Weil am Rhein

149 SANAA (Kazuyo) Sejima and (Ryue) Nishizawa
150 and Associates: Production Building Marking and 30 Years of Vitra Campus, 2006-2012, Charles Eames-Strasse 2

151 Nicholas Grimshaw: Vitra Furniture Factory, 1981, Charles Eames-Strasse 2

152 Tadao Ando: Vitra Conference Pavilion, 1992–1993, Charles Eames-Strasse 1

153 Frank O. Gehry: Vitra Design Museum, 1988–1989, Charles Eames-Strasse 1

154 Álvaro Siza da Vieira: Vitrashop Factory Hall, 1992–1993, Charles Eames-Strasse 2

155 Herzog & de Meuron: Frei Photo Studio, 1981–1982, Riedlistrasse 41

156 Zaha M. Hadid: Trinational Environmental Centre (previously Baden Württemberg Pavilion at National Garden Show "Grün 99"), 1996–1999, Mattrain 1

Illustration Index of Projects and Maps
Index of Architects and Companies
Index of Building Types and Uses

ORGANIZATION AND USE

The projects presented in this architectural guide are distributed across three national borders and many local and regional areas. We have therefore organized the entries in accordance with existing administrative and planning entities. The interconnected urban area between Hésingue and St. Louis in the west (France), Dornach and Arlesheim in the south (Switzerland), Muttenz and Birsfelden in the east (Switzerland), and Lörrach and Weil am Rhein in the north (Germany) has been divided into thirteen urban districts, or chapters. Preceding each chapter is a map of the district, which locates the buildings for visitors.

The order of the chapters follows the borders of the local land registry offices in the case of the self-governing municipalities in France and Switzerland. The canton of Basel-Stadt was subdivided according to the official documents of the department of public housing and planning (Residential Neighbourhoods and Statistical Districts in Canton Basel-Stadt). Annexed communities and satellite districts as they exist in Lörrach were disregarded for the purposes of this book, since they are separate and some distance from the city proper.

The sequence from chapter to chapter and from project to project within each chapter approximates a route that reflects the geographic proximity between buildings in one and the same district while at the same time taking care to establish links between chapters. Neighbouring projects in adjacent districts are also marked in the map section preceding the relevant chapter; sometimes, they are also cross-referenced in the text.

This architectural guide can also be used in other ways, facilitated by means of two indices at the back: an index of names, which includes the names of architectural firms (e.g., Herzog & de Meuron) and an index of building types and uses, a valuable tool for planners and architects.

The region of Basel has an excellent public transportation system. In addition to parking zones, the maps that accompany each chapter indicate the relevant bus and tram lines and the stops closest to the various projects listed in the guide. This information – updated in Spring 2014 – is also contained in the general data given for each project beneath the address.

THE STAR IS THE CITY

This Book's Foundations, Boundaries, Criteria, and Selection

"It is not the triumph of urban living that awaken the prophetic wrath of a Jeremiah, a Savonarola, a Rousseau, or a Ruskin." (Lewis Mumford: The Culture of Cities, 1938)

This book deals with a city as a built reality made up of buildings, streets, monuments, and spaces. This city, the "actual city", has emerged through a historical and contemporary process of designed utilization by its inhabitants and investors. This book is set in the year 2000 and the city it deals with is located at the geographical interface between Switzerland and the borders it shares with France and Germany in the High and Upper Rhine region. Basel forms the centre of this region. This centre is supplemented by a patchwork of twenty cities and communities spread over three countries. In some cases these communities constitute political units (such as Basel, Riehen, and Bettingen in the Basel-Stadt canton) but the majority of them are not defined in political terms. In May 2013 this actual city, which can also be called "Basel and the trinational city"[1] had 454 851 inhabitants.[2] Every locality in this city can be reached from its historic centre, formed by the Münsterhügel (Cathedral Hill) with the Basler Münster (Basel Cathedral) and the Martinskirche (St. Martin's Church), on foot without having to leave coherently built-up streets or paths.[3] The parts of this actual city can be experienced as elements of a whole that are separated, as it were, by mental, communal, and national boundaries.

The city that is the subject of this book is understood as a material (built), structural (inhabited and operated), and empirical (lived) city. The material city determines a geographical space comprising built elements exhibiting highly diverse forms and dimensions. These buildings serve both everyday and spiritual life and their organization. The structural city determines, steers, and develops within the material city a static and simultaneously mobile economic, political, demographic, and social texture that is constantly thickening and expanding. This texture deploys and utilizes the space. The empirical city combines these two categories and, ideally, is able to dovetail them. This is the case when texture and space within the framework of time and movement facilitate this everyday or spiritual utilization in a physiological sense and simultaneously activate or promote them for the general good in a socioeconomic and cultural sense. The first of these three factors is "immobile". The two others are subject to constant change. Together these factors form the cultural city.

THE CONCEPT OF THE CITY

From the time of the oldest known treatise on architecture, Vitruvius's (Marcus Vitruvius Pollio's) De architectura libri decem (circa 33–22 BCE),[4] systematic reflection on the material and structural city was long a domain of architects, engineers, and politicians, observed by philosophers, poets, and representatives of other art forms.[5] From 1800 onwards, the growth and industrialization of Western cities led to a diversification of the humanities in their universities and the emergence of the social sciences. The theme of architecture became the subject of an increasingly complex field of study and assumed a multifactorial character. The concept of "the city" which had always eluded lexical definition, was approached by means of circumscription. When in 1938 Lewis Mumford published The Culture of Cities, one of the first attempts to develop a synthetic view of the city as a phenomenon of human culture, he began in an essayistic style: "The city … is the point of maximum concentration for the power and culture of a community."[6] Mumford unfurls a historical panorama that investigates the development and role of the city with reference to anthropological and economic-historical sources, theories of consciousness and perception, the interaction of mechanical forces and social structures (markets and money), and cultural identity and aesthetics. Mumford's concept of the city as a cultural-historical phenomenon extends back to the development of settlements in agrarian society (the dependence of the city on the land for food and raw materials). The author presents the city as a place where the phenomenon of time becomes visible in the forms of art and architecture, a place in which different forms of life exist simultaneously. With a focus on Europe and North America, Mumford describes and analyses the city as a fascinating but only partially explicable fact. In his view, the city and language represent humanity's greatest artworks.[7] Here, the city is a total work of art, where structural and empirical, and peripherally also material, factors flow into one another.

THE STRUCTURAL AND EMPIRICAL CITY

In his treatise "Die Stadt" (The City), which was published in 1921, Max Weber[8] links this term with the factors of economy, autonomy, and power. The sociologist analyses and develops the concept of the city in southern and northern Europe with reference to the political and economic structures of cities in India, China, and Japan. Weber's development of a typological and structural analysis of his theme is largely limited to the city of antiquity and the Middle Ages, only occasionally addressing the city in the twentieth century. His work is almost completely devoid of considerations relating to human geography, anthropology, and in particular architectural culture. According to Weber, size (the number of buildings and inhabitants) is not decisive. Central to the character of the city is the autonomous exchange of goods on a local market (daily or weekly) or even a market for long-distance trade (annual fair): "the city … is a market settlement."[9] On Weber's chronological axis, the Ackerbürgerstadt, the city of agricultural producers, becomes the industry, merchant, consumer, and producer city, which in turn gives rise to modern cities (Paris, London, Berlin, Düsseldorf) dominated by national and international financiers, big banks, joint stock companies, and the operational headquarters of cartels. This development is broadly positioned within the associated history of politics and law.

In the face of the increasing internationalization of the circulation of money and capital, Weber's text, which was first published not long after the end of the First World War, reaches the limits of its analytical applicability. However, the economic primacy of the author's concept of the city in "the theory he develops of social action and its successive generation of ever more comprehensive social structures"[10] retains its validity. "It is not my intention here," writes Weber, "to present a further specialization and casuistry, which would be required of a strictly economic theory of the city. It hardly needs to be stated that empirical cities almost always represent mixed types and can therefore only be classified according to their respectively predominant economic components."[11]

In his book Die Stadt im Altertum (The City in Antiquity, 1984), the historian Frank Kolb supplements Weber's sociological typology of cities with the criteria "topographical and administrative coherence", "diversity of built volumes", and "urban lifestyle." The author also distinguishes his own approach from a political-historical and "cultural-morphological" view of the city, such as found in the work of Mumford.[12] Kolb draws on archaeological research and written sources to examine the city as a form of human organization and an aspect of settlement geography in Asia Minor, the Middle East, North Africa and south-eastern, southern and north-western Europe. Citing the example of a building boom in western Asia Minor during the Roman period (first to third centuries), where a municipal, hybrid building policy resulted in the right (granted by the emperor) to bear the title of "metropolis",[13] the author draws an analogy with the marketing character of today's metropolitan discourse. In both Weber's and Kolb's analyses, the emphasis is on the structural city.

In the work of sociologist Georg Simmel, the "empirical city", as Max Weber calls it, is expanded to include the dimension of so-called modern life. This concept is developed in Simmel's essay "Die Grossstädte und das Geistesleben" ("The Metropolis and Mental Life"), which was published in 1903.[14]

The sociologist Hartmut Häussermann writes that an important aspect of
this text is its structural-theoretical content: "the refinement of the division of
labour by way of competition in a restricted space, the promotion of eccen-
tricity, the metropolis as a place of economic and cultural innovation as
the consequence of extreme heterogeneity under conditions of high physical
density. These structural-theoretical observations are genuine examples
of urban or spatial sociology."[15] Yet, similarly to Weber, in his urbanistic texts
Simmel constantly retains a focus on the monetary and financial economy.
Indeed, it was around this time that Simmel also produced his seminal study on
the central societal role of the economy, Philosophie des Geldes (The Philosophy of Money, 1900/1907).[16]

Research around the beginning of the twenty-first century inspired by Simmel's
work has led to the urban studies by Stanley Milgram (The Experience of
Living in Cities, 1970) and Saskia Sassen (Metropole: Grenzen eines Begriffs,
1995; The Global City, 2001) and underscores the continuing relevance of
this author when considering the function and development of a metropolitan
civilization.[17] The interesting question has been raised in relation to Simmel's
essay "Soziologie des Raumes" ("The Sociology of Space", 1903) as to whether
a genuinely ethnic (and not only social) segregation of the city actually
exists.[18] Simmel's observations in and of the city view it as an empirical laboratory: "One seldom realizes," writes Simmel, "how wonderfully the extensity
of the space accommodates the intensity of sociological relationships, how the
continuity of the space, precisely because it does not objectively incorpo-
rate an absolute boundary, everywhere allows for the constitution of a subjective one."[19] In this context, the sociologist Heike Delitz points to the
possibility, misunderstanding, and questionability of a liberalization of the city,
its space, and terminology at the level of the individual body.[20]

Georg Simmel's intellectual existence and his sociology of the city were sus-
tained by the phenomenon of individual isolation within the entropic diffusion

of social forces that shaped all Western metropolises in the late nineteenth and twentieth centuries. Heterogeneity, density, and mobility are Simmel's descriptive terms for an urbanization of forms of life in the large city around 1900. And Simmel composed his texts against the background of his experience of Berlin. He was born there in 1858 in a city that in 1819 still had a population of only 200 000, a number that passed the one million mark in 1877 and reached four million in 1914 prior to the outbreak of the First World War.[21] Between 1880 and 1920 the introduction of electrification in European and North American metropolises ushered in a process of modernization that, with new forms of commuter transport, the medium of cinema, and inventions such as the elevator, the telephone, the radio, and electrical household appliances, radically affected the character of everyday perceptions and action.[22] Simmel's linguistic abstraction and his empirical analysis of the new and unprecedented were based on his own biography and the coordinates of his lifetime. Simmel died in 1918.

Some eighty years later, from around 1990 onwards, the development of computer technology, the possibilities it has opened up for research and communications, its influence on mobility and transport, its supposed—not actual—diminution of spatial distance, and its transformative processes in industry (environment, energy, health, food), transport logistics, and distribution appears to have generated a situation analogous to what was happening during Simmel's lifetime. But Simmel was also a sociological subject of his time. Can his empirical perception, description, and analysis of the city and its space claim the timelessness attributed to it in the urban sociological discussion?

Both Simmel's "totalization of the concept of life"[23] and the conceptual proximity of his homogenization of modern urban existence to totalitarian structures of the twentieth century[24] are open to question. In the current discourse on the city, this "totalization of the concept of life" has led to a one-sided focus on the empirical city as compared with its material and structural cha-racter.[25] Moreover, the current sociological discourse barely takes into account the fact that Simmel's empirical thought and the modernity of his spatial perception are anchored in the paternalisms of the nineteenth century.[26] In the wake of the catastrophes of the twentieth century, an approach that unre-servedly superimposes the coordinates of Georg Simmel's history of ideas onto the city and its metropolitan form in the twenty-first century therefore seems questionable.

THE CULTURAL CITY

Lewis Mumford begins The Culture of Cities with the fairly straightforward observation, "The city … is the point of maximum concentration for the power and culture of a community." However, the approach he subsequently adopts to the complex constituted by his subject involves intellectually circling his theme by addressing questions relating to physicality, technology, supply and administration, communications, sociality, and—peripherally—aes-thetics. Mumford sees the city as an integral phenomenon of a material, struc-tural, and empirical situation. He constructs a conceptual network whose complexity is encompassed by the idea of the cultural city.

In his book L'architettura della città (1966) Aldo Rossi takes as his theme the material existence of the Western, occidental city, its origins, its form, and its architectural development. The comprehensive study of the material and structural city by Leonardo Benevolo (1975) is conducted against the back-ground of empirical analysis.[27] In his 1991 publication Spiro Kostof incorpo-rates Mumford's ideas with a total of nine definitional features in a comparative, cultural overview.[28] In 2010 Vittorio Magnago Lampugnani, who supplements the "history of the city" with the differentiating concept of the "history of the architecture of the city", formulated a syntheses: "The history of the architec-ture of the city is inseparable from the history of society, its ideological superstructure, its power relations, its economic laws, its utilization structures, its production techniques and its culture."[29] He also specifies the simultaneous operation of the factors that are constitutive for the city or the architecture of the city in a written presentation.

According to Magnago Lampugnani, these factors "must of course only be drawn on insofar as they serve to explain the form of the city. They may not function as one-sided, let alone exclusive, explanatory dispositives. The conditions that shape the city project in history do so in an idiosyncratic and variable fashion. In one case it is a philosophical or religious principle that becomes the formative factor of a certain form of city; in another it is social relations that propel a fundamental renewal of the urban structure; in another it is the structure of ownership, the mechanisms of the social utilization of landed property and the juridical instruments that regulate this utilization that lead to a forma urbis; in another it is the preconditions for its technical production that determine it; and in another the city is the materialization of an intellectual, literary, and artistic vision. It is nearly always the case that all conditions exert an influence at the same time but to different degrees and with different levels of transparency."[30] Here, the different aspects of this book, the material (architectural), and the structural and empirical (urban developmental), are unified.

BASEL: BEGINNINGS, FOUNDATION, EARLY ARCHITECTURE

The genesis, dating, and form of the city that forms the focus of this book are subjects of ongoing early-historical and archaeological research and its scholarly discussion.[31] The first traces of settlement in the current urban area date from the Late Neolithic Period (around 5500–5000 BCE). The fragments of a Late Neolithic wooden post that was found on the Novartis Campus and has been radiocarbon-dated to 3200 BCE has been identified by archaeologists as a "building structure" and is thus currently the oldest element of human architecture in the actual city of today. In 1550 BCE a settlement was established on the Low Terrace (Niederterrasse) between the Rhine and a right tributary, the Wiese. Today this site is the location of the district of Kleinhüningen and the two basins of the Rhine Harbor. The beginnings of settlement in the historic centre of today's city date back to the late Bronze Age. Around 1300 BCE a village-like settlement is thought to have existed on the right bank of the Rhine, and evidence has been found of a strongly fortified settlement on the left bank about 40 metres above the river on the Martinskirchsporn, the northern tip of the Münsterhügel plateau.[32]

The first city-like structure emerged in the Late La Tène Period (Late Iron Age) between 150 and 80 BCE somewhat further to the north-west of the Münsterhügel in an area now known as Basel-Gasfabrik. The Basel-Gasfabrik settlement has yielded finds that indicate trade in goods via and with the Rhône Valley and with Massalia (Marseille), which was founded in 600 BCE, as well as the importation of wine from central Italy. On the approximately fifteen-hectare area of this Celtic settlement of the Raurici tribe, buildings were constructed of wood and clay that formed a right-angled network of paths and streets. A similar large settlement existed at the same time in Breisgau (Hochstetten) on the right bank of the Rhine.

From the middle of the first century BCE onwards, settlement and building on the site of the future city were first influenced then determined by the Roman Empire. The process of Romanization in the Upper and High Rhine region centring on the Münsterhügel is a focus of internationally renowned research.[33] Romanization began in the wake of Julius Caesar's Gallic campaign and the victory over Vercingetorix at Alesia in 52 BCE.[34] In 44 BCE, L(ucius) Munatius Plancus, Caesar's lieutenant and the Roman governor in Gaul, established the "Colonia Raurica".[35] Scholars are still debating whether this "Colonia Raurica" was implanted in an existing oppidum on the Münsterhügel,[36] what strategic intentions and structural changes were associated with its establishment, and how it was linked with the Colonia Augusta Raurica, the construction of which commenced in 15–10 BCE around ten kilometres east of the current city centre (this site now lies in the Swiss municipalities of Augst in the Basel-Landschaft canton and Kaiseraugst in the Aargau canton).[37] With Caesar's murder and the transition to the reign of Augustus, Rome's internal politics defined the historical coordinates of the city's foundation.[38]

We can assume that the plans for a new principal town on the Upper and High Rhine were based on a good knowledge of the local geography among the leadership of the Roman army. Munatius Plancus probably never visited the region but we know that Caesar was present in nearby Upper Alsace. It is clear that a settlement already existed on the Münsterhügel when the Roman military stationed soldiers there. Soldiers were also deployed in the building of the Colonia Augusta Raurica (from 15 BCE onwards) ten kilometres away.[39] The Münsterhügel settlement (in present-day Basel) and Augusta Raurica (in present-day Augst and Kaiseraugst) were thus linked in terms of transport and possibly also military strategy. The criterion of the structural city (inhabited and operated) can thus be seen as operational at this time between the two locations. Since both belonged to the Imperium Romanum, there was also a currency union. But apart from road building, there was no built (material) homogeneity, and there is no—or barely any—evidence in historical sources suggesting the realization of the criterion of the lived (empirical) city.

The earliest known written source relating to the actual city is an inscription made on the grave of L. Munatius Plancus between 20 and 15 BCE near Gaeta in central Italy.[40] The name "Basel," rendered as "Basilia", was first used in 374 BCE in a Roman historical work,[41] and Augusta Raurica, which around 200 CE had up to 18 000 inhabitants, which numbered among the Roman Empire's larger cities,[42] is first registered as a name on a milestone by the abbreviation "Aug Raur" dating to around 139 CE.[43]

The first buildings in Augusta Raurica were wooden constructions (the earliest dendrochronologically determined date is 6 BCE). In contrast to Vindonissa (now the Windisch municipality in the canton of Aargau), which was forty kilometres away and built as a military camp, Augusta Raurica had a civilian character due to its settlement by army veterans. The ground plan of the new city was based on a right-angled road system defined by the longitudinal (Cardo Maximus) and a lateral axis (Decumanus Maximus) of a cross.[44] In high summer, when the area is dry, this ground plan of the ancient city is partially visible from the air.[45] It has long been thought that Roman construction on the site (from 15 BCE onwards) could have drawn on Vitruvius's treatise on architecture (circa 33 to 22 BCE) and a Vitruvian influence on the design is not implausible.[46] Celtic influences are also thought to have played a role in the geographical orientation of the ground plans of both Augusta Raurica and the settlement on the Münsterhügel.[47] Around 40–70 CE, housing began to be built of stone in Augusta Raurica. Stone was also used to build two theatres, two bridges over the Rhine, three thermal baths, and the first religious building.[48] In the fourth century Basel was accorded the status of a civitas (township).

With the introduction of fortress architecture in the Late Roman period, the two locations acquired parallel uses. Around 300 CE, sections of the lower part of Augusta Raurica were encircled by wall to create a fort (Castrum Rauracense).[49] Around the same time, a Roman fortification wall replaced a Celtic fortification (the Murus Gallicus, circa 80–50 BCE).[50] This construction remained the growing city's protective wall until a ring wall was built in the High Middle Ages. The construction of a religious building proved particularly influential on the city's development. In 343/346, Augusta Raurica (Augst/Kaiseraugst) was first recognized as the seat of a bishop (based on participation in a synod in Cologne), and in 350 the first early Christian church was built there.[51] With the end of the Western Roman state (476), the use of the church and its administration were limited or even interrupted for a time, but this was followed by a continuum that proved decisive for growth and development. Records show that Augst/Kaiseraugst and Basel shared a bishop in the seventh century,[52] while references to the first Bishop of Basel date back to the eighth century.[53] It was while Bishop Haito (805–823), an advisor to Charlemagne, was in office that the first Münster (cathedral) was constructed. The building, which measured some 50 metres in length, necessitated the alteration of the street line, still visible today between Rittergasse, Münsterplatz, and Augustinergasse. It has been shown that a narrow building 30 metres long stood on this site during the Late Roman period.

In 1019, on the same site, a new church building (Heinrichsmünster) was consecrated, which from the twelfth to the end of the fifteenth century exhibited the late Roman and Gothic form that can still be seen and experienced today in the building's ground plan and layout.[54] During this period, this sacral building experienced and "survived" destruction wrought by war (917, destruction of the "Haito" cathedral and its replacement by a new building on the same site), damage by fire (repaired in 1285), and damage and partial destruction due to an earthquake (reconstruction and enlargement in 1356). Over a period of almost eighteen years (1431–1449), the Münster constituted the architectural and spiritual focus of a synod and in 1529 of the reformation of the city. During these seven centuries, Basel formed part of the Carolingian Empire, the kingdom of Upper Burgundy, and subsequently the Holy Roman Empire. In 1501 it joined the Swiss Confederation, becoming part of what is now Switzerland.

The Martinskirche, which is located about 350 metres west of the Münster, was built at the turn of the eleventh to twelfth centuries (and first given its name in 1101/03). At almost the same time the Church of St. Leonard was built in the southern part of the city (1160–1118, see project 1). In the eastern part of the city and on the other side of the Rhine the churches of St. Alban and St. Theodor were built (both circa 1100), while in the western part St. Peter's church, like the first Münster building, dates back to the Carolingian period.[55] At the beginning of the twenty-first century, the Münster and the churches of

St. Martin, St. Leonhard, St. Alban, St. Theodor, and St. Peter represent the actual city's oldest pieces of architecture that have been constantly used in accordance with their original purpose.

BASEL: GROWTH AND URBAN SPACE

Basel's transport topography dates back to Celtic and Roman times.[56] The campus of the Vitra firm (see projects 149–153) is located on Römerstrasse[57] in the northern town and commune of Weil am Rhein, which lies on the Roman highway that once led from Augusta Raurica across the Rhine to Wyhlen and from there to Cambete (Kembs) in the north-west. The Pfaffenhof Meadow (in present-day Riehen), which is also located on this highway, was the site of a temple in Roman times. Since 1950 it has been the site of a Christian sacral building.[58] And in the north-western part of the city, parallel to the road that led from Augusta Raurica via Basilia to Argentorate (Strasbourg), lies Fabrikstrasse, the main axis of the developing Novartis Campus (see projects 37–51). And below this campus lies the city-like Basel-Gasfabrik settlement that dates back to the Late La Tène Period (Late Iron Age). In Basel, Rittergasse, Augustinergasse, Martinsgasse and Bäumleingasse on the Münsterhügel all point to Celtic or Roman uses as do St. Alban-Vorstadt to the east and in particular Freie Strasse. Today, Gundeldingerstrasse and Holeestrasse lie on the route of the former highway from Augusta Raurica to Vesontio (Besançon).[59]

Basel developed on the area around the Roman fortification wall (third century), initially to the west, near the mouth of the River Birsig, which flows into the Rhine, and on its left embankment (the delta around the mouth of the river was canalized at the end of the nineteenth century). Here, buildings were constructed of wood and stone, the ground plans and layout of which represent the form of the Late Roman city.[60] Around 1080–1100, some 800 years after the construction of the Roman wall, a larger fortification ring 1.7 kilometres long and enclosing an area of 37 hectares was built.[61] It was commissioned by Bishop Burkhard von Fenis, who was also responsible for the construction to the east of the first Cloister of St. Alban in 1083, which owned lands on the right bank of the Rhine that included the settlement of "Lorracho" (now Lörrach).[62] In the years 1200–1250 the wall was extended and, between 1220 and 1230, the first bridge over the Rhine was constructed (now known as the Mittlere Brücke). A small settlement around the Church of St. Theodor on the right bank of the Rhine now became an integrated and fortified part of the town (Kleinbasel). From 1200 to 1348, a period in which the population grew from 4 500 to 12 000 (by around 1360 it had sunk again to 6 000 due to epidemics, in particular the Black Death[63]), the city experienced a building boom that produced both religious (cloisters) and non-religious buildings (residence towers and courts of the nobility, town hall) and engineering constructions (canals for industrial handcraft production).[64] By the Late Middle Ages, the city had around three dozen churches, chapels, and cloisters as well as 2 000 houses.[65] The architecture and access roadways that emerged from the thirteenth century onwards shaped the inner-city cadastral structure until the late nineteenth century and still make up much of the old town's structural core today (see projects 3, 5, 12).[66]

The city recovered relatively rapidly from an earthquake and the fires it ignited in 1356: of the original five towers on the Münster, two were rebuilt. In 1361 work began on a 4.1-kilometre-long wall that amply enclosed the city such that enough space was left for Basel's architectural growth well into the nineteenth century. It also enclosed the cloister complex of St. Alban to the east, where in the late fifteenth century (during and after the Basel Synod of 1431–1449) the first industrial zone developed for the production of paper. This infrastructure remained in use until 1956 (see projects 92, 93).

From the Late Middle Ages until the middle of the nineteenth century, the cityscape was recorded in all genres of the pre-photographic image.[67] The ground plan of the inner city and the appearance of individual buildings (e.g. facades and roof shapes) can still be seen in copperplate engravings of elevated views of the city from the north and the south by Matthäus Merian der Ältere (1615–1642). Numerous residential, administrative, and public buildings still used today bear witness to Late Gothic, Renaissance, Baroque, and Classicist architectural cultures and the period from 1450 to 1850.[68] From the sixteenth to the nineteenth century, buildings that would ultimately shape the layout of the city were constructed outside the town walls in what are today Gundeldingen, Wettstein, and Hirzbrunnen, and in the municipalities of Arlesheim, Münchenstein, Riehen and Bottmingen.[69] In the seventeenth century, what is now the French part of the actual city developed out of a fortress on which construction was begun in 1679 and which led to the establishment of Village-Neuf and Saint Louis (1684).[70]

When the first census was conducted in Basel in 1778, the city had around 15 000 inhabitants. Since the middle of the fourteenth century, when its population had been 12 000, it had grown erratically and almost imperceptibly.[71] By the time of the first Swiss census in 1850, its population had reached 27 000. For the construction of the first railway station, which was erected in 1845 on the western edge of the city on the Strasbourg-Basel line, the city wall was extended. In 1861 the dismantlement of the fortifications dating back to the fourteenth century was begun to accommodate the city's growing population and its structural expansion.[72]

The expansion of the city in the second half of the nineteenth century saw the construction of the Gundeldingen district in the south, St. Johann in the west and Rosental and Matthäus in the north. In the period leading up to the beginning of the First World War in 1914, the districts of Breite, Bachletten, and Iselin emerged on the left side of the Rhine. Building density increased in the St. Alban and Ring districts. On the right side of the Rhine, a similar increase in density took place in the districts of Wettstein, Klybeck, and Kleinhüningen, the latter of which had been part of Basel since 1640. The main emphasis was on residential building, since between 1888 and 1910 the population had increased from 70 000 to 130 000[73] (in 1899 the 100 000 mark was passed in Basel; in 1892 in Zurich; and in 1898 in Geneva) and specifically the construction of cooperatively and privately financed multifamily dwellings. Up until around 1950, this building program was accompanied by infrastructural construction for education, public administration, health, and recreation (schools, university, hospitals, halls, and swimming pools; see projects 6, 9, 57, 95, 103). There was also an intensive increase in building for industry, transport, and commerce.[74] From the middle of the nineteenth century onwards, the buildings now used by the international companies Novartis and Hoffmann-La Roche were constructed (projects 37–51, 73/74, 129). In 1919 construction began on the basins of the northern Rhine harbour (the St. Johann Rhine harbour was built in 1906). After the Second World War, the transport infrastructure provided by the large southern railway station serving Switzerland and France (1907, project 98) and the northern station serving Germany (1913, project 68) was supplemented by the Basel-Mulhouse (1946) airport in the west of the city. This development has been examined in detail by the architectural historian Dorothee Huber.[75]

The actual city of this book has emerged over the last fifty years. The structural expansion during the first boom following the Second World War led in the late 1950s and 1960s to a growth in terms of area of the villages and towns forming a ring around the core of the city of Basel. Open areas disappeared and architectural zones began to approach, abut, and dovetail one another with varying degrees of intensity. This led to a diminishment of the population in the core city. In 1970 Basel had around 213 000 inhabitants. Currently (2013), around 170 000 people live in the city and 194 000 in the Basel-Stadt canton. The actual city has a little over 450 000 inhabitants.[76]

THIS BOOK'S PROJECTS AND THE CRITERIA GOVERNING THEIR SELECTION
The following projects have supplemented, extended, and increased the density of the actual city of this book since 1980. The criteria of the material, struc-

tural, and empirical city have been manifested over the last thirty-three years in very different ways. The empirical, lived city has only figured peripherally because in the everyday context new buildings have hardly had to prove themselves. Even where a technical or aesthetic quality is discernible, its influence on the building's use can only be guessed at. The structural city is the used city as manifested in its existing structural substance and morphology. Here, the situation is similar because new architecture can offer very little or nothing in the way of experiential value. Nevertheless, a solution for the typology and site of the new architecture can be comprehensible in urban planning terms or a vitalizing potential can be identified on the basis of the existing situation. The radical step of creating a new architecture following demolition can also be seen from this perspective. For when earlier planning was too tied to its particular time, resistance to a change in use can be directed against the city and its interests. In this situation the extent to which the interests of the administered city (by authorities and organs of government) and those of its economic users (investors, planners, and architects) contribute to the quality of the material city needs to be carefully weighed up. This gain in substance has been decisive for the selection made for this book.

Artistic architecture in the city can be compared with the artistic form of language, with literature,[77] although literature has a far greater degree of autonomy than architecture. Works of literature (and of art) "come from a subject and go to a subject", as Alfred Döblin put it.[78] By contrast, the artistic building links subjective art with collective use. Words form sentences and sentences plots. Building types form structural ensembles, which form contexts of use. Literature emanates from the interest of the individual, his experiential capacity with the power of the word, in "his time." Architecture in the city emerges as a collective process of those involved in its planning, financing, and realization within the network of rules and interests of "a time."

The artistic aspect of architecture is limited in these circumstances.[79] A build-ing—like an aphorism or a work of poetry—can embody its own reason for existing, for example, when its design at a site in the city is unquestionable but evokes a reaction that ranges from benevolent to enthusiastic or disap-proving to abrasive, but is never indifferent. However, language and literature emerge in an intellectual-ideational space, whereas architecture and the city develop in a physical one. Literature can represent an individual aggre-gation of observations, feelings, experiences, or ideas in a world. Prose (novella, novel, epic) can capture an episode, a social panorama, or even an epoch. Architecture in the city is always part of a structure that supports and perhaps facilitates individual and social action, but always creates only the basic form and space of a present to serve its needs. This function of architecture is primary and forms the material or architectural city. And the material, the built city is therefore also the primary criterion of this book.

Around 1980 a changed dialogue between contemporary architecture and the city and its history could be detected in Basel and the actual city.[80] That this return to the historical city was connected with the seminal impact of urban theorist and architect Aldo Rossi's book L'architettura della città (1966)[81] is unproven but is possible and probable.[82] Rossi's book is a manifesto for the city in the continuum of its history.—The author took an emphatic—and courageous—stand against a functionalist dogma informing new architectural theory from around 1830 onwards.[83] Here, his concept of the typological city is contained in the categories of the material and empirical city.[84]

This book aims to extend the history of the architecture of the city of Basel and the actual city into the present. And since Basel seems to be a city in which memory is ever-present, the cultural city with its more than 2000-year history plays a decisive role. The star of this book is the city that, in Max Weber's words, is an element of the "non-legitimate domination"[85] in human society. Weber hereby assigns an autonomous authority to the existence of this

phenomenon that has no legislative or executive power but possesses a force
that crosses generations and epochs. And because in the architectural city
the "architecture of a time" can accumulate in the form of a continuum of use,
a city can also communicate phenomena of spoken and written language
such as a meaningful silence, speaking without words, or the slowing down
of time.[86]

How this history of the city continues in an age of explosive world-popula-
tion growth (empirical city), the computer-based organization of the world and
financial economy (structural city), and the post-industrial future of the
continent of Europe and the Swiss nation-state (structural and empirical city)
is the everyday theme of politics and its interest groups on international,
national, and local levels. This book cannot and does not aim to anticipate this
history. After all, the author is always aware of the subjectivity shaped by
his own historical circumstances.

1   See Lutz Windhöfel, **Drei Länder, eine Stadt. Neueste Bauten im grenzübergreifenden Stadtraum Basel**, ed. Ernst Spycher and Lutz Windhöfel (Basel et al.: Birkhäuser, 1997).

2   Population statistics of the connected national segments in Switzerland, Germany, and France based on figures compiled by the Statistics Office of the canton of Basel-Stadt in April 2013 and the Wikipedia entries for the relevant communes as of 29 May 2013. The urban area in Switzerland consists of the canton of Basel-Stadt (Basel: 172 145 inhabitants; Riehen: 20 810; Bettingen: 1186) and municipalities in the canton of Basel-Landschaft (Allschwil: 19 864; Arlesheim: 9066; Binningen: 14 867; Birsfelden: 10 427; Bottmingen: 6213; Muttenz: 17 426; Therwil: 9860; Münchenstein: 11 839; Oberwil: 10 715 and Reinach: 18 701), and Dornach (6375), in the canton of Solothurn. The urban space in Germany consists of Lörrach (48 626 inhabitants), Weil am Rhein (30 011) and Grenzach-Wyhlen (14 122); and in France, of St. Louis (19 995), Huningue (6664), Village-Neuf (3501) and Hésingue (2438).

These figures include so-called frayed settlement sections that barely or do not belong to the actual city. The suburban community of Bettingen very loosely borders Riehen (and Basel) in structural terms. The situation is similar for the districts of Tüllingen and Salzert in Lörrach and Haltingen in Weil am Rhein. In Lörrach Brombach, Haagen, and Hauingen are separated from the urban space by a large bridge viaduct (part of the High Rhine Autobahn) but connected by the Grüttpark, which was built for the state horticultural show in 1983. Aesch is a marginal case, since it is directly connected with Dornach on the ground plan of the actual city but is separated from the urban area by the River Birs, a tributary to the Rhine, and a parallel highway (Basel – Jura canton). The structural contact points between the actual city and Grenzach-Wyhlen, Hésingue, and Village-Neuf also constitute only a partial homogeneity of urban space. On the other hand, during the Roman period, Wyhlen, when it lay opposite Augusta Raurica on the other side of the Rhine (and was connected to it by bridges), was the site of a temple district and an aristocratic estate, and was connected to the actual city by the road to Cambete (Kembs) and the "Landauer" villa complex. See Archäologische Bodenforschung Basel-Stadt and Historisches Museum Basel (eds.), **Unter Uns – Archäologie in Basel** (Basel: Christoph Merian, 2008), 225ff. Today the Charles Eames-Strasse on the Vitra campus in Weil am Rhein branches off from this ancient road.

For a long time it seemed that what are today clearly separated municipalities such as Aesch (next to Reinach), Biel-Benken (next to Therwil) and Pratteln (next to Muttenz) in the south and east (all in Switzerland) would soon be part of the actual city. Happily, current political and urban planning tendencies, building density, and landscape protection measures are placing a question mark over this development. Augst begins around a kilometre north-east of Pratteln. The ancient city of Augusta Raurica, which in 200 BCE had some 18 000 inhabitants and was one of the Imperium Romanum's larger cities (Frank Kolb, **Die Stadt in Altertum** [Düsseldorf: Patmos/Albatros, 2005], 176, 191–192), began on what is today the municipal area of Pratteln; see Eckhard Deschler-Erb, "Der Anteil des Militärs an der frühen Entwicklungsgeschichte von Augusta Raurica", in **Genese, Struktur und Entwicklung römischer Städte im 1. Jahrhundert n. Chr. in Nieder- und Obergermanien**, Xantener Berichte 9, ed. Gundolf Precht

(Mainz: Philipp von Zabern, 2001), 203, n.2.

3   The buildings at the Basel-Mulhouse airport, which lies on French territory, are connected directly to the urban body by a road but isolated from it by a strip of land and are therefore not taken into consideration here.

4   **Vitruv Baukunst**, ed. Beat Wyss, 2 vols. (Zurich and Munich: Artemis, 1987). The edition includes the translation from the Latin by August Rode (Leipzig: Göschen, 1796), a scholarly essay by George Germann on the history and reception of the edition (pp. 7–26), updated explanatory notes by Andri Gieré (pp. 323–330), and a selection of illustrations from editions of Vitruvius from the sixteenth to eighteenth centuries.

5   Hanno-Walter Kruft, **Geschichte der Architekturtheorie**, 4th ed. (Munich: C. H. Beck, 1995); and Vittorio Magnago Lampugnani, Katia Frey, and Eliana Perotti (eds.), **Anthologie zum Städtebau**, vol. 1 (2 books): **Von der Aufklärung zur Metropole des industriellen Zeitalters** (Berlin: Gebr. Mann, 2008).

6   Lewis Mumford, **The Culture of Cities** (London and Bradford: Secker & Warburg, 1946), 3.

7   "With language itself, it [the city] remains man's greatest work of art", ibid., 5. In relating architecture to language Mumford also refers to Vitruvius. See Vittorio Magnago Lampugnani, "Städte erschreiben, Städte entwerfen", in **Stadt & Text. Zur Ideengeschichte des Städtebaus im Spiegel theoretischer Schriften seit dem 18. Jahrhundert**, ed. Vittorio Magnago Lampugnani, Katia Frey, and Eliana Perotti (Berlin: Gebr. Mann, 2011), 13–14. By "grammar" Vitruvius means both the written and the spoken forms of language (**Baukunst** 1:24, note by August Rode; see note 4).

8   The posthumously published text "Die Stadt" by Max Weber (1864–1920), in **Archiv für Sozialwissenschaft und Sozialpolitik** 47 (1921): 621ff. The first paragraph, "Begriffe und Kategorien der Stadt", is also in **Die Stadt des Mittelalters** vol. 1, ed. Carl Haase (Darmstadt: Wissenschaftliche Buchgesellschaft, 1969), 34–59. The complete text appears as "Die nichtlegitime Herrschaft (Typologie der Städte)", in **Wirtschaft und Gesellschaft. Grundriss einer verstehenden Soziologie**, 5th ed., ed. Johannes Winckelmann (Tübingen: Mohr, 1972), 727–814.

9   Weber, **Wirtschaft und Gesellschaft**, 728 (see note 8).

10   Johannes Winckelmann, foreword to the 5th edition, in Weber, **Wirtschaft und Gesellschaft**, xi (see note 8). Weber's city typology ascertains an economically based "illegitimate domination" that—particularly in Europe—becomes the forerunner of the rational state constitution and "legitimate domination". The text therefore also figures in Weber's economic history and his political writings (Ibid., xix, n. 86). In 2012, based on Weber's transnational scholarly orientation, the Stiftung Deutsche Geisteswissenschaftliche Institute im Ausland (Bonn) was renamed the Max Weber Stiftung – Deutsche Geisteswissenschaftliche Institute im Ausland. Weber's study of the city thus assumes a normative character (Ibid., n. 84).

11   Haase, **Die Stadt des Mittelalters** 1:40 (see note 8).

12   Frank Kolb, **Die Stadt im Altertum** (Düsseldorf: Patmos / Albatros, 2005), 15ff. The author distinguishes his own approach from literature on the city of antiquity as an element of political history (Martin Hammond, **The City of the Ancient World** [1972]) and on the "cultural-morphological" city (Oswald Spengler, **Der Untergang des Abendlandes** [1918/1922]; Arnold J. Toynbee, **A**

Study of History [10 vols., 1934–1954]; and Mumford, **The Culture of Cities** [see note 6]). The Roman establishment of Augusta Raurica that was so important for Basel is not taken into account in the discussion of the western Roman provinces (Gaul and North Africa).

13 Ibid., 176.

14 Georg Simmel, "Die Grossstädte und das Geistesleben", in **Georg Simmel Gesamtausgabe** vol. 7, **Aufsätze und Abhandlungen 1901–1908**, vol. 1, ed. Ottheim Rammstadt et al. (Frankfurt am Main: Suhrkamp, 1995), 116–131.

15 Hartmut Häussermann, "Georg Simmel, der Stadtsoziologe. Eine Einführung", in **Georg Simmel und die aktuelle Stadtforschung**, ed. Harald A. Mieg, Astrid O. Sundsboe, and Majken Bieniok (Wiesbaden: VS Verlag für Sozialwissenschaften, 2011), 15–27; quote, 25.

16 Georg Simmel, **Philosophie des Geldes**, vol. 6 of **Georg Simmel Gesamtausgabe**, ed. David Frisby and Klaus Christian Köhnke (Frankfurt am Main: Suhrkamp, 1989). The text refers to the "second, expanded edition" of 1907, which, like the first edition (1900), was published by Duncker & Humblot in Leipzig and Munich.

17 See Harald A. Mieg, "Simmel – Milgram – Sassen: Metropolen als Orte der Zivilisationsproduktion", in **Georg Simmel und die aktuelle Stadtforschung**, 41–52 (see note 15); and Majken Bieniok, Reinhard Beyer, Elke van der Meer: "Aktualität Simmels in der Wahrnehmung von Metropolen", in ibid., 53–72.

18 Astrid O. Sundsboe, "Simmel Reloaded: Ein klassischer soziologischer Blick auf die aktuelle Erforschung ethnischer Segregation", in **Georg Simmel und die aktuelle Stadtforschung**, 115–146 (see note 15).

19 Georg Simmel, "Soziologie des Raumes", in **Georg Simmel Gesamtausgabe**, 132–183; quote, 139 (see note 14); see also Sundsboe, "Simmel Reloaded", 117–121 (see note 18).

20 Heike Delitz, "Soziologie der gebauten 'Haut' der Gesellschaft: Georg Simmels Architektursoziologie", in **Georg Simmel und die aktuelle Stadtforschung**, 245–267, especially 247, 256 and 259 (see note 15).

21 Ibid., 247, 258–259; and Vittorio Magnago Lampugnani, **Die Stadt im 20. Jahrhundert. Visionen, Entwürfe, Gebautes**, 2 vols. (Berlin: Wagenbach, 2011), 1:279.

22 Wolfgang Schivelbusch, **Lichtblicke. Zur Geschichte der künstlichen Helligkeit im 19. Jahrhundert** (Munich: Hanser, 1983), 67–78.

23 Uwe Justus Wenzel, "Denken in Beziehungen. Die ersten Bände der Simmel-Gesamtausgabe", **Neue Zürcher Zeitung** 167, (21/22 July 1990), "Literatur und Kunst" section, 62.

24 Markus Bernauer, **Die Ästhetik der Masse** (Basel: Wiese, 1990), 50–58.

25 See Silke Steets, **Wir sind die Stadt! Kulturelle Netzwerke und die Konstitution städtischer Räume in Leipzig** (Frankfurt am Main: Campus, 2008); Daniel Wiener (ed.), **Wir sind die Stadt. Das Beispiel Werkstatt Basel** (Basel: Christoph Merian, 2001); or Mark Shepard (ed.), **Sentient City – Ubiquitous Computing, Architecture and the Future of Urban Space** (Cambridge, MA: MIT Press, 2011). The futuristic, empirically based city model by MVRDV (Rotterdam) for the IBA Emscher Park (conurbation between Duisburg and Dortmund in Germany) was accompanied by the exhibition (with catalogue) **Talking Cities. The Micropolitics of Urban Space/Die Mikropolitik des urbanen Raums** (Basel et al.: Birkhäuser, 2006).

26 See the discussion of "Frauenkauf" in Simmel, **Philosophie**

des Geldes, 506–510 (see note 16).

27 Leonardo Benevolo, **Storia della città** (Rome/Bari: Laterza, 1975). The 3rd expanded edition was translated as: **The History of the City**, trans Geoffrey Culverwell (London: Scolar Press, 1980)

28 Spiro Kostof, **The City Shaped** (London: Thames and Hudson, 1991).

29 Lampugnani, **Die Stadt im 20. Jahrhundert**, 1:8 (see note 21).

30 Ibid., 8–9.

31 See Archäologische Bodenforschung Basel-Stadt and Historisches Museum Basel (eds.), **Unter Uns – Archäologie in Basel** (Basel: Christoph Merian, 2008). The publication by sixteen academic authors presents the history of archaeology as a scholarly discipline in Basel from the early sixteenth century onwards and its historiography. On the Bronze Age see also Dieter Holstein, "Die bronzezeitlichen Funde aus dem Kanton Basel-Stadt", **Materialheft Archäologie Basel** 7 (1991). The archaeological part of this manuscript owes much to Nobert Spichtig, deputy canton archaeologist of the Archäologische Bodenforschung Basel-Stadt, for his many tips and critical reading.

32 Ibid., 94f, 98. The identification of the village-like settlement on the right side of the Rhine is based on an excavation in 2011 at Utengasse 15/17 (on the construction site of the new Jazz Campus).

33 Most recently Eckhard Deschler-Erb, **Der Basler Münsterhügel am Übergang von spätkeltischer zu römischer Zeit**, 2 vols. (Basel: Archäologische Bodenforschung des Kantons Basel-Stadt, 2011).

34 In 2012 the "Centre d'interprétation du Muséo Parc Alésia", designed by the architect Bernard Tschumi, was built in Alice-Sainte-Reine/Burgund to mark this central event in the history of France.

35 **Unter Uns**, 205 (see note 31).

36 Here, a southern Mediterranean influence (in the form of technical know-how) has been identified in road building around 80 BCE, and an "Augustan road" has been found dating to 30–20 BCE. See **Unter Uns**, 209–210 (see note 31).

37 Deschler-Erb, **Das Basler Münsterhügel**, 1:20–21 and 1:231–241 (see note 33).

38 See Ludwig Berger et al., **Führer durch Augusta Raurica**, 7th ed. (Basel: Schwabe, 2012), 17ff; and Deschler-Erb, **Das Basler Münsterhügel**, 1:230, fig. 263

(see note 33). In the year the "Colonia Raurica" was founded (44 BCE) Caesar was murdered in the Roman senate. In 30 BCE his successor, Octavian, following his victory in a civil war, became sole ruler. In 27 BCE the Roman senate awarded him the honorary title of Augustus. With the definitive conquest of the foothills of the Alps under Augustus (circa 15 BCE), a Roman building campaign was instituted in the area of the Upper and High Rhine and began with the construction of the Colonia Augusta Raurica. For a comprehensive scholarly bibliography on Augusta Raurica, see Berger et. al., **Führer durch Augusta Raurica**, 357–368.

39 Deschler-Erb, "Der Anteil des Militärs", 203–216 (see note 2).

40 **Unter Uns**, 205 (see note 31).

41 Ibid., 21 and 197; see also Casimir Hermann Baer, **Die Kunstdenkmäler des Kantons Basel-Stadt** vol. 1 (Basel: Birkhäuser, 1971), 17–26.

42 Estimates for the late imperial period around 200 CE lie between 9000 and 18 000: Peter-Andrew Schwarz et al., "Zur Einwohnerzahl von Augusta Raurica", **Jahresberichte aus Augst und Kaiseraugst** 27 (Basel: Schwabe, 2006), 67–108; Berger et al., **Führer durch Augusta Raurica**,

23 (see note 38). See also "Eine rekonstruierte Isometrie der Gesamtanlage von Augusta Raurica", in Alex R. Furger, **Kurzführer Augusta Raurica, Augst** (Römerstadt: Augusta Raurica, 1997), 14; and Jean-Claude Golvin, **Metropolen der Antike** (Stuttgart: Theiss, 2005), 145. Between 150 and 200 CE Augusta Raurica reached its greatest size with 106 hectares of settled area and a Rhine bank extending 800 metres. It was somewhat larger than Aventicum (today Avenches, 80 hectares) and somewhat smaller than the Colonia Claudia Ara Agrippinensium (Cologne, 110 hectares) and the Colonia Augusta Treverorum (Trier, 150 hectares); see Furger 1997, as in note. 38, 9).

43 Berger et al., **Führer durch Augusta Raurica**, 20 (see note 38).

44 Ibid., 49 and 54.

45 See aerial photo in Dorothee Huber, **Architekturführer Basel. Die Baugeschichte der Stadt und ihrer Umgebung** (Basel: Architekturmuseum in Basel, 1993), 19.

46 On Vitruvius's influence, see Hans Stohler, "Über die Orientierung der Stadtpläne von Augusta Raurica und Basilia Romana", **Basler Zeitschrift für Geschichte und Altertumskunde** 37 (1938), 295–297. While

writing his treatise (33 to around 22 BCE), Vitruvius received an annuity through the sister of Octavian (from 27 BCE, the sister of the emperor) and the treatise was dedicated to the Roman Imperator Augustus (63 BCE–14 CE); see Georg Germann, "Vitruv, Vitruvianismus und Rodes Übersetzung", in: **Vitruv Baukunst**, 7 (see note 2). The emperor, who gave the new city on the High Rhine its name, was therefore possibly familiar with Vitruvius's treatise. And in 27 BCE, L. Munatius Plancus, who had founded the Colonia Raurica in 44 BCE, tabled the motion in the Roman senate to give Octavian the name Augustus, which was subsequently accepted; see **Der Kleine Pauly. Lexikon der Antike**, vol. I (Munich: Deutscher Taschenbuch Verlag, 1979), column 749. It is therefore possible that Munatius Plancus and Augustus knew each other personally. The influence of Vitruvius's ideas has been identified in the framework construction of a residential building on the Münsterhügel; see **Unter Uns**, 219–221 (see note 31).

47 Rolf d'Aujourd'hui, "Zur Geometrie des Stadtplans von Augusta Raurica – Mit einem Exkurs zum Belchensystem", in **Mille Fiori – Festschrift für Ludwig Berger** (Augst: Römermuseum, 1998), 19–32.

In the academic discussion this theory is also seen as a modern projection unsupported by historical evidence.

48 On the building boom around 200 CE see Berger et al., **Führer durch Augusta Raurica**, 23–24 (see note 38).

49 Ibid., 26–27, 317–327.

50 **Unter Uns**, 140, 193–194 (see note 31); and Deschler-Erb, **Das Basler Münsterhügel**, 1:235ff (see note 33).

51 **Unter Uns**, 251 (see note 38); and Berger et al., **Führer durch Augusta Raurica**, 32, 335–340 (see note 38). In the year 313 CE (Tolerance Edict of Emperor Constantine) Christianity became the official Roman religion. In 380 CE it became the state religion under Emperor Theodosius.

52 Around 630/40 a Bishop Ragnachar from Augst/Kaiseraugst was appointed provost of Basel's churches. His diocese was under the control of the Archbishop of Besançon, just as the late Roman Augusta Raurica had belonged to the province Maxima Sequanorum, the capital of which was Vesontio (Besançon). Until the Late Middle Ages the Bishopric of Basel belonged to the Archdiocese of Besançon; see **Unter Uns**, 246 (see note 31).

53 Disputed between Walaus (around 730) and Baldobert (740–762); see **Unter Uns**, 251 and 254 (see note 31).

54 Dorothea Schwinn Schürmann, "Baugeschichte", in **Das Basler Münster**, ed. Stiftung Basler Münsterbauhütte (Basel: Schwabe, 2008), 12–17.

55 François Maurer, **Die Kunstdenkmäler des Kantons Basel-Stadt** vol 4, **Die Kirchen, Klöster und Kapellen**, part 2 (Basel: Birkhäuser, 1961), 312ff and 146ff (an older building is thought to be underneath St. Martin's); Gesellschaft für Schweizerische Kunstgeschichte (ed.): **Die Kunstdenkmäler des Kantons Basel-Stadt** vol 3, **Die Kirchen, Klöster und Kapellen**, part 1 (Basel: Birkhäuser, 1941), 43–46 and 81–92. The construction of St. Leonhard's between 1060 and 1118 is disputed. François Maurer, **Die Kunstdenkmäler des Kantons Basel-Stadt** vol. 5, **Die Kirchen, Klöster und Kapellen**, part 3 (Basel: Birkhäuser, 1966), 15–16 and 31ff; and, for a summary, Guido Helmig and Udo Schön, "Die Stadtbefestigung am St. Alban-Graben und am Harzgraben", **Jahresbericht der archäologischen Bodenforschung des Kantons Basel-Stadt** 1994 (Basel: Archäo-logische Bodenforschung des Kantons Basel-Stadt, 1997), 78.

56 See Furger, **Kurzführer Augusta Raurica**, 10–11 (see note 42); and Cornel Doswald, **Historische Verkehrswege im Kanton Basel-Stadt** (Bern: Astra, 2004), 11ff.

57 The name of Weil am Rhein is first referred to as "Willa" in a document from the Cloister of St. Gallen from 786. In 1958 archaeological evidence of a farmstead dating to the Roman period was found south of Weil-Haltingen (Wikipedia entry on Weil am Rhein, accessed 11.06.2012).

58 On the building, see Huber, **Architekturführer Basel**, 11ff and 344–345 (see note 45). The entire complex of the ancient temple in a historical landscape simulation with the highway in Guido Helmig, "Gallorömische Tempel in Riehen", **z'Rieche**, **Jahrbuch** (Riehen: Stiftung z'Rieche, 2009), 38.

59 Martin Steinmann, "Von der frühen Besiedlung bis zur ersten Blüte der Stadt", in **Basel – Geschichte einer städtischen Gesellschaft**, ed. Georg Kreis, and Beat von Wartburg (Basel: Christoph Merian, 2000), 16.

60 Ludwig Berger, **Die Ausgrabungen am Petersberg in Basel** (Basel: Helbing & Lichtenhahn, 1963).

61 **Unter Uns**, 300ff (see note 31).

62 The oldest reference to the name "Lorracho" is found in a cloister document dating from 1102 (Wikipedia entry on Lörrach, accessed 11.06.2012).

63 Population statistics for the city of Basel from 1100 to 2000 in Kreis and von Wartburg (eds.), **Basel**, 410 (see note 59).

64 See Werner Meyer, "Basel im Spätmittelalter", in Kreis and von Wartburg (eds.), **Basel**, 38ff (see note 59). Meyer refers to the source research by Rudolf Wackernagel, **Geschichte der Stadt Basel**, 3 vols. (1907–1924).

65 **Unter Uns**, 288 (see note 31).

66 See Anne Nagel, Martin Möhle, Brigitte Meles, **Die Kunstdenkmäler des Kantons Basel-Stadt** vol. 7, **Die Altstadt von Grossbasel I – Profanbauten** (Bern: Gesellschaft für Schweizerische Kunstgeschichte, 2006); and Thomas Lutz, **Die Kunstdenkmäler des Kantons Basel-Stadt** vol. 6, **Die Altstadt von Kleinbasel – Profanbauten** (Bern: Gesellschaft für Schweizerische Kunstgeschichte, 2004).

67 See "Das Stadtbild von Basel", in **Die Kunstdenkmäler des Kantons Basel-Stadt** vol. 1,

83–141 and 739–740 (see note 41).

68 Representation to scale in Huber, **Architekturführer Basel**, 42ff (see note 45). An informative overview with numerous illustrations is in Hans Eppens, **Baukultur im alten Basel**, 5th ed. (Basel: Frobenius, 1974).

69 Huber, **Architekturführer Basel**, 58–59, 82–85, 88–89, 92–93, 108–109, 111, and 128–129 (see note 45).

70 Wikipedia entries, accessed 11.06.2012. Hüningen is first referred to in a document from 828 as a gift to the Cloister of St. Gallen.

71 **Die Kunstdenkmäler des Kantons Basel-Stadt** vol. 1, 66, 72, and 74 (see note 41); and the population statistics in Kreis and von Wartburg (eds.), **Basel**, 410 (see note 59).

72 See chronologies, statistics, and the list of the chronological building inventory with names and streets ordered alphabetically (and pictured) in Othmar Birkner and Hanspeter Rebsamen, "Basel", in: **INSA Inventar der neueren Schweizer Architektur 1850–1920** vol. 2, **Basel, Bellinzona, Bern**, ed. Gesellschaft für Schweizerische Kunstgeschichte (Zurich: Orell Füssli, 1986), 25–241.

73 Kreis and von Wartburg, **Basel**, 410 (see note 59); see Rose Marie Schulz-Rehberg, **Architekten des Fin de Siècle. Bauen in Basel um 1900** (Basel: Christoph Merian, 2012); and Rolf Brönnimann, **Basler Bauten 1860–1910** (Basel et al.: Helbing & Lichtenhahn, 1973).

74 See Rolf Brönnimann, **Basler Industriebauten 1850–1930. Die Entstehung und Entwicklung der Industriearchitektur in Basel und Umgebung** (Basel: Basler Zeitung, 1990).

75 Dorothee Huber's **Architekturführer Basel. Die Baugeschichte der Stadt und ihrer Umgebung** (see note 45) presents the architectural history of the city in the nineteenth and twentieth centuries thematically and chronologically, with introductory texts for each chapter and monographic contributions (text, image, and/or plan) relating to all individual buildings, settlements, and use ensembles. The publication includes an index of people and places, a city-map insert, and traces an arc stretching from Celtic settlement to the beginning of the 1990s. On residential building in the twentieth century, see Rebekka Brandenberger, Ulrike Zophoniasson, and Marco Zünd, **Die Baumgartnerhäuser Basel 1926–1938** (Basel et al.: Birkhäuser, 2002).

76 Kreis and von Wartburg, **Basel**, 410 and n. 2 (see note 59).

77 See note 7.

78 Alfred Döblin, "Kunst, Dämon und Gemeinschaft", **Das Kunstblatt** 10, no. 5 (1926), 184.

79 See Christoph Baumberger (ed.), **Architekturphilosophie. Grundlagentexte** (Münster: mentis, 2013).

80 See Baudepartement Basel-Stadt (ed.), **Neues Wohnen in der alten Stadt. Die Sanierung staatlicher Liegenschaften in der Basler Altstadt 1978–1990** (Basel: Basler Zeitung, 1991). This architectural and urban-planning development of the actual city is presented in the introduction to the previous editions of this book (2000, 2004, 2008) from a personal and structural perspective.

81 Aldo Rossi, **L'architettura della città** (Padua: Marsilio, 1966), translated into German as **Die Architektur der Stadt. Skizze zu einer grundlegenden Theorie des Urbanen**, Bauwelt Fundamente 41 (Düsseldorf: Bertelsmann, 1973).

82 See Lampugnani, **Die Stadt im 20. Jahrhundert**, 2:813–847 (see note 21).

83 Peter Collins, **Changing Ideals in Modern Architecture 1750–1950** (London: Faber and Faber, 1965); 2nd ed., with a foreword by Kenneth Frampton (Montreal et al.: McGill-Queen's, 1998).

84 Rossi's "typological city" differentiates the built reality of the city into monuments (mostly for collective use) and additive buildings (mostly for individual use) and thereby develops a structural logic of architectural design. Although Rossi refers to Max Weber (see note 8), he develops the concept of the "typological city" parallel to Weber's older terminology. Rossi approaches the typology of buildings (i.e. the material city) in an applied manner and as a norm and strategy of the artistic and, in terms of urban planning, responsible work of the architect. Max Weber's terminology is more fundamental for the existence of the city (see note 10). In this book, the artistic construction of the material city is therefore considered in context with the empirical city.

85 See note 10.

86 See Georg Mörsch, "Der Münsterplatz in Basel – Gebrauch oder Verbrauch eines Stadtdenkmals", in **Konfliktzone Münsterhügel – Bewahren oder beanspruchen** (Basel: Freiwillige Basler Denkmalpflege 2012), 9–15, and Gerhard Vinken, "Mut zur Lücke. Kontrast und Gegensatz in Basels Stadtbild", in ibid., 17–26.

Architect:	Morger & Degelo, Basel
	Now: Morger & Dettli, Basel, www.morgerdettli.ch and
	Degelo Architekten, Basel, www.degelo.net
Client:	Canton Basel-Stadt, Department of civil services and environment,
	Planning department, Basel
Dates:	project planning 1996, construction 1997–1999

MUSEUM OF MUSIC

Im Lohnhof 9, 4051 Basel | Tram 3: Musik-Akademie | Tram 3 6 8 11 14 15 16 17: Barfüsserplatz

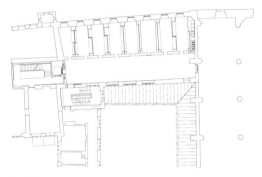

Second floor

The Lohnhof is a thousand-year-old complex, which Morger & Degelo have converted into a museum. Originally, the site was occupied by a church (founded in 1002) to which other sacred buildings were added over the years. After some time, these were used as a jail. As far back as the twelfth century, the complex was incorporated into medieval fortifications. The modern conversion has created apartments, a hotel restaurant, and cultural facilities. For the first time, there is space to exhibit the Museum of History's collection of musical instruments. Within strict preservation regulations, an exhibition space (600 m^2) across four storeys has been created in the former prison wing. The minimal, sparse atmosphere is an ideal environment for the exhibitions.

Entrance courtyard

Architect:	Gmür / Vacchini, Basel
	Now: Silvia Gmür Reto Gmür Architekten, Basel; www.gmuerarch.ch
Client:	Papyrus AG, 4001 Basel
Dates:	project planning 1997, construction 1999

RETAIL BUILDING CONVERSION

Freie Strasse 43, 4001 Basel | Tram 3 6 8 11 14 15 16 17: Barfüsserplatz

Stairwell across four floors

Sixth floor

Fourth floor

Ground floor

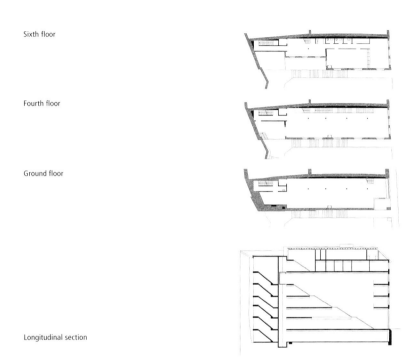

Longitudinal section

In recent years, monumental stairs have become an important motif in Basel's contemporary architecture: the most recent example is Silvia Gmür's and Livio Vacchini's design for a paper and art supply store on Freie Strasse. Narrow, single-file stairs connect four floors in a stairwell placed next to the building's right fire wall. Each landing leads to a different department, which are accentuated with muted but deep colours. From the street the added stairwell is visible only on the first two floors, which are fully glazed. This is a rigorous modernization of this narrow building, originally designed by Suter & Burckhardt in 1911.

Architect:	Mathias E. Frey Architekten, Basel; www.mathiasefrey.ch
	Associates Beni M. Hänzi, Patrik Strasser
Client:	Basel-Stadt Department of civil services and environment,
	Planning department, Basel
Dates:	project planning 2009, construction 2010–2012

TAXIDERMY FACILITIES AND WORKSHOPS
OF THE NATURAL HISTORY MUSEUM

Stapfelberg 2/4, Schlüsselberg 3+5, 4051 Basel | Tram 6 8 11 15 16: Marktplatz

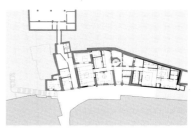

Ground plan of the ground floor with the buildings
"Zum Fälkli" (left) and the new taxidermy hall (far right).

On the Münsterhügel Mathias E. Frey collaborated with the historical preservation authority on a multipartite architectural intervention for the Natural History Museum that involved three historic buildings ("Zum Fälkli", name first recorded in 1394; "Zum Venedig", 1486; "Zum Weissen Bär", 1395). The building complex on Stapfelberg and Schlüsselberg developed in stages over 600 years, during which time it had residential, commercial, and industrial uses (from 1871 onwards it housed a printing business) and has been part of the museum since 1918. The last previous architectural intervention, an insensitive renovation of offices and repositories, had been undertaken in 1955/56. The new project entailed the installation of taxidermy facilities (maceration and dissection rooms, hygiene zone, laboratories) and workshops (carpentry, painting, fitting) through a process of remodelling and new building on an area of 1620 m². The original spatial structure was partially restored, doors and windows on the perimeter of the remodelled area were renewed, and a highly sensitive infrastructure for building utilities and hygiene facilities was installed. Striking features of the project include the roofing over of a former courtyard to create a restoration room and the addition on the southern street side of a washed concrete taxidermy room equipped with an underground lift.

The taxidermy hall with windows facing Schlüsselberg.

The late Gothic facade of the building "Zum Weissen Bär" merges with a new concrete facade.

Architect:	Rüdisühli Ibach Architekten, Basel; www.ri-ag.ch
	in collaboration with Stauffenegger + Stutz Visuelle Gestaltung, Basel; www.st-st.ch
Client:	Basel Transport Services, Basel
Dates:	competition 2005/2006, prototypes and construction since 2008,
	Kunstmuseum tram stop 2009

"PARAPLUIE" TRAM SHELTER AT "KUNSTMUSEUM"

St. Alban-Graben, Basel | Tram 2 15: Kunstmuseum

The tram stop on St. Alban-Graben.

The "Kunstmuseum" tram stop on St. Alban-Graben features two tram shelters. The street lies on the boundary between the old town and the eastern suburbs, and the design of the shelters by Rüdisühli Ibach and Stauffenegger + Stutz, which as of December 2013 has been erected at 46 tram stops is called "Parapluie" (umbrella). The design features a modular structure and an additive character and does not entail any site-specific reference. It has been developed for use throughout the city and its functions are rigorously and palpably bundled. The basic element of the delicate structure is a slender, 2.6-metre-high and 3.8-metre-long steel support frame displaying graphics in the corporate-identity green of Basler Verkehrsbetriebe, a local transport operator. The structure's glass roof projects out 1.5 metres. The back wall consists of glass plates (12 mm ESG panels) with serigraphs (bird protection) and a display case for travel information or advertising. A bench or a rail made of oak can be installed on the front of the wall. Glass walls on the sides provide protection from rain and wind, and lighting units provide security at night.

The new tram shelters in front of the Basel Kunstmuseum portico.

The "Duplex" model
of "Parapluie".

The "Mono" model of "Parapluie"
and the side elevation of the
2.6-meter construction
(from the left).

Architect:	Silvia Gmür, Basel
	Now: Silvia Gmür Reto Gmür Architekten, Basel; www.gmuerarch.ch
	Associate Christoph Butscher
	in collaboration with Vischer Architekten, Basel; www.vischer.ch
Client:	Canton Basel-Stadt, Department of civil services and environment,
	Planning department, Basel
Dates:	construction 1986–1990

UNIVERSITY INSTITUTE IN THE ENGELHOF

Nadelberg 4, 4051 Basel | Tram 3, Bus 34: Universität | Tram 6 8 11 14 15 16 17: Marktplatz

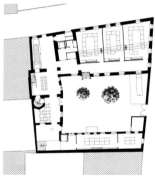

Ground floor

The history of the Engelhof goes back to the eleventh century. Its current shell dates mostly from the sixteenth century. The interior, however, has undergone a radical change in this conversion of the building into seminar facilities for the University of Basel. Metal stairs, fine carpentry in clean forms, and prototype lighting fixtures give the building a contemporary look. Perhaps no other conversion or modification in the building's long history has had a comparable impact: the result is a profound visual harmonization of the space. One would have to travel far to find another library that is as tranquil, focused, and contemporary. A tranquil, focused and modern library stretches over two floors beneath the gable roof.

Band of skylights in reading area

Two-storey library

Architect:	Fierz Architekten, Basel; www.fierzarchitekten.ch
Client:	Canton Basel-Stadt, Department of civil services and environment,
	Planning department, Basel
Dates:	project planning 2000, construction 2001–2003

UNIVERSITY ADMINISTRATION BUILDING

Petersplatz 1, 4003 Basel | Tram 3, Bus 30 33: Spalentor | Bus 34: Universität

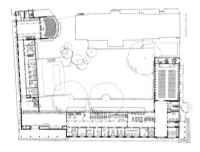

Ground floor plan

The main administration building of the University of Basel on the Petersplatz – designed by Roland Rohn and opened for occupation in 1939 – has been restored (lighting fixtures, furniture), renovated (windows, sanitary installations, building services) and converted (administrative area, basement level). Fierz Architekten have preserved the dignity of the important historic building, reinvigorated the bright interior and the imposing exterior. Half of the eighteen lecture halls were restored and modernized: most of the chairs by Häfeli, Moser, and Steiger were preserved. The glass front overlooking the garden runs parallel to the internal corridor in the north wing. The interior space (with the new café-restaurant) is now linked to the enclosed courtyard park at several points. An open-plan space with PC workstations was created in the basement level. A simplified, discrete lighting scheme once again allows the 70-metre-long ribbon of windows on the upper floor to come into full effect. The same is true for the elegant spiral staircase with skylight, which connects the U-shaped ensemble on the Petersgraben side.

Foyer with spiral staircase

A conference room on the upper floor

Architect:	Naef, Studer & Studer, Zurich
Client:	Canton Basel-Stadt, Department of civil services and environment,
	Planning department, Basel
Dates:	conceptual competition 1979, project competition 1980, construction 1984–1988

UNIVERSITY INSTITUTE IN THE ROSSHOF

Petersgraben 49/51, 4051 Basel | Tram 3, Bus 34: Universität | Tram 6 8 11 14 15 16 17: Marktplatz

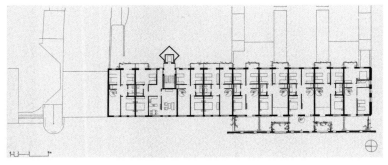

Fifth floor

The construction of the new Rosshof was a hot political topic for years and the very fact that it was finally realized makes it significant in terms of urban planning. Naef, Studer & Studer erected a complex cubature whose formal aesthetics and physicality are convincing. The new complex provides 5000 square metres of floor space for the university's Institute of Economics. The six-storey building on Petersgraben also contains sixteen apartments ranging from 2.5 to 5.5 rooms. Two shops as well as some 400 underground parking spaces round out the building program. In one corner of the lot, a wing that contains a lecture hall cleverly integrates an historic fifteenth-century building into the complex.

Courtyard with historic building

Facade overlooking Petersgraben

Architect:	Herzog & de Meuron, Basel; www.herzogdemeuron.com
	Project management Mario Meier
Client:	Canton Basel-Stadt, Department of civil services and environment,
	Planning department, Basel
Dates:	competition 1984, construction 1987–1988

COURTYARD RESIDENTIAL BUILDING

Hebelstrasse 11, 4056 Basel | Bus 30 33: Bernoullianum | Tram 3, Bus 34: Universität

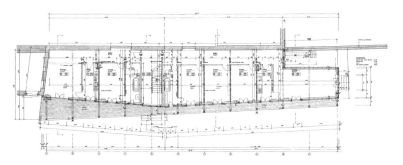

Ground floor

A small residential building, which lies parallel to a dividing wall in a courtyard on Hebelstrasse, has fascinated the public ever since it was first completed. The three-storey building with oak siding is raised on Japanese-style wooden supports. It contains six apartments in this quiet urban location. The project brought international attention to the architects. The verandahs are accessible from all the interiors in a sophisticated integration of interior and exterior space. The ground-floor verandah is reached via two steps. This building seems to float above the ground, reminiscent of sacred wooden architecture in the Far East. Bamboo in the gravel-covered yard reinforces this association.

Oak facade

Slim volume against wall

Architect:	Gmür / Vacchini, Basel
	Now: Silvia Gmür Reto Gmür Architekten, Basel; www.gmuerarch.ch;
	for Klinikum 1 Ost (East),
	in collaboration with Kurt Nussbaumer, Toffol + Berger, Suter + Suter (all in Basel)
Client:	Canton Basel-Stadt, Department of civil services and environment,
	Planning department, Basel
Dates:	project planning and construction 1989–2003

KLINIKUM 1, CANTONAL HOSPITAL RENOVATION

Spitalstrasse 21, 4056 Basel | Tram 11, Bus 30 33 36 38: Frauenspital

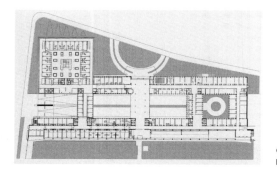

Ground-floor plan with new annex
by Gmür / Vacchini (top left)

Basel's university hospital was fully renovated over the course of fourteen years. Silvia Gmür and Livio Vacchini were the signatory architects of a consortium of architects. Hermann Baur, the architect of the original building, completed in 1945, placed particular emphasis on the human scale. Respecting this philosophy, the architects have nevertheless thoroughly modernized the building. The massive complex is 180 metres long, with two wings (three storeys and nine storeys high). Thanks to sliding fire doors, the unbroken interior lines of the building can be fully experienced. Beauty in form and material was paramount in all the upgrades (sanitary and electrical installations, signage, transportation, furnishings). The architects added the new women's clinic (project 10) to the west wing.

Entrance atrium

The nine-storey main building

Architect:	Gmür / Vacchini, Basel
	Now: Silvia Gmür Reto Gmür Architekten, Basel; www.gmuerarch.ch
Client:	Kantonsspital Basel, Basel
	Canton Basel-Stadt, Department of civil services and environment,
	Planning department, Basel
Dates:	project planning 1994–1999, construction 2000–2003

WOMEN'S CLINIC WITH OPERATING THEATRES

Spitalstrasse 21, 4031 Basel | Tram 11, Bus 30 33 36 38: Frauenspital

Waiting area in the corridor next to facade

Although Gmür / Vacchini added the new Women's Clinic of the university to the structure designed by Hermann Baur (project 9), the cube with the simple glass facade has the presence of a detached building. The architects attached a square with a side length of 40 metres and three storeys to the west wing of the historic ensemble, organizing the comprehensive spatial programme around two courtyards and restoring the ideal, rectangular geometry of the ensemble on the Schanzenstrasse elevation. The facade, composed of filigree concrete rods and floor-high glass panels, transforms the interior spaces (in combination with the light falling into the building from the courtyards) into patient- and staff-friendly environments. The furnishings, prototypes designed by the architects, the high-quality exposed concrete and a colour palette ranging from lime-green to yellow and blue (especially in the flooring) correspond to the high requirements for hygiene, and also reflect a design approach that is a harmonious blend of skilful execution and aesthetic-psychological perception.

Elevation seen from the intersection of
Schanzenstrasse/Spitalstrasse

Ground plan with courtyards

Architect:	Herzog & de Meuron, Basel; www. herzogdemeuron.com
	Project management Mathis S. Tinner
Client:	Canton Basel-Stadt, Department of civil services and environment,
	Planning department, Basel
Dates:	project planning 1995, construction 1997–1999

ROSSETTI BUILDING, CANTONAL HOSPITAL

Spitalstrasse 26, 4056 Basel I Tram 11: Johanniterbrücke I Bus 30 33 36 38 603 604: Frauenspital

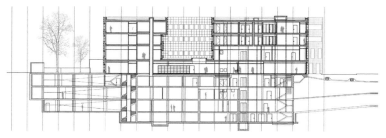

Longitudinal section

On a 7000-square-metre property surrounded by historic buildings from the last 270 years, Herzog & de Meuron erected the new Institute for Hospital Pharmaceutics. The four-storey building rises from an underground structure that dates back to the 1960s. The basic dimensions of the plan were thus predetermined. The facade design – glazing with a screen-printed pattern of bottle-green dots – was inspired by glass objects in the city's pharmaceutical museum. This has resulted in a 1500-square-metre glass sculpture on the edge of the city's downtown. At the main entrance, a section of the glass has been replaced by an ivy-covered honeycomb wall.

Facade on courtyard side

Facade on Spitalstrasse

Architect:	LOST Architekten, Basel; www.lost-architekten.ch
Client:	Ackermannshof AG, Basel
Dates:	invited competition 2009, construction 2010–2011

REMODELLING AND RENOVATION OF THE "ACKERMANNSHOF"

St. Johanns-Vorstadt 19–21, 4056 Basel | Tram 11, Bus 30: Johanniterbrücke

Ground floor layout with the "path space" leading from the street (bottom left) to the old "Setzerei" (top right).

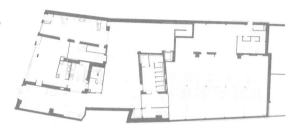

An 800-year-old ensemble of buildings was restored, renovated, and remodelled by LOST Architekten and the historical preservation authority. The earliest written source relating to the site (1325, death of the owner, Heinrich Ackermann) is reflected in the name "Ackermannshof" (the oldest cellar section dates to around 1230). The last phase of construction (1669/70) resulted in the height of the courtyard entrance being raised (by a Rococo drawing room), a shared facade, and the installation of a Rococo staircase. Between 1750 and 1950, industrial buildings were added on the courtyard side and at different times housed a textile factory and a printing business. From 1997 onwards a number of the spaces were converted into studios, a theatre, and restaurants. Careful and sensitive demolition conducted by the architects returned a readable form to the courtyard. An S-shaped "path space" now leads from the street entrance and provides access to all the buildings. The "Setzerei" (1872), the old typesetting building, was equipped with large windows looking onto the courtyard and an open stairway. The ground floor was remodelled on the street side to house a restaurant and bar. Medieval wall and ceiling paintings discovered during the remodelling process were restored.

Courtyard view of the buildings on
St. Johanns-Vorstadt with lighted passage.

The new stairway of
the old "Setzerei".

Courtyard facade of the old
"Setzerei" with large windows.

Architect:	Nussbaumer Trüssel Architekten und Gestalter, Basel; www.nussbaumertruessel.ch
	Associate Daniel Hammans
Client:	Canton Basel-Stadt, building authority, Basel
Dates:	competition 2001, construction 2003–2004

DESIGNING THE RHINE PROMENADE UNDERNEATH THE MITTLERE BRÜCKE

Unterer Rheinweg / Oberer Rheinweg, 4057/4058 Basel | Tram 1 6 8 14 15 17, Bus 34: Rheingasse

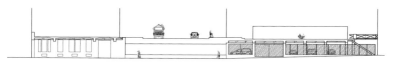

East-west section

The Mittlere Brücke, a granite bridge erected in 1905 (first bridge structure in 1225) is 192 metres long and 18.8 metres wide. Six of the seven arches span the river, while the domed vault of the last arch on the right bank arcs over the Rhine promenade below. The terraces on both sides of the bridgehead extend the arched tunnel into an underpass of a total length of 70 metres. Lack of light, multiple uses and leaks in the ceiling rendered this popular underpass into an inhospitable locale for a long time. Nussbaumer Trüssel Architects have redesigned this situation. The nine ceiling slabs beneath the terrace structure were clad in polyester resin panels tinted in a blue green and backlit. With the bridge arch bisecting these fields, at night the ceiling is transformed into two minimal art fields of light that cover a total area of 448 square metres. Underneath the arch, the stone curb of the sidewalk was replaced by a light strip. This serves to illuminate the arch and link the light fields. The minimal intervention increases safety for users (pedestrians, cyclists, and motorists) and renders heterogeneous structures experiential as a cohesive unit. A glass strip that was inserted at the interface to the terrace on the downriver side also makes it visually perceptible at bridge level.

In daytime, the Rhine is reflected in the ceiling sections on Obere Rheinweg.

The ceiling sections at night and the light strips in the sidewalk looking upstream along the Rhine

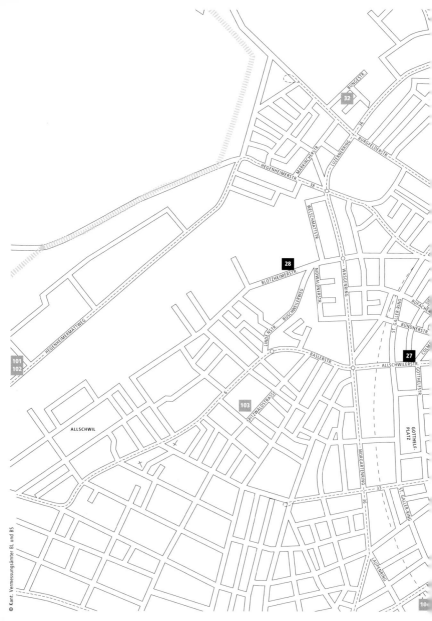

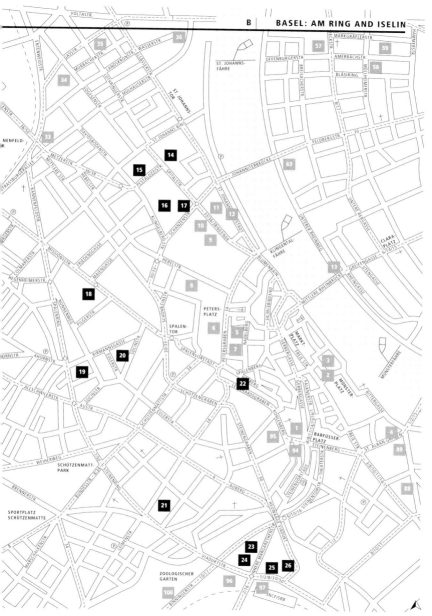

Architect:	Diener & Diener Architekten, Basel; www.dienerdiener.ch
Client:	Canton Basel-Stadt, Department of civil services and environment,
	Planning department, Basel
Dates:	construction 1992–1996

VOGESEN SCHOOL

St. Johanns-Ring 17 / Spitalstrasse, 4056 Basel | Tram 11: St. Johanns-Tor |
Bus 30 33 36 38 603 604: Frauenspital

Standard floor plan, second to fourth floor

The first phase of the Vogesen School construction by Diener & Diener was completed in 1994, the second phase in 1996. Increased student enrolment and school reforms led to higher standards for the school facilities in Basel from the 1980s onwards. In 1994, Diener & Diener's project was the first new school building to be constructed in the city in twenty years. The elegant four-storey tiered-concrete building accommodates a total of forty classrooms, a gym, and extensive ancillary facilities. The entranceway, as well as the entire access area, are finished in Onsernone granite from the Ticino Mountains. The facade is composed of green-tinted poured concrete slabs. The classrooms, with windows reaching almost from floor to ceiling, have an inviting atmosphere.

East-west section

Facade on courtyard side

Classroom on second floor

Architect:	Fierz & Baader, Basel
	Now: Fierz Architekten, Basel; www.fierzarchitekten.ch and
	Baader Architekten, Basel; www.baader.ch
Client:	Canton Basel-Stadt, Department of civil services and environment,
	Planning department, Basel
Dates:	competition 1989, construction 1993 –1996

INSTITUTE OF ANATOMY, UNIVERSITY OF BASEL

Pestalozzistrasse 20, 4056 Basel | Bus 30 33 36 38 603 604: Frauenspital | Bus 36 38: Metzerstrasse |
Tram 11: St. Johanns-Tor

Section of lecture and dissection
hall (left), of Anatomical Museum
(centre), and facade of historic
building (right).

The Institute of Anatomy at the University of Basel has been extensively transformed, renovated, and enlarged by a new addition. Architects Peter Fierz and Stefan Baader placed an asymmetric cube next to the Art Nouveau building from 1921, lowered the new lecture hall (and the dissection facility above it) into the ground, and created new rooms for the Anatomical Museum. The former lecture hall was converted into a library and a photo studio. Exposed concrete, granite, and oak and beech parquet flooring demonstrate the high quality of the materials used in the construction. To create a column-free open space for the new lecture hall, the architects laid a massive brace across the cube, whose square plan was modified into a diamond shape. This project is a prime example of successful dialogue between the old and the new.

The asymmetric cube of the lecture
and dissection hall

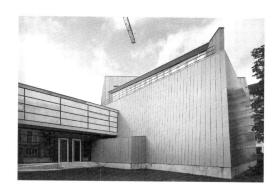

The dissection hall

Architect:	Andrea Roost Architekt, Bern; www.aroost.ch
	Associates Andreas Kaufmann and Heiri Tannenberger
Client:	Canton Basel-Stadt, Department of civil services and environment,
	Planning department, Basel
Dates:	graduate study commission 1987/1988, construction 1996–2000

BIO-PHARMAZENTRUM OF THE UNIVERSITY

Klingelbergstrasse 50–70, 4056 Basel | Bus 36 38: Metzerstrasse | Bus 30 33: Frauenspital

Ground floor

The facade of the new Pharmazentrum on Klingelbergstrasse is covered in a square grid of exposed concrete rods. This ideal geometry and the nine-storey height have redefined the streetscape: the structure is a self-assured focal point for all neighbouring buildings. The labyrinthine entrance hall, reaching from the ground floor to the third floor, is the core element of the building. The foyer is executed in expertly handled exposed concrete and finished in granite. With columns, stairs, galleries, and landings, the design has resulted in a space that opens up sightlines in all directions and from all perspectives, reminiscent of Piranesi's fantastical etchings.

Facade on Klingelbergstrasse

Three-storey-high entrance atrium

Architect:	Stump & Schibli Architekten BSA, Basel; www.stumpschibliarch.ch
	Construction management: Proplaning AG, Basel
	Landscape architect: Berchtold Lenzin, Liestal
Client:	Canton Basel-Stadt Department of building and transport, town planning and
	architecture, Building department, Basel, and Basel-Landschaft building
	and environment authority, Building department, Liestal
Dates:	two-stage competition 2004, project planning 2004–2006, construction 2007–2010

UNIVERSITY PAEDIATRIC HOSPITAL OF BASEL (UKBB)

Spitalstrasse 33, 4056 Basel | Bus 30 33 36 31/38 603 604 607: Kinderspital UKBB

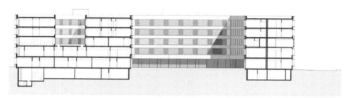

West-east section of courtyard.

The University Paediatric Hospital of Basel (UKBB) was constructed by the architects Stump & Schibli at the intersection of Schanzenstrasse and Spitalstrasse. The building measures 100×85×20 m (length, width, height / 116 000 m³), and is built on a U-shaped ground plan around an atrium. The facade of the five-storey clinic is lent rhythm by ribbon windows and coated glass. Windows facing the streets are double-layered. The colour of the glazing depends on the angle of view and varies between green, yellow, and red, projecting an identity in keeping with a clinic for children. The precision with which this appearance of playfulness, friendliness, and lightness is created extends to the spatial design (comfortable, child-friendly facilities / high-tech medical care) of the entire complex (26 000 m²): access areas (reception area, cafeteria, stairways, and corridors), medical treatment areas (emergency, polyclinic, therapies, surgery, IPS, and radiology), and areas used by staff and patients (physician and care areas, research, and administration). Patients' rooms (100 beds) look out onto the greenery of the interior courtyard. Eight open balconies provide play and recreation areas and overlap with atriums on the fourth and fifth levels.

Ground plan of ground floor.

Entrance hall on Spitalstrasse.

Projecting facade on
Schanzenstrasse.

Architect:	Urs Gramelsbacher Architekt, Basel; www.gramelsbacher.ch
Client:	Protestant Baptist Congregation, Basel
Dates:	construction 1993–1995

RESIDENTIAL BUILDING WITH MEETING HALL

Missionsstrasse 37, 4055 Basel | Tram 3: Pilgerstrasse | Tram 1: Hegenheimerstrasse

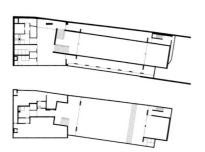

Floor plan of meeting hall (below)
and mezzanine

Facade on Missionsstrasse

For the Baptist congregation in Basel, Urs Gramelsbacher designed a residential building with a meeting hall. On the narrow and angled lot, the low-lying volume of the hall abuts the four-storey residential unit. The floor plans are based on a 6×36 metre grid that creates harmonious proportions in the rooms and on the facade. The prayer hall lies on the same level as an underground car park would and is structured like a basilica. Light falls into the space through a skylight and a light well, which is positioned much like an apse. The hall – designed for a capacity of 200 people – has an understated and serene atmosphere. There are no overt sacred symbols, merely an abstract cross composed of four window squares at the far end.

Entrance area of residential building

Architect:	Atelier Gemeinschaft (Michael Alder, Hanspeter Müller, Roland Naegelin), Basel
	Now: Atelier Gemeinschaft (Hanspeter Müller, Roland Naegelin), Basel
Client:	Basel Association for the Mentally Handicapped, Basel
Dates:	project planning 1995/1996, construction 1997

HOME FOR THE MENTALLY HANDICAPPED

Birmannsgasse 37, 4055 Basel | Tram 1: Birmannsgasse | Tram 3, Bus 30 33: Spalentor

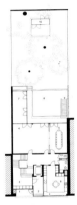

Ground floor

Facade on Birmannsgasse

On Birmannsgasse the architects' cooperative designed a building for the Association for the Mentally Handicapped. This five-storey building is a bright, friendly, and attractive structure, unusual for an institutional building. The materials are especially beautiful: the facades are characterized by finely formed exposed concrete and large glazed surfaces framed in oak. The communal and dining areas on the raised ground floor have light-coloured French limestone floors. The window sills and counters in both kitchens are made of sanded and polished granite. The furnishings, designed by the architects in collaboration with two specialty design shops, are equally elegant. The panoramic view from the fifth-floor patio is a visual treat.

Facade overlooking garden

Architect:	Brogli & Müller Architekten, Basel; www.broglimueller.ch
	Associates Rosmarie Schwarz and Adrian Weber
Client:	Gesellschaft für das Gute und Gemeinnützige (GGG), Basel;
	Willi + Carola Zollikofer Foundation, Basel
Dates:	competition 1987/1988, construction 1988–1991

LINDENHOF NURSING HOME

Socinstrasse 30/Eulerstrasse, 4051 Basel | Tram 3, Bus 30 33: Spalentor | Tram 1 6, Bus 50: Brausebad

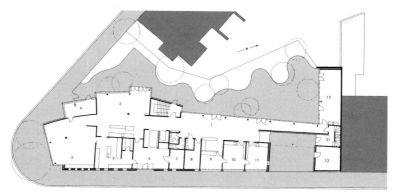

Ground floor

On the periphery of the downtown core, architects Esther Brogli and Daniel Müller built a home for twenty-seven seniors. The linear structure, with rhythmically arranged windows, follows the contour of the street on one side of the acute-angled lot composed of trapezoids and triangles. On the courtyard side, balconies, ribbons of windows on the ground floor, and the moderate height – a mere three storeys – emphasize the human scale of this architecture, as does Samuel Eigenheer's landscape design. The former Lindenhof Nursing Home, which used to occupy this site, was nondescript and went largely unnoticed. The new building has retained the name but is far more expressive, introducing an urban accent to this residential neighbourhood.

Facade on Euler- and Socinstrasse

Architect:	Alioth Langlotz Stalder Buol, Basel
	Now: Langlotz Architekten, Basel; www.langlotzarchitekten.ch,
	Stalder & Buol Architekten, Zurich; www.stalderbuol.ch
	with Diener & Diener Architekten, Basel; www.dienerdiener.ch
Client:	Holbeinhof Foundation, Basel
Dates:	construction 2000–2002

"HOLBEINHOF" SENIORS RESIDENCE AND NURSING HOME

Leimenstrasse 67, 4051 Basel | Tram 6, Bus 33 34: Schützenmattstrasse | Tram 1 8: Zoo Bachletten

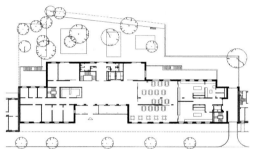

Ground floor

When the Leimenstrasse was constructed around 1870, it was designed as a suburban boulevard with rows of two- and three-storey homes. With its five storeys, the Holbein-hof seniors residence and nursing home, planned and constructed by the architects Alioth Langlotz Stalder Buol in collaboration with Diener & Diener, is a symbol of the urbanization of the now inner-city location. The home for 111 seniors is a Jewish-Christian pilot project that is unique in Switzerland. The ground floor contains the reception area, living-, dining- and other communal spaces, with the openness and generosity of an intimate hotel setting. The clever layout of the building form creates a piazza in the exterior space and provides the interior with a varied and interesting floor plan. Twelve planted squares in front of the facade bearing the names of the months in Yiddish and German declare the interfaith philosophy of the project.

Facade on Leimenstrasse

Stairwell with skylight

Architect:	Vischer Architekten + Planer, Basel; www.vischer.ch
	Project management Lukas Stutz, Silvio Martignoni
Client:	Foundation for the Basel Music Academy, Basel
Dates:	planning 2006–2008, construction 2008–2009

VERA OERI LIBRARY / BASEL MUSIC ACADEMY

Leonhardsgraben 40, 4051 Basel | Tram 3: Musik-Akademie

Entrance pavilion (left back) with reading
room on the recessed ground floor.

In 1954 the "Allgemeine Musikschule" (founded 1867) merged with the Conservatorium (founded 1905) and the Schola Cantorum Basiliensis (founded 1933) to form the Basel Music Academy, which joined the University of Applied Sciences and Arts North-western Switzerland (FHNW) in 2008. Since 1903 the institute has been located on Leonhard-strasse, where an academy campus has emerged between Leonhardsgraben, Auf der Lyss, and Steinengraben. On the western side of this campus Vischer Architekten built a library (for 150 000, Switzerland's largest music collection). The main entrance, which is made of exposed concrete, is located in a pavilion that can be accessed via a passage from Leonhardsgraben 40. The main building is a three-storey cube (26.6×16.5 m) recessed into the ground and houses the loans section, a reading room, offices, and special media rooms. The structure's panoramic windows (on the northern side) and skylight (on the southern side) flood the interior with light. The repository is located on the two lower floors (sheet music, reference works, old media, CDs, LPs, and DVDs) and is accessed via a single-flight, cascade staircase 13 metres long. Natural light provided by a skylight in the garden. The library is named in honour of Vera Oeri-Hoffmann, a patron of the academy for many years, whose foundation financed the building.

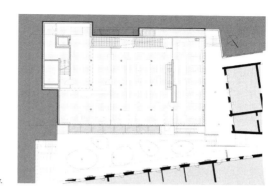

Ground plan of first lower floor.

Cascade stairway with
skylight in the ceiling.

Architect:	Wilfrid and Katharina Steib, Basel
Client:	Canton Basel-Stadt, Department of civil services and environment,
	Planning department, Basel
Dates:	construction 1991–1995

PUBLIC PROSECUTOR'S OFFICE AND MUNICIPAL JAIL

Binningerstrasse 21/Innere Margarethenstrasse 18, 4054 Basel | Tram 1 2 8 16: Markthalle |
Tram 6 10 16 17: Heuwaage

Corridor between public prosecutor's office (right) and municipal jail (left)

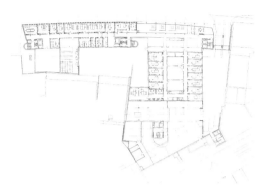

Ground floor

Facade on Binningerstrasse

The new building for the public prosecutor's office and the municipal jail stands on a challenging site: between the streets that surround the property, the terrain drops by as much as the equivalence of three storeys. The shape of the lot is composed of two rectangles, one trapezoid, and several triangles. On this property the architects erected a building with a total of 26 000 square metres in floor space. The structure is divided into two sections, which correspond to its separate functions as prosecutor's office and jail. The former is housed in the section at the bottom of the property, while the jail section is integrated into the hillside. An elegant, convex curved facade of more than 100 metres in length is one of the outstanding architectural features of this building.

Architect:	Richard Meier & Partners, New York; www.richardmeier.com
	Project management Bernhard Karpf
Client:	Credit Suisse, Zurich
Dates:	project planning 1990–1993, construction 1995–1998

EUREGIO OFFICE BUILDING

Viaduktstrasse 40–44, 4051 Basel | Tram 1 2 8 16: Markthalle | Tram 6 10 16 17: Heuwaage

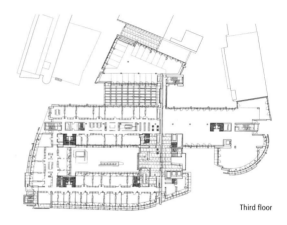

Third floor

Richard Meier's first building in Switzerland is clad in white aluminium sheeting. The eleven-storey structure (five storeys on the south-facing Viaduktstrasse and eleven on the west-facing Binningerstrasse) has a total floor space of over 35 000 square metres. The white of the walls and the grey of the granite floor combine to create a professional and harmonious atmosphere in the office spaces. The location of the building is noteworthy. Diagonally across from Meier's new building lies a residential development from 1915 in traditional "fin de siècle" style. On the valley side, the new building is neighbour to a structure from 1934 in the International Style, while the UBS training and conference centre (project 96) across the street exemplifies the new simplicity in contemporary architecture.

Facade on Viaduktstrasse

Conference area on third floor

Architect:	Blaser Architekten, Basel; www.blaserarchitekten.ch
	Associates Christian W. Blaser, Sonja Proksch, Isabell Palkowitsch, Corina Llamera,
	Martin Egger, Samuel Meier, Mauro Pausa
Client:	Allreal Markthallen AG, Zurich
Dates:	competition 2005, planning 2006–2008, construction 2009–2012

MARKET HALL RESTORATION AND REMODELLING

Steinentorberg / Innere Margarethenstrasse / Viaduktstrasse, 4051 Basel | Tram 1 2 8 16: Markthalle

The pillared hall on the lower
level is now linked with the domed hall
via an atrium and escalators.

Built in 1929 on the valley slope above the River Birsig, the Market Hall was a wholesale outlet until 2004. Since then the 9000 m² area with its domed roof and perimeter buildings along three streets has remained unused. In 2005 Blaser Architekten won a competition to renovate and remodel the area. Their approach emphasized the preservation of the structure while also opening it up. The thin-walled, 28-metre-high dome spanning 60 metres (3000 m²) was painstakingly restored and renovated. The historic building, the dome of which was only outrivaled by the Centennial Hall in Breslau (1913, 65 m) and the Market Hall in Leipzig (1929, 75 m), was largely restored to its original condition. On the lower level, a 4.7-metre-high and 5700 m² pillared hall with floor-to-ceiling glass walls was converted into shops and linked with the domed hall by an atrium with escalators. A glass portal provides access to and from the valley slope (Steinentorberg). On the eastern side, the building is linked to the inner city by a 27-metre-long (and 6.8-metre-wide) cascading staircase. Demolition on Viaduktstrasse restored the historical situation of the main entrance (Steinentorberg). In the case of the perimeter buildings the roofs were renovated and the shop areas modernized.

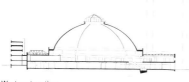

West-east section.

Ground plan of the dome with
main entrance on Viaduktstrasse (centre below)
and peripheral buildings.

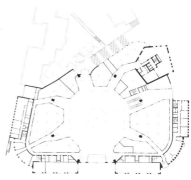

The round hall with its 28-meter-high dome.

Architect:	Diener & Diener Architekten, Basel; www.dienerdiener.ch
Client:	Allreal, Generalunternehmungen AG, Zurich
Dates:	planning and construction 2007–2012

TOWER BLOCK AT THE MARKET HALL

Steinentorberg 18, 4051 Basel | Tram 1 2 8 16: Markthalle

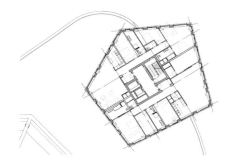

Ground plan of residential levels.

On the valley slope of the Market Hall plot, Diener & Diener built a new tower block 50 metres high with a volume of 27 180 m³. The design was conceived as supplementing and gently overhanging the hall's striking dome (project 25). The tower comprises twelve residential levels, two commercial levels (entry halls on the ground and first upper levels) and parking space (two underground levels). The ground plan forms an irregular pentagon (with sides 15 to 20 metres long), which functions as a variation on the octagon of the dome and is connected to the hall it encloses by a walkway on the first upper level. The forty-six apartments are between 70 and 100 m² (eleven have 2.5 rooms, thirty-three have 3.5 rooms) and between 170 and 190 m² (one has 4.5 rooms, one has 5.5 rooms). The load-bearing elements comprise a concrete core (containing a staircase and two lifts) and steel supports in the facade. This design allows for an orientation of the floor plans to the large windows and panoramas of the inner city. The floors are made of smoked oak (tongue-and-groove wooden flooring) and anthracite-coloured stoneware (wet rooms). The entrance halls and lift forecourts have stone-grey cement floors. The facade of the tower block is completely clad in raw glass panels that give off a greenish shimmer.

Panoramic view through a large window.

The 50-meter tower block on Steinentorberg.

Architect:	Herzog & de Meuron, Basel; www.herzogdemeuron.com
	Project management Annette Gigon
Client:	Horat Generalunternehmung AG, Basel
Dates:	competition 1985, construction 1987–1988

RESIDENTIAL AND OFFICE BUILDING

Allschwilerstrasse 90 / Sierenzerstrasse / Colmarerstrasse, 4055 Basel | Tram 6: Allschwilerplatz |
Bus 36: Morgartenring

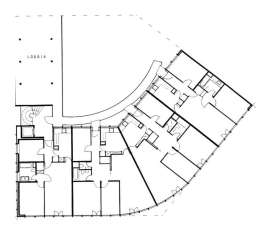

Second to fifth floor

The first large building designed by Herzog & de Meuron to be built in Basel is located
on Allschwilerstrasse. The rectangular lot is slightly curved along its length. The main
facade follows this curve, as does the facade that overlooks the courtyard. Access
balconies lead to eight 3.5-room and twelve 4.5-room apartments on all five upper
floors. The ground floor features generous windows and is predominantly reserved for
retail use. The pretinted concrete slabs of the facade point to a characteristic element
in later projects by this creative architectural team: the sculptural external skin.

Facade on Allschwiler- and
Colmarerstrasse

Access balconies on courtyard facade

Architect:	Zinkernagel Architekten, Basel
Client:	Canton Basel-Stadt, Department of civil services and environment,
	Planning department, Basel
Dates:	project planning 1993, construction 1994–1995

WASGENRING SCHOOLHOUSE EXPANSION

Blotzheimerstrasse 82, 4055 Basel | Bus 36: Buschweilerweg | Bus 38: Thomaskirche | Tram 6: Lindenplatz

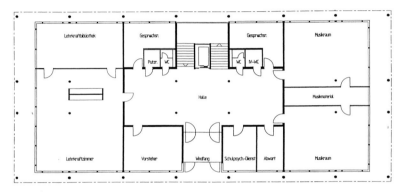

Ground floor

The large school complex on Wasgenring dates from 1951. It was recently expanded with a new addition designed by Peter Zinkernagel. Bruno and Fritz Haller's original concept for the multi-stream elementary school was an ensemble of free-standing pavilions, which were completed in two building phases: 1951–1955 and 1958–1962. Zinkernagel chose to pick up on the established pattern by placing a slender slab along the north-south axis. He successfully combines New Building aesthetics with contemporary building technology and a 1990s philosophy of education by means of large glass surfaces, simple floor plans, and a green-tinted glazed facade between the ribbons of windows. The artist Renate Buser was commissioned to etch the glazing on the east side.

The new school building (left) with
its predecessors from 1962

Site plan

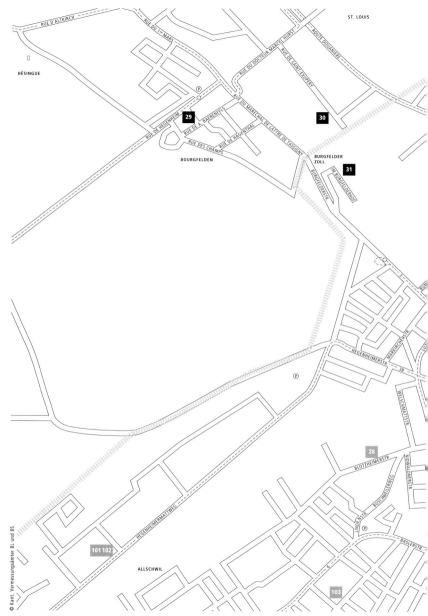

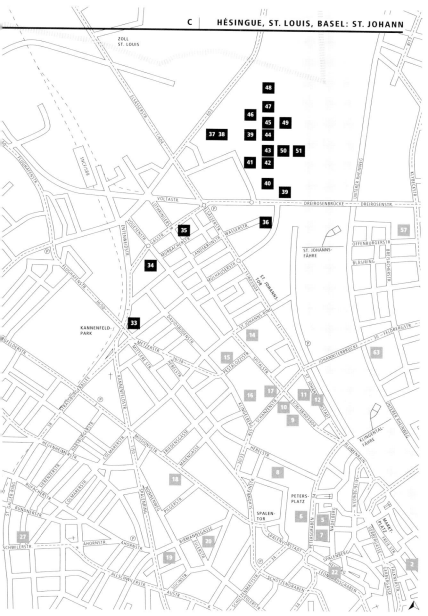

Architect:	Daniel Stefani & Bernard Wendling, St. Louis
Client:	Municipality of St. Louis, City Hall, St. Louis
Dates:	construction 1992–1993

KINDERGARTEN AND CLUB HOUSE

rue Anne de Gohr / rue de A. Baerenfels, F-68300 St. Louis | Bus 601 602: Bourgfelden Centre |
Tram 3: Burgfelden Grenze | Bus 50: Friedrich Miescher-Strasse

The gym bathed in light

The kindergarten against the back-
drop of 1960s housing blocks

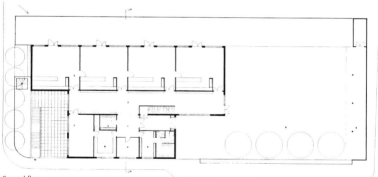

Ground floor

Daniel Stefani & Bernard Wendling built a kindergarten in Burgfelden, a central neighbourhood in St. Louis dominated by large housing blocks from the 1960s and a busy
traffic artery. A roofed arbor, with slate slabs mounted to the inside, protects against
noise and emissions. It also serves as a drawing surface for the children. In the large
gym, the architects arranged the windows in a zigzag pattern. This results in optimal
natural light and creates an invigorating, even euphoric, feeling in the interior space.
The basement level contains meeting rooms for local clubs and associations. This kindergarten building is topped by a roof terrace.

Architect:	Herzog & de Meuron, Basel; www.herzogdemeuron.com
	Project management Eric Diserens
Client:	Bürgerspital Basel, Basel
Dates:	project planning 1989/1990, construction 1992–1993

PFAFFENHOLZ SPORTS COMPLEX

5, rue de St. Exupéry, F-68300 St. Louis | Tram 3: Burgfelden Grenze |
Bus 50: Friedrich Miescher-Strasse

Site plan: the Swiss border is to
the right

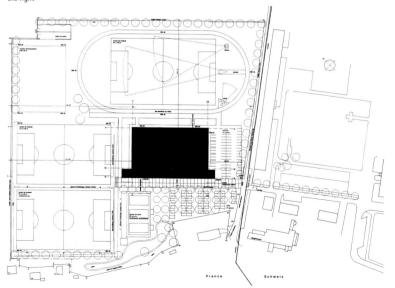

The sculptural glass skin

Exposed concrete surfaces define
the interior

Herzog & de Meuron's sports complex, featuring a large indoor gym and an open-air
oval track, is located at the border between Switzerland and France. Since the service
ducts are hidden behind the glass facade, the interior is exposed concrete. The entrance
area is dominated by a clear-span roof that runs the full length of the building and is
its most monumental feature. The interior and exterior are linked by light: daylight
creates bright channels throughout and vistas that stretch up to 70 metres. The gym
floor was sunk into the ground, allowing for an external shape that is almost flat. The
facade glazing, tinted dark with screen prints, gives the building an almost sacred air.
The Centre for Paraplegics (project 31) is located on the other side of the border fence.

Architect:	Planning: Herzog & de Meuron, Basel: www.herzogdemeuron.com
	Construction planning: Proplaning AG, Basel
Client:	REHAB Basel AG, Basel
Dates:	competition 1998, project planning 1998–1999, construction 1999–2002

REHAB – SWISS CENTRE FOR PARAPLEGICS, BASEL

Im Burgfelderhof 40, 4025 Basel | Tram 3: Burgfelden Grenze | Bus 50: Friedrich Miescher-Strasse

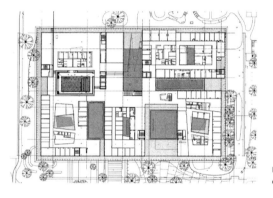

Floor plan of 2nd storey with main
entrance (top centre)

On the border between Switzerland and France, the new Swiss Centre for Paraplegics
(REHAB) has been realized on a lot of 144 by 86 metres. In this building created for the
rehabilitation of paraplegics and brain-injured, Herzog & de Meuron emphasise the
horizontal. The structure comes alive through the use of concrete, timber and glass,
making it very bright in the interior and giving it a very light appearance on the exterior.
The architects have structured the facade as well as the network of paths connecting
the 9500 m² floor area in the building with five large and four small courtyards. As a
result there is an abundance of light channels and numerous rooms with aquatic plants
(designed by landscape architect August Künzel). In this western city, the new building
appears like the pavilion of an East-Asian temple or palace ensemble. The Pfaffenholz
sports complex (project 30) is located on the other side of the border fence.

South-west elevation

View from the foyer on the upper
storey into two courtyards

Architect:	Michael Alder, Associate Hanspeter Müller, Basel
	Now: Atelier Gemeinschaft (Hanspeter Müller, Roland Naegelin), Basel
Client:	Basel civil servants pension fund, Basel
	Neue Wohnbaugenossenschaft, Basel
Dates:	competition 1989, construction 1991–1993

LUZERNERRING HOUSING DEVELOPMENT

Bungestrasse 10–28, 4055 Basel | Tram 3, Bus 36: Luzernerring

Verandahs and balconies
on Bungestrasse

Standard floor plan, second to fifth floor

Michael Alder created a "residential street" between Luzernerring and Bungestrasse with six units and ninety-eight apartments. The spacious apartments are intended predominantly for large families. Nearly every room opens onto outside spaces such as balconies or enclosed porches, which are generously proportioned for a social housing project at 20 square metres. The ground-floor units have small gardens. Each of the six buildings includes a common room complete with kitchen on the ground floor, a covered bicycle stand in the courtyard, a sandbox, and a fruit tree. Residents also enjoy access to the 200-metre-long rooftop covered in gravel, yet another outdoor space.

Architect:	Voellmy Schmidlin Architektur, Zurich; www.voellmyschmidlin.com
Client:	Galerie von Bartha, Basel
Dates:	planning and construction 2008–2009

CONVERSION OF AN AUTO SHOP INTO AN ART GALLERY

Kannenfeldplatz 6 / Entenweidstrasse 8+10, 4056 Basel | Tram 1, Bus 31/38 36 50: Kannenfeldplatz | S-Bahn S1: Bahnhof St. Johann

View through the exhibition hall to the entrance on Kannenfeldplatz.

Around 1945, an auto shop with shed roofs was built onto the back of two residential buildings (both from around 1905) in Entenweidstrasse. The construction in the back courtyard was extended to Kannenfeldplatz, where a filling station was installed. From 1970 onwards the ground and basement levels on Entenweidstrasse were also taken over by the company running the garage complex. In 2005 the garage (though not of the filling station) was shut down. On this 1400 m² site, Voellmy Schmidlin implanted an art gallery, including a loading dock, an office, storerooms, a kitchen, and a studio apartment. The petrol pumps on Kannenfeldplatz (the main entrance) recall the site's former use. A hard concrete floor was installed in the 640 m² hall with its 51-metre front wall. The varying room heights (3.2 to 3.7 metres) across the sloping space, which broadens from 10 metres at the entrance to 23.5 metres at the back, are offset by a ramp. In the areas lit by skylights in the seven shed roofs, the hall reaches a height of 6.4 metres. The entrance area (170 m²) was equipped with a square skylight. The walls and ceilings were plastered and painted. The dark colour used for the facade serves to visually connect the structural elements on Entenweidstrasse and Kannenfeldplatz as an ensemble.

Ground plan with entrances on Entenweidstrasse
(bottom) and Kannenfeldplatz (far right).

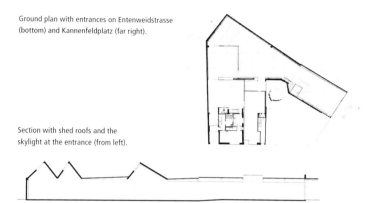

Section with shed roofs and the
skylight at the entrance (from left).

Entrance with petrol pumps

Architect:	Erny, Gramelsbacher, Schneider, Basel
	Now: Erny & Schneider, Basel; www.ernyschneider.ch and
	Urs Gramelsbacher Architekt, Basel; www.gramelsbacher.ch
Client:	Christoph Merian Foundation, Basel; Helvetia Patria Insurance Group, Basel
Dates:	competition 1987, construction 1989–1991

IM DAVIDSBODEN HOUSING DEVELOPMENT

Gasstrasse / Vogesenstrasse, 4056 Basel | Tram 1: Gasstrasse / Bahnhof St. Johann |
Tram 11, Bus 603 604: Voltaplatz

Site plan

With 155 apartments, three kindergartens, clinics, studios, workshops, a library, and an auditorium, the Davidsboden development has changed the face of St. Johann, a neighbourhood characterized by a blend of residential and industrial use. Close to the French border, it creates an urban marker as Diener & Diener's Hammer 1 development (project 60) did ten years earlier. The four- to six-storey structure meets the requirements of social life in an urban setting by providing wintergardens and creating a child-friendly environment. Glazed projections create rhythmical divisions in the large volume. Fair-face brickwork and linear forms emphasize friendliness and serenity. The covered walkways fulfil two roles: circulation paths within the development and outdoor meeting places.

Facade on Gasstrasse

View into a courtyard

Architect:	Urs Gramelsbacher, Basel; www.gramelsbacher.ch
Client:	Marc Stutzer, Basel
Dates:	project planning and construction 2006–2011

WOODEN TOWN HOUSE

Lothringerstrasse 98a, 4056 Basel | Tram 1 21: Bahnhof St. Johann | Tram 1 11 21, Bus 603, 604: Voltaplatz

Ground plan of first upper level.

Section from the street (left) to the garden side with terraced upper levels.

The wooden town house was built by Urs Gramelsbacher on a 100 m² plot between the buildings at number 96 (built 1904 on the eastern side) and number 98 (1907 on the western side). The new building has the same ridge height (20 metres) as its neighbouring structures, is 7 metres wide, and contains 149 m² of living area spread over five levels (with flooring made of 30-centimetre-wide Oregon pine). The upper floors have balconies and / or terraces, which cover a total area of 56 m². A single-run staircase (in Oregon pine) was built against the firewall to the building at no. 96. On the side adjacent to the building at number 98, with which the new building shares energy and water connections, the entrance, the windows of the kitchens on each floor, and the projecting hipped roof had to be integrated in a way that met building regulations. An elegant solution was found in the form of a path from the street, a separate wooden door in the facade, and – on the garden side – an open space at ground level as well as a 1.2-metre-wide light gap. Terracing the new building resulted in two kitchens in the old building gaining additional balconies. Large sliding windows open the building to the terraces and the garden. The street facade features large picture windows set in a slatted frame wall (spruce / pine), lending the structure a minimalistic austerity.

Facade on Lothringerstrasse.

Architect:	Miller & Maranta, Basel; www.millermaranta.ch
Client:	Canton Basel-Stadt, Department of civil services and environment,
	Planning department, Basel
Dates:	competition 1996, construction 1999–2000

VOLTA SCHOOL

Wasserstrasse 40 / Mülhauserstrasse, 4056 Basel | Tram 1: Novartis Campus |
Tram 11: Mülhauserstrasse | Bus 603 604: Voltaplatz

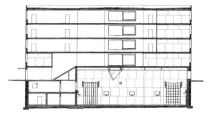

East-west section

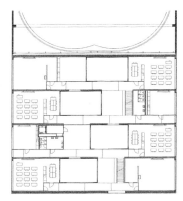

Third to fifth floor

Facade on Wasserstrasse

When a fuel depot located on busy Mülhauserstrasse was demolished, space became available for a new building for the Volta School. Architects Quintus Miller and Paola Maranta moved the entrance to Wasserstrasse, an adjoining dead-end street, to make it safer for children. Four open light wells are central features of the structure. They are distributed across four of the five storeys in a zigzag formation. Large glazed surfaces open up views into all the interiors, the rooms that are not located along the outside of the building are thus provided with sufficient daylight. An atrium for school recess is located just inside the main entrance. All common rooms are located above the two-storey gym.

Architect:	Vittorio Magnago Lampugnani, Studio di Architettura, Milan; www.gta.arch.ethz.ch
	Associates Jörg Schwarzburg, Fiona Scherkamp, Fleur Moscatelli,
	Markus Mangler, Francesco Porsia
	Landscaping Peter Walker, PWP Landscape Architecture,
	Berkeley, CA; www.pwpla.com
Client:	Novartis International AG, Basel
Dates:	design 2000–2001, construction since 2003

NOVARTIS CAMPUS MASTER PLAN

Between Voltastrasse / Elsässerstrasse / the Swiss-French border / Schiffmühlestrasse,
and the Rhine | Tram 1 21: Novartis-Campus | Tram 11, Bus 603 604: Voltaplatz

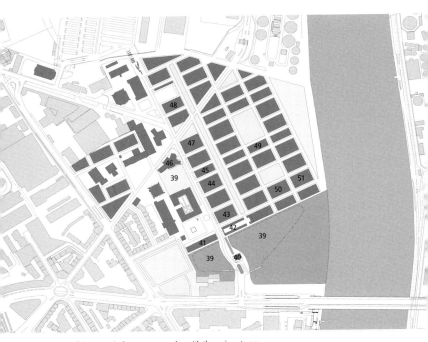

Ground plan of the Novartis Campus master plan with the main entrance
on Voltastrasse and the central axis formed by Fabrikstrasse.

The master plan for the headquarters of Novartis AG (est. 1996) on the left bank of the Rhine (on the site of the "Chemischen Fabrik, Kern & Sandoz" founded in 1886) was created by Vittorio Magnago Lampugnani and his Studio di Architettura. The task was to transform a 115-year-old industrial site, where expansion had been characterized for a long time by pragmatism without strategy, into an urban environment that cohesively combined research and development, administration and interaction, knowledge exchange, functionality, and an atmosphere amenable to productive entrepreneurial endeavours in the life science sector.

The result is the plan for the Novartis Campus. The 600-metre-long Fabrikstrasse on which the main administration building was erected in 1939 was and remains the central axis of the site, which covers more than 200 000 m². Building lots up to 60 metres deep and ranging from 18 to 36 metres in width were created within an orthogonal network of roads (between 10 and 20 metres wide) and squares. With the exception of a few high-rise structures, all buildings are to reach a maximum height of 23 metres, with the structures on the north-eastern edge of Fabrikstrasse also incorporating a 4×6-metre arcade. Wherever possible, existing structures are being preserved and integrated. The master plan envisions the creation of a total of around 350 000 m² of new gross floor area.

The basic structure of the master plan is based on urban models from Mesopotamia and Ancient Greek Asia Minor (Milet) as well as the orthogonal ground plan of the late Celtic settlement that once stood on this site (circa 150–80 BCE, the first city-like forerunner of present-day Basel). With its right-angled network of roads, the master plan also establishes a reference to the Roman settlement of Augusta Raurica, the construction of which commenced in 15 BCE on the Rhine around eleven kilometres from the campus, and the design of which is thought to have been influenced by Vitruvius's De architectura libri decem (circa 33–22 BCE) (see p. 23).

The birch forest (Betula utilis Doorenbos) in the "Forum 1"
administration building courtyard.

Working in consultation with the architects, Peter Walker (PWP Landscape Architecture)
created a landscaping design for the entrance area on Voltastrasse, a treed area parallel to the arcade side of Fabrikstrasse and treed areas on its branch and parallel roads,
as well as a design for the underpass at the end of Fabrikstrasse (leading to the parking
area in France). The inner courtyard of the main administration building (designed by
Brodbeck & Bohny in 1939) and the Forum square (between the Forum 1 main administration building and the new Forum 3 building, project 41) were also designed by PWP.

The design of the Forum 1 interior courtyard (49.5×24.5 m) features an ornamental pool (26×2.6 m) with semicircular ends, which lies along the longitudinal axis and is planted on both sides with birches (Betula utilis Doorenbos). A ring of hornbeams (Carpinus betulus) and boxwood hedges (Buxus sempervirens) invests the path running diagonally through the courtyard with rhythm. On the Forum square a 40×40-metre block of 35 pin oaks (Quercus palustris) encloses a 12×12-metre fountain. This minimalistic forest is bordered by White Moncini slabs. A double row of tulip trees (Liriodendron tulipifera) has been planted on Fabrikstrasse opposite the arcade. All the branch and parallel roads (which bear names such as Asklepios, Banting, Unna, and Virchow) are being planted with columnar tree types: hornbeam (Carpinus betula 'Frans Fontaine'), cypress oak (Quercus robur 'Fastigiata Koster') and sweet gum (Liqudambar styraciflua).

The Forum square with its block of
pin oaks (Quercus palustris).

Architect:	Vogt Landschaftsarchitekten, Zurich; www.vogt-la.ch
	Project management Lars Ruge
Client:	Novartis International AG, Basel
Dates:	construction 2004 and 2009

THE CAMPUS PARK AND THE GREEN

Fabrikstrasse, 4056 Basel I Tram 1 21: Novartis-Campus I Tram 11, Bus 603 604: Voltaplatz

The Campus Park was successively constructed by Vogt Landschaftsarchitekten based on a design that reflects the geological character of the landscape along the Rhine between its source and Basel. The park begins on the flat terrain either side of Fabrik-strasse (25 000 m² of which lie on top of the underground garage, project 40), which has been planted with a forest of 15 000 trees made up of oak, beech, cherry, birch, maple, lime (with trunks up to 60 cm thick) and hornbeam. These are interspersed by ferns, grasses, bulbs, and shrubs. North-east of the forest, on the gently terraced area leading down to the Rhine, the structure of the landscape changes to a mixture of thickly vegetated embankments, meadows, and trees (apple, quince, Tartarian maple, and wintersweet).

The Green is situated next to the glass structure designed by Frank Gehry and above the auditorium (project 46). Here the landscape architects have used an 8000 m² area to create an image of a karst landscape and its characteristic features. Between a lime-stone terrace and an open lawn area (with moveable seating) crookedly growing bushes and trees are interspersed with shrubs, grasses, mosses, and ferns. The Green is traversed by 90-centimetre-wide bands of limestone and vegetation.

In the Campus Park forest.

Ground plan and planting plan of the Campus Park with Voltastrasse (bottom) and the Rhine (right).

Architect:	Marco Serra, Architect Novartis, Basel
Client:	Novartis Pharma AG, Basel
Dates:	design 2002, project planning 2003, construction 2005–2007

RECEPTION PAVILION AND UNDERGROUND CAR PARK

Fabrikstrasse 2, 4056 Basel | Tram 1 21: Novartis-Campus | Tram 11, Bus 603 604: Voltaplatz

The glass pavilion with its cantilevered roof.

On Fabrikstrasse in the midst of the Campus Park stands the reception pavilion built by Marco Serra over an underground car park. The glass building (ground plan 17.6×12.4 m), whose elegant roof (21.6×18.5 m) protrudes on all sides, is the firm's main entrance, and is in use 24 hours a day. The interior is a rectangular space measuring 195 m² enclosed by 4-metre-high glass elements. These support a roof made of glass-fibre-reinforced plastic that varies between 7 and 62 centimetres in thickness. Its form suggests a detached wing tip with three narrow edges and one lens-shaped side. Above the reception desk, textile ribbons have been woven into the ceiling construction and are illuminated by interior up lights to create an evenly lit surface. The pavilion floor is paved with Giallo Siena (semi marble). The garage is 300 metres wide and 100 metres deep, and offers 1200 parking spaces (150 for guests) over two levels (21 000 m²). It forms the interface between motorized transport and the surface constructions and pedestrian areas on the firm's premises. Inside the garage, a combination of exposed concrete and so-called light walls (floor-to-ceiling stainless steel panels lit by LED strips) create a sense of security and comfort.

View from the pavilion in the Campus Park "forest".

Architects:	General planning Diener & Diener Architekten, Basel; www.dienerdiener.ch,
	in collaboration with Helmut Federle and Gerold Wiederin, Basel
Client:	Novartis Pharma AG, Basel
Termine:	study commission 2002, construction 2003–2005

NOVARTIS CAMPUS: FORUM 3

Forum 3, 4056 Basel | Tram 1 21: Novartis-Campus | Tram 11, Bus 603 604: Voltaplatz

The spiral staircase made of walnut starts on the second floor.

Diener & Diener Architects erected a five-storey office and conference building – the first new structure of the Novartis Campus. The 83.5-metre-long, 22.5-metre-wide and 22-metre-tall structure abuts on Fabrikstrasse and forms the "entrance gate" together with the Sanaa building on the opposite side (project 42). On the side overlooking the Forum square, the upper storeys are cantilevered by eight metres across the entire length of the building, creating an elegant entrance canopy for the "Pharma-Development" and a rain-sheltered zone for the square. The ground floor (1200 m²) is six metres high and features black, Greek marble flooring (Chios Brown). The four office floors above (6000 m²) are linked by oval-shaped stairs in walnut. Vogt Landschaftsarchitekten have created a full-height atrium with a tropical garden (1400 trees, shrubs and groundcover plants from Thailand) on the southwest side. For the design of the facade of the upper floors, the architects collaborated with artist Helmut Federle and the architect Gerold Wiederin. Mounted on a filigree load-bearing structure, 1200 glass panels (in 21 colours and 25 different formats) are assembled into a structural image, which – were it un-folded – would cover an area of 18×12 metres.

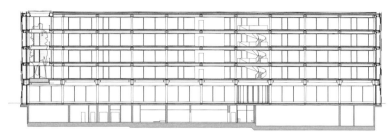

West-east section with tropical
atrium (extreme left)

Facade facing the city

Architect:	SANAA / Kazuyo Sejima + Ryue Nishizawa, Tokyo; www.sanaa.co.jp
	project management: Nicole Kerstin Berganski; Associates: Takayuki Hasegawa,
	Isao Shinohara, Yuka Nishiyama
Client:	Novartis Pharma AG, Basel
Dates:	construction 2005–2006

NOVARTIS CAMPUS: FABRIKSTRASSE 4

Fabrikstrasse 4, 4056 Basel | Tram 1 21: Novartis-Campus | Tram 11, Bus 603 604: Voltaplatz

The thin ceilings are clearly visible in
the glass facade.

Second floor plan with a connecting
building bridge

Elevation of facade with
arcade space on Fabrikstrasse
(extreme left)

Longitudinal section of atrium with
connecting building bridges

The six-storey office building by Sanaa Architekten is the second "gate structure" of the Novartis campus and lies next to Diener Federle Wiederin's house (project 41) on the right side of Fabrikstrasse. Both buildings feature the same facade axis and are nearly identical in proportion. Ground and second floor of the Sanaa building are slightly recessed from the street. This marks the area set aside for an arcade (4 m wide / 6 m high) that will create a "covered" promenade along the entire length of the north-east side of the street in the near future. The building is constructed like a ship. With dimensions of 84×22.5×22 metres (length / width / height), the structure is hollowed out by an atrium at the centre (72,1×11,3 metres; length / width). The "external walls" vary in width from 5.6 to 6.3 metres and are glazed from floor to ceiling on the facade and courtyard sides. The thin poured concrete ceilings were realized by means of incorporating "displacement bodies" (balloons) in the formwork. Despite the considerable floor area (4300 m²), the building has an ethereal air. On the second, third and fifth floor one single-storey and two two-storey bridges span the interior courtyard (see also project 129).

Architect:	Märkli Architekt, Zurich; www.maerkliarchitekt.ch
	Project management Caspar Oswald
Client:	Novartis Pharma AG, Basel
Dates:	competition 2002–2003, construction 2004–2006

NOVARTIS CAMPUS: FABRIKSTRASSE 6
(VISITOR CENTRE)

Fabrikstrasse 6, 4056 Basel I Tram 1 21: Novartis-Campus I Tram 11, Bus 603 604: Voltaplatz

Facade on Fabrikstrasse
with the display by Jenny Holzer

Architect Peter Märkli created the Visitor Centre of the pharmaceutical company parallel to the Sanaa building (project 42). The new building incorporates the arcade of the
master plan. The 13 200 square metres of floor space are spread across a comb-like,
elongated rectangular building surrounding a central atrium that links all six floors.
Reception, a lounge and a cafeteria / restaurant are housed on the ground floor of the
visitor centre beneath a coffered yew ceiling. Two sets of stairs lead down to the presentation and conference hall in the basement with 124 lobby chairs by Charles and Ray
Eames. The second floor accommodates guest offices. The floors above house internal
offices and communication areas complemented by private rooms for meetings and
focused work as well as open-plan kitchens. On the ground floor and the large stairs,
the floors are seamlessly covered in white Carrara marble; the floors on the upper
storeys are covered in dark blue fitted carpeting. The marble stairs and the atrium are
equipped with a raw cast aluminium balustrade with olive wood handrails (design by
Alex Herter); the aluminium facade panels are champagne-hued. On the street elevation,
a display by Jenny Holzer is exhibited in the upper half of the arcade.

Ground floor plan with arcade
on Fabrikstrasse (left) and atrium
(centre)

View into atrium

Cross-section with seminar
and conference hall (bottom) and
atrium above

Architect:	Yoshio Taniguchi, Austin, Texas; www.taniguchi-arch.com
Client:	Novartis International AG, Basel
Dates:	design and project planning 2005–2009, construction 2007–2009, opening 2010

LABORATORY BUILDING WITH SHOP AND PHARMACY

Fabrikstrasse 10, 4056 Basel | Tram 1 21: Novartis-Campus | Tram 11, Bus 603 604: Voltaplatz

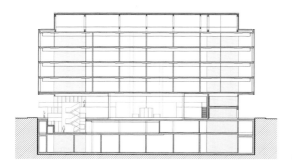

Axial section

The laboratory building by Yoshio Taniguchi continues the arcade facade on Fabrikstrasse (projects 42, 43), with a recessed ground floor. The arcade is covered by projecting upper levels without external supports and runs around the four building cores on which the "floating box" is suspended at a height of 23.5 metres. This cube (50 metres long, 17 metres high) houses laboratories and offices on four levels, is clad with glass panels (each 4×1.7 m) and by day exhibits an opaque, white surface, lending this large building (14 916 m² of floor area) the appearance of a minimalistic pavilion. On the ground floor, the four building cores (each of which is independent in terms of access systems, statics, and utilities connections) are clad in matt black granite and frame the space housing the exhibition laboratory, where visitors can gain an insight into the research being carried out in the facility. The laboratory, which is encased in a square "cabinet" with walls made of 6-metre-high glass panels, is traversed by a 42-metre-long mezzanine bridge, which leads to a pharmacy. A stairway running parallel to Fabrikstrasse leads into a courtyard recessed 3.8 metres into the ground, where a shop is located. The mezzanine bridge and courtyard are linked by a stairway featuring Cresciano granite, which can also be found on the walls and floors at ground level and in the outside area.

The "floating box" spanning
four floors on Fabrikstrasse.

Exhibition laboratory on the ground floor (top)
with the recessed courtyard on Fabrikstrasse and
the shop (bottom).

Architect:	Vittorio Magnago Lampugnani, Studio di Architettura, Milan;
	www.gta.arch.ethz.ch
	Project management Jens Bohm
	Rooftop garden August Künzel AG, Basel
Client:	Novartis International AG, Basel
Dates:	design and project planning 2005, construction 2006–2008

ADMINISTRATIVE BUILDING WITH DODICI RESTAURANT

Fabrikstrasse 12, 4056 Basel | Tram 1 21: Novartis-Campus | Tram 11, Bus 603 604: Voltaplatz

Second upper level ground plan.

The building at Fabrikstrasse 12 is the Novartis Campus's prototypical structure. Featuring an arcade formed by a five-section colonnade, the building was designed by Vittorio Magnago Lampugnani in accordance with the master plan. With an eaves height of 22.46 metres, the office block and restaurant contains 4794 m² of floor space. The facade of the reinforced concrete construction is made of Carrara marble, recalling the architecture of the "Novecento milanese". The entrances to the lobby and the bar and restaurant are located under the arcade. The upper levels and the rooftop, can be accessed via lifts from the lobby (which features marble floors, walnut wood walls, and Murano lamps). A walnut wood staircase (32.4 metres long, 2.4 metres wide) leads to the fourth upper level. This monumental flight of stairs (supports and balustrades in walnut) ascends through an open space extending to the top of the building, creating a residential atmosphere. The offices are naturally ventilated and the windows can be opened individually. The desks and lamps are prototypical designs, while the tables and seating furniture combine elements drawn from the history of design. A garden is located on the roof. The restaurant and bar area (seating 300) extends the length of the ground floor (50 metres) and has a square cross-section of 6×6 m metres.

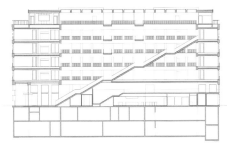

Axial section with 32.4-meter-long
cascade staircase.

The facade on Fabrikstrasse with
its five-section colonnade.

The floor-to-roof space
for the stairs.

Architect:	Gehry Partners, Los Angeles; www.foga.com
	Construction planning and management Arcoplan / Nissen Wentzlaff
	Architekten, Basel
Client:	Novartis International AG, Basel
Dates:	project and construction 2003–2009

ADMINISTRATIVE BUILDING WITH AUDITORIUM WSJ-242 / WSJ-243

Fabrikstrasse 15, 4056 Basel I Tram 1 21: Novartis-Campus I Tram 11, Bus 603 604: Voltaplatz

The sculptural glass building by night.
Right: The Green (project 39).

Frank O. Gehry's sculptural glass architecture represents an exception on the new campus. His above-ground administrative building (with offices, seminar rooms, and a reading room) is connected with an underground auditorium (which can be subdivided and offers total seating for 630) located beneath the garden on the Green (project 39). The building has a total floor area of 19 500 m² and a volume of 92 000 m³. The glass building, which includes a restaurant on the ground floor (seating 250), bulges and branches over five levels, reaching a height of 35 metres (on Fabrikstrasse). The steel construction (embedded in a concrete bearing structure) forms five volumes, which flow into one another and are clad in polygonal discs. None of the software-generated "biomorphic" discs (between 0.3 and 6.2 m², with an average size of 2.5 m²) on the external surface (just under 8000 m²) is identical. Access is provided by outside staircases (two), enclosed stairways (two), lifts (two) and a flight of stairs leading into the auditorium. The ground and underground levels have floors made of limestone and red oak; the upper levels are carpeted. The building's atrium allows daylight to reach into the foyer of the auditorium.

The 630-seat underground auditorium.

The five-storey glass building is up to 35 meters high.

Architect:	Architekt Krischanitz, Vienna; www.krischanitz.at
	in collaboration with Birgit Frank (2004–2007), Berlin
Client:	Novartis Pharma International AG, Basel
Dates:	project and construction 2003–2008

LABORATORY BUILDING WSJ-152 WITH AUDITORIUM AND KNOWLEDGE CENTRE

Fabrikstrasse 16, 4056 Basel | Tram 1 21: Novartis-Campus | Tram 11, Bus 603 604: Voltaplatz

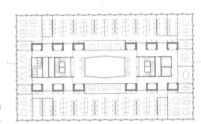

Ground plan of upper levels 3 and 4
with the atrium in the middle.

The laboratory building by Krischanitz and Frank with its enclosed interior courtyard is visually dominated by a central atrium (6×12×29 m) equipped with illuminated balustrades; 55 metres long and 34.5 metres wide, the building has two access cores (stairs/lifts), a total area of 15 517 m² and a narrow concrete arcade. Steel supports in the shaft and on the exterior (over all levels), which are linked on the roof, allow for an airy interior and a flexible ground plan. The 6-metre-high ground floor is glazed from floor to ceiling around the courtyard and contains three meeting rooms, an auditorium (with seating for 95) and five monumental chandeliers (5.5×3.6 m) positioned along each of its long sides. The biology and chemistry laboratories on the four upper levels are arranged in series with a shared structure and abut the folded, clear-glass facade. The natural rubber floors in the research areas change colour (blue, yellow, red, and green) with each floor. The 119 laboratory work modules are prototypes. The ground floor, stairways, and corridors have terrazzo/Jura limestone floors. The atrium and entrance foyer feature works by the artists Gilbert Bretterbauer and Sigmar Polke.

The building with its folded glass facade
seen from the west.

Enfilade against the facade
in the upper-level labs.

Architect:	David Chipperfield Architects, Berlin; www.davidchipperfield.co.uk
	Project management Alexander Schwarz
Client:	Novartis Pharma International AG, Basel
Dates:	design and project planning 2006–2007, construction 2007–2010

LABORATORY BUILDING WITH CHA CHA RESTAURANT

Fabrikstrasse 22, 4056 Basel | Tram 1 21: Novartis-Campus | Tram 11, Bus 603 604: Voltaplatz

Axial section

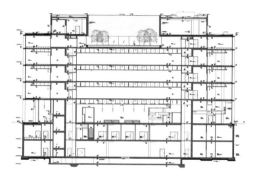

Eastern facade

The "Molecular" garden in the atrium on the fourth upper level.

David Chipperfield's building for the Novartis Institutes for BioMedical Research (NIBR) boasts an ingenious supporting structure. The five-storey building is supported by a 23.9-metre-high facade with concrete supports and two service cores (stairs, lifts, sanitation, building services). The open atrium on the fourth upper and attic levels is supported by a structure that begins on the ground floor. Five concrete supports, from which the interior ceilings are suspended, stretch 27 metres between the two cores. This design has allowed the architect to create areas free of pillars around the facade, where the laboratories (upper levels 1–3) and the offices with the atrium (upper level 4) form luminous suites (total floor area 4412.3 m²). In the north-west of the building, an open stairway made of biomorphic, honey-yellow, fibreglass segments (designed by Ross Lovegrove) is suspended between all the upper levels. The sedate facade, which is composed of concrete elements and floor-to-ceiling windows (6 metres high behind the arcade) is atmospherically extended into the interior through the use of light-coloured wood (ash), light-coloured walls, and floors in grey (laboratories) or natural stone (Xango Red in the foyer and restaurant). There are plans to extend the building with an L-shaped structure and an internal courtyard open to Fabrikstrasse.

Architect:	Maki and Associates, Tokyo; www.maki-and-associates.co.jp
Client:	Novartis Pharma AG, Basel
Dates:	design and planning 2006–2007, construction 2007–2009

OFFICE BUILDING

Square 3, 4056 Basel | Tram 1 21: Novartis-Campus | Tram 11, Bus 603 604: Voltaplatz

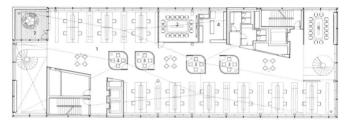

Ground plan of upper levels 2 and 4.

The pristine white facade of the office building by Fumihiko Maki features both transparent and opaque elements (glass fibre system) and a geometrical clarity that lends it a character that is both sacral and welcoming; 18 metres wide, 22 metres high, and 51.4 metres long, the building has a floor area of 6150 m² (five upper and two basement levels) and 160 work stations. The building is accessed via two diagonally positioned cores (each with stairs and a lift), between which thin concrete ceilings (using aerated concrete, see project 42) rest on steel girders (facade) and supports. The open, hall-like floors are punctuated by glass cabins (private rooms), sloped by aluminium panels in the ceilings along the diagonal axis (2.8–3.3 metres, centre / facade), and in combination with the ribbon windows appear light and intimate. The elegant spiral staircases (with 1.2-metre-wide steps) located in double-height atriums behind panoramic windows allow for easy movement on foot through the radially symmetric levels (upper levels 1–4). The top floors of the atriums include outside terraces with larch wood flooring. The use of maple and teak creates a reference to the future park in the Large Square that is to be built to the north-west.

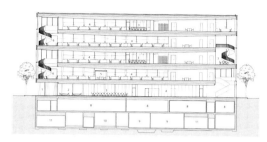

Axial section

Western facade

Architect:	Eduardo Souto de Moura, Porto
Client:	Novartis International AG, Basel
Dates:	design 2005, construction 2007–2011

LABORATORY BUILDING / TECHNICAL RESEARCH AND DEVELOPMENT (TRD)

Physic Garden 3, 4056 Basel | Tram 1 21: Novartis-Campus | Tram 11, Bus 603 604: Voltaplatz

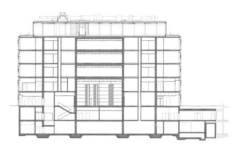

Axial section

Located adjacent to the Physic Garden modelled by Thorbjörn Andersson on a seventeenth-century pharmaceutical garden, Eduardo Souto de Moura's Technical Research and Development (TRD) building points to both the present and the future. The building accords with the dimensions specified in the master plan (51 metres long, 31 metres wide, 28 metres high) and houses four special laboratories for pharmacological research. Access is provided by a central entrance foyer extending over two storeys (ground and first upper level, 9.6 metres high). The foyer is separated from two conference rooms by large glass walls and is lent solidity by three cruciform brick steles by the artist Pedro Cabrita Reis. The laboratories face the southwest, are arranged on top of one another, and are separated by corridors from the offices (which offer a view of the Physic Garden from the third storey upwards). The structure is supported by the access cores (reinforced concrete) and the facade supports, allowing the interior to be free of pillars. On the inside, the two-part glass facade provides an insulating climatic boundary and includes a second layer of light green and grey, vertically moveable elements (sub panels). The facade, the colours of which provide a reference to the pharmaceutical garden, allows for sunlight to be completely blocked out when required (video conferences, screen presentations). Next to the building is an annex designed by Álvaro Siza (project 51).

Ground plan of ground floor

Northern facade detail

Western facade at the
Physic Garden.

Architect:	Álvaro Siza da Vieira, Porto; www.alvarosizavieira.com
Client:	Novartis International AG, Basel
Dates:	Design 2005, construction 2008–2010

LABORATORY BUILDING

Virchow 6 3, 4056 Basel | Tram 1 21: Novartis-Campus | Tram 11, Bus 603 604: Voltaplatz

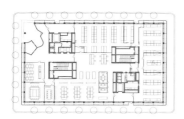

Ground floor

Axial section

The laboratory building by Álvaro Siza is connected with the building by Eduardo Souto de Moura (project 50) both in terms of use and utilities connections. The architects have cultivated an interplay between their works in Basel, an approach already seen in their work on the light rail system in Porto (1999–2005). Siza's first building in Switzerland, with its north-western corner abutting the Physic Garden and north-eastern facade looking over the Rhine, is elegant in terms of its appearance, discreet in terms of its materials, and virtuoso in the way it is crafted. The building is 51.4 metres long, 31.2 metres wide and 28 metres high. It comprises five upper and two basement levels and its technical facilities are housed on the roof. The four cores in the middle of the reinforced concrete construction and supports in the facade allow for floor plans uninterrupted by pillars. The facade is made of beige-white Estremos marble and features a second layer comprising a steel structure with clear glass (without visible frames) suspended from the roof 90 centimetres from the inner surface. The corner entrance on the Physic Garden features 4.5-metre-high convex and concave glass panels under a mirrored ceiling. The floors on the ground level, laboratories, offices, and conference rooms are surfaced with beige-coloured natural rubber. Internally located bearing elements, fire escapes, balustrades, and sanitary spaces are clad in beige Meleanos limestone (quarried between Porto and Lisbon).

The facade seen from the Physic Garden.

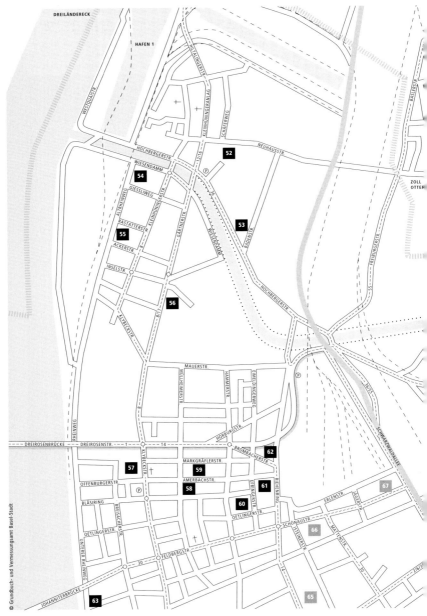

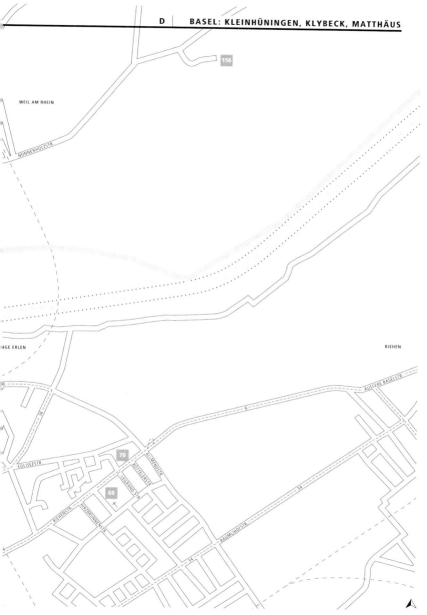

WEIL AM RHEIN

NONNENHOLZSTR

GE ERLEN

RIEHEN

156

AUSSERE BASELSTR

6

EGLISEESTR

70

ALMENDSTR

ROTTLERSTR

LEGRANDSTR

34

69

REHENSTR

HIRZBRUNNENSTR

BAUMLIHOFSTR

14

Architect:	Luca Selva AG Architekten; www.selva-arch.ch
	Project management Roger Braccini; associates Melanie Camenzind,
	Gian-Andrea Serena, Sigrid Vierzigmann
	Landscape architecture August und Margrith Künzel, Basel
Client:	Densa Immobilien AG, Basel
Dates:	competition 2007, planning 2008–2009, construction 2009–2012

DENSA PARK HOUSING DEVELOPMENT

Neuhausstrasse 28–36 and Salmenweg 12–16, 4057 Basel | Tram 8: Kleinhüningen | Bus 36: Stücki

Site plan

On a former industrial site on Neuhausstrasse, Luca Selva Architekten erected two large residential buildings. The building on the northern edge is L-shaped, follows the course of the street (over 54 metres), and includes two wings that enclose an interior courtyard. Building S abuts this courtyard on the north-south axis. Both buildings have six storeys (and 2630 m² of floor area), contain 99 apartments, and share a parking garage (178 parking spaces). The buildings are made of reinforced concrete and their facades have been meticulously clad with Wittmunder clinker bricks. The obtuse and right angles of the floor plans, of which there are thirty-five variations, lend vibrancy to the structure of the thirty 2.5-room (58–68 m² of living area), forty-six 3.5-room (78–91 m²) and twenty-three 4.5-room (85–127 m²) apartments (the attic apartments have up to 177 m²). All the units on the upper levels feature loggias or terraces. The floors are made of Jura limestone (kitchen, bathroom) or parquet. The eight access cores (five stairways with lifts in Building L, three in Building S) feature asphalt plates and oak handrails. Paths through the surrounding area and garden (5414 m²) are bordered by hedge-like vegetation.

Ground plan of upper levels 1 to 4.

Courtyard view from
the southwest.

Visual axis and terrace
of an attic apartment.

Architect:	Diener & Diener Architekten, Basel; www.dienerdiener.ch
	Landscape architecture Vogt Landschaftsarchitekten, Zurich,
	with Fahrni and Breitenfeld Landschaftsarchitekten, Basel
Client:	Tivona Eta AG, Basel and Swiss Prime Site AG, Olten
Dates:	competition 1999, planning 2000–2006, construction 2007–2009

STÜCKI SHOPPING CENTRE WITH HOTEL

Hochbergerstrasse 68 and 70, 4057 Basel | Tram 8: Kleinhüningen | Bus 36: Stücki

Western shopping-centre facade with fire escapes and plant shelves.

View into shopping street.

Ground plan of the
367-metre-long complex
with the shopping centre
(top and middle)
and hotel (bottom right).

The Stücki service centre was built by Diener & Diener between the Deutsche Bahn complex on the border to Switzerland and an avenue running along the shore of the River Wiese, a tributary of the Rhine. The large building (367×110×15 metres, total area 107 589 m²) comprises a two-storey shopping centre (120 shops and 15 food outlets), a six-storey hotel (144 rooms), a car park (824 parking spaces), and a children's playground. The volume is structured by four towers (each 38 metres high), which mark the entrances to the complex and house building services. The white, 367-metre-long facade facing Badenerstrasse visually interacts with the serially planted birches, ash trees, poplars, and willows and the narrow windows on the hotel to create a gigantic, surreal image. The side facing the square on Hochbergerstrasse features panoramic glazing and "plant shelves" (balconies in front of windowless walls covered with ivy, wild vines, and flowering shrubs). The shopping streets are between 6 and 12 metres high and exhibit the profile of a basilica with colonnades (made of black, sanded concrete pillars). Natural light is provided by nineteen light domes. The position of the shops and their lighted showcases has been coordinated with the colonnades.

Western facade elevation

Architect:	Wilfrid and Katharina Steib, Basel
	in collaboration with Bruno Buser & Jakob Zaeslin, Basel
Client:	Basel civil servants pension fund, Basel
Dates:	competition 1980, construction 1983–1986

WIESENGARTEN HOUSING DEVELOPMENT

Wiesendamm / Altrheinweg / Giessliweg, 4057 Basel | Tram 8, Bus 12 16 36: Kleinhüningen

Third to sixth floor

With 168 apartments ranging in size from 1.5 to 5.5 rooms, the Wiesengarten development was the most important project of its kind in the 1980s in the northern section of Basel. Studio and commercial spaces were included, stipulating mixed use from the very beginning. The complex consists of seventeen buildings situated on a tributary of the Rhine (the Wiese), with Kleinhüningen harbour nearby and a short bicycle ride away from a large nature and recreation area (Lange Erlen). The architects varied the building heights and set architectural circle segments against the facade, giving the large volume a pleasing rhythm and structure. The interiors are finished to very high standards.

The housing development seen from the north with the facade overlooking the Wiese River

A residential street on the courtyard side

Architect:	Ackermann & Friedli, Basel
	Now: Ackermann Architekt, Basel; www.ackermann-arch.ch
Client:	Canton Basel-Stadt, Department of civil services and environment,
	Planning department, Basel
Dates:	project development and planning 1994, construction 1995–1996

ACKERMÄTTELI SCHOOL

Rastatterstrasse 32, 4057 Basel | Tram 8: Wiesenplatz, Inselstrasse | Bus 36: Kleinhüningen

Access at ground-floor level

The neighbourhoods in the north and north-west of Basel are residential and industrial districts. Architects Ackermann & Friedli erected a new school in this sector of the city, in the Klybeck neighbourhood. It is situated in a grassy area bordered by trees and separated from the Rhine by a train track and docks. The new Ackermätteli School provides not only a valuable new educational facility for the district, it also improves the urban layout of the area: the L-shaped building frames the heterogeneous residential buildings to the east, creating a cohesive block. The rows of windows in the four-storey building produce a tranquil geometry and transform the grassy area into a small park. The architecture is an important urban marker at this location.

Third and fourth floors

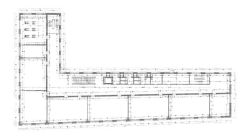

Facade on Altrheinweg

Architect:	Barcelo Baumann Architekten, Basel; www.barcelobaumann.ch
Client:	Erbengemeinschaft Bollag, Nutzer Genossenschaft Bollag-Areal, Basel
Dates:	planning 2007–2008, construction 2008–2009

BOLLAG STUDIO COMPLEX

Gärtnerstrasse 50, 4057 Basel | Tram 8: Wiesenplatz | Bus 36: Stücki

Ground plan of upper level 3.

In the district of Klybeck on Gärtnerstrasse and directly on Wiesenplatz, Jordi Barcelo and Katrin Baumann erected a building for use by artists and firms working in the creative industries (including architecture, film, sound, and graphic design). The Bollag studio complex, which is used as a cooperative, was built to replace a building that was integrated into the site of the Novartis Campus (projects 37–51). The building has six storeys, is 23 metres high, and its cubic form features large windows (upper levels 1–4, 3.3×3 m meters, aluminium on wood and metal frames) in a silver-coloured facade. It contains forty-one studios over an area of 2952 m² comprising single rooms measuring 21 m² (smallest unit) and combined spaces (average area 71 m²). The storeys are 3.4 metres high, include corridors 2.85 metres wide and 27 metres long parallel to the long facades, and are accessed via two stairways as well as a lift for people and goods (basement to upper level 5). The concrete on the walls has been left raw or painted white. The floors are made of hard concrete (sealed in the kitchens and painted with water-resistant paint in the wet rooms). The ground floor contains a meeting room with a kitchen (80 m²), a wood workshop (48 m²) and an exhibition space (68 m²).

A studio flooded with light
by 3.3×3 meter windows.

West-east section

Bollag studio complex on Gärtnerstrasse

Architect:	Morger & Degelo, Basel
	Associates Marianne Kempf, Lukas Egli
	Now: Morger & Dettli, Basel; www.morgerdettli.ch and
	Degelo Architekten, Basel; www.degelo.net
Client:	Canton Basel-Stadt, Department of civil services and environment,
	Planning department, Basel
Dates:	construction 1990–1996

DREIROSEN SCHOOL EXPANSION

Breisacherstrasse 134 / Klybeckstrasse 111–115, 4057 Basel | Tram 1 8 14: Dreirosenbrücke

Facade overlooking Dreirosen Park

On Klybeckstrasse, next to the small park at the Dreirosenbrücke, Morger & Degelo have expanded an existing school and erected a new residential building. On the street side, the residential building relates to the five-storey structure of a Neo-Baroque church by August Hardegger (1902). The architects retained the vertical volume of the original school building designed by K. Leisinger (1906), but have gained an additional floor by decreasing the floor height at each level. A large underground gym beneath the school-yard as well as workshop spaces and studios for art courses are linked to the original structure by a 90-metre-long enclosed colonnade, which also shields the school from the noisy street. There are many large bands of windows. The residential building consists of twenty-nine units ranging from two to four rooms in size.

Courtyard with lit squares from
the underground gym

Site plan: the new buildings are
to top left

Architect:	Morger & Degelo, Basel
	Associate Lukas Egli
	Now: Morger & Dettli, Basel; www.morger-dettli.ch and
	Degelo Architekten, Basel; www.degelo.net
Client:	Canton Basel-Stadt, Department of civil services and environment
	Planning department, Basel
Dates:	competition 1989, project planning and construction 1990–1993

HOUSING CO-OP

Müllheimerstrasse 138/140, 4057 Basel │ Tram 8: Bläsiring │ Bus 30: Hammerstrasse

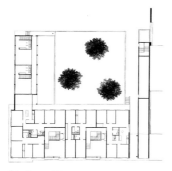

Raised ground floor

The housing co-op on Müllheimerstrasse had a similar impact in north-west Basel as did the nearby Hammer 1 housing development (project 60). The twenty-six four- to five-room apartments are distributed across one raised ground floor and five upper floors. The kindergarten is located on the "base" floor, just below the raised ground floor. Reddish brown panels of cement-bound wood lend a sculptural tone to the structure and enter into a dialogue with the brickwork of the neighbouring buildings, which date back to the late nineteenth century. At the same time, the wraparound balconies and patios on the upper floors established a new typology for residential buildings in the city. Since the "windows" onto these balconies or patios are in fact floor-to-ceiling French doors, the interior of the building is suffused with light.

Elevator shaft and stairwell

Architect:	Degelo Architekten, Basel; www.degelo.net
Client:	abilia wohnen begleiten leben, Basel; www.abilia.ch
Dates:	planning and construction 2006–2010

BONIFACIUS RESIDENTIAL BUILDING

Amerbachstrasse 37, 4057 Basel | Tram 1 8: Dreirosenbrücke

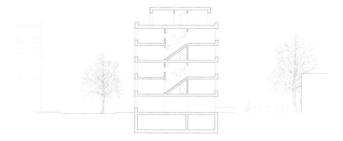

Section from Amerbachstrasse (left). The stairs are used to make levels 2 and 3 as well as 4 and 5 into maisonettes.

On a row plot (455 m²) on Amerbachstrasse, Degelo Architekten built a five-storey residential building for mentally disabled people. Featuring an almost square elevation (17.3 metres high, 16.9 metres wide) and ribbon windows running the width of the facade, the building radiates an atmosphere of harmony and openness towards the street and allows ample light to enter the interior. The structure is supported by a central core that contains stairs and a lift providing access to the pillar-free storeys between the firewalls. This allows for optimal flexibility in terms of floor plans. Four storeys are additionally connected in pairs by stairs to maisonettes. Levels two and four and levels three and five therefore have identical floor plans. The ribbon windows spanning 15.7 metres on the garden and street facades feature wooden frames (2.85 metres long, 1.8 metres wide) and curtains that provide sun protection. The changing colours between floors energize the building's appearance from the street. Both facades are completely clad in anthracite-coloured clinker strips. On the inside as on the outside of the building all materials have been used in their inherent colours in order to deal with heavy use. The plaster on the walls and the wood on the floors are therefore also waxed, and the entrance door is made of brass.

Facade on Amerbachstrasse.

A 15.7 metre ribbon window to the garden.

Architect:	Diener & Diener Architekten, Basel; www.dienerdiener.ch
Client:	Baselland civic servants pension fund, Liestal
Dates:	construction 1978–1981

HAMMER 1 HOUSING DEVELOPMENT

Hammerstrasse / Bläsiring / Efringerstrasse, 4057 Basel | Tram 14: Musical-Theater |
Bus 30: Hammerstrasse

Site plan with new building
(left) and the historic buildings on
Oetlingerstrasse (right)

The apartments, studios, and retail shops created by Diener & Diener in the late 1970s in a small housing development catapulted Basel's contemporary architecture to an international level. The five-storey structure, bordered on three sides by different streets – thereby nearly defining a city block – was designed with six-storey-high projections at two intersections. Square wood-framed windows create tranquil geometrical facades. Most of the apartments have wintergardens on the courtyard side, supported by a bold metal construction. The studio buildings in the courtyard are accessible via covered walkways. The architects treated the facade in an unusually poetic manner by using painted bricks.

Facade and wintergardens on
courtyard side

Architect:	Diener & Diener Architekten, Basel; www.dienerdiener.ch
Client:	Baselland civic servants pension fund, Liestal
Dates:	planning and construction 1980–1985

HAMMER 2 HOUSING DEVELOPMENT

Efringerstrasse / Amerbachstrasse / Riehenring, 4057/58 Basel | Tram 14, Bus 30: Riehenring

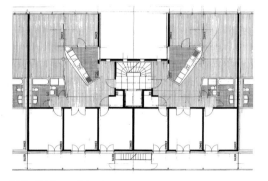

Third to fifth floor on Riehenring

The Matthäus neighbourhood, developed in the last quarter of the nineteenth century as a residential, commercial, and industrial district, shifted decisively towards modernity with the construction of Diener & Diener's Hammer 1 and Hammer 2 housing developments. Another high-impact residential structure was created to the north (project 66), and the new Fair Hall (project 65) is located on the same street (Riehenring). Only a few city blocks separate Hammer 2 from a new residential building (project 58). Diener & Diener divided the facade of the large building into squares. The linear floor plans are generous in size and the building also features large patios and roof gardens. Retail stores and a supermarket help to give the development the feeling of a neighbourhood.

The projection at the corner of
Amerbachstrasse and Riehenring

Architect:	(Efringerstrasse) B. Trinkler + H.R. Engler Architekten, Basel,
	supervision Giovanni Ferrara, (Riehenring)
	Trinkler Engler Ferrara Architekten, Basel, executive partner Giovanni Ferrara
	Now: TrinklerStulaPartner Architekten, Basel; www.trinklerstulapartner.ch
	englerarchitekten, Basel; www.englerarchitekten.ch
	Ferrara Architekten, Basel; www.ferrara-architekten.ch
Client:	(Efringerstrasse) Homeowner consortium Efringerstrasse 96
	(Riehenring) Canton Basel-Stadt, Central office for public real estate transactions
	(ZLV); building authorities, construction and planning authority, Basel
Dates:	(Efringerstrasse) planning and construction 1997–1998
	(Riehenring) competition 2001, planning and construction 2001–2004

RESIDENTIAL AND MULTI-FAMILY BUILDING
WITH KINDERGARTEN, DAYCARE AND SEMI-PUBLIC PARK

Efringerstrasse 96 and Riehenring 199/201, 4057/4058 Basel | Tram 14: Brombacherstrasse
and Musical-Theater

Two buildings for two different clients were created on two parcels and in two construction stages above the northwest ramp to the underground freeway (northbound). Yet these structures constitute an urban renewal and a cohesive unit both with regard to planning and design and material aesthetics. A six-storey house (850 m² floor area) with five loft apartments was erected on Efringerstrasse. The floor plans of the ground floor units (kitchen, dining, bedrooms, bathrooms) and a room running the full width of the building with a concrete floor and ceiling are arranged around the access area (facade centre). Street and rear elevations are fully glazed. The facades of the building on the Riehenring (3000 m² floor area) are similarly transparent. The six-storey structure accommodates sixteen apartments (third to sixth floors), a daycare and a kindergarten (ground floor and second floor). Conceived as a "minenergy" pilot project (photovoltaic installation), the building is nearly self-sufficient. Windows and sliding doors in thickly varnished fir/spruce combined with fair-faced concrete constructions provide the material and aesthetic cohesion between the two buildings. By demolishing an old structure, additional space was created for a nearly 1000-square-metre semi-public park with covered parking between Efringerstrasse and Riehenring.

Floor plan (Efringerstrasse) of 2nd
to 5th floor

Facade on Efringerstrasse

Site plan with new buildings on
Efringerstrasse (top) and Riehenring
(bottom) with sketched in curve of
the underground highway (northern
arterial road)

Facade overlooking the park on Riehenring

Architect:	Wilfrid and Katharina Steib, Basel
Client:	Community of heirs Unterer Rheinweg, Basel
Dates:	competition 1993, construction 1994–1996

RESIDENTIAL BUILDING ON THE WATER'S EDGE

Unterer Rheinweg 48–52, 4057 Basel | Bus 30: Erasmusplatz | Tram 8: Feldbergstrasse

Facade on the Rhine

Wilfrid and Katharina Steib have erected a six-storey building with forty-eight units (3- to 5.5-room apartments and three penthouse units) on grounds formerly occupied by an 1878 villa. In 1910, a large residential building in the Art Nouveau style was erected on the lot adjoining the villa grounds. At the time, the construction considerably increased the density of this central location. The facade of the new building is completely glazed on the sides that overlook the Rhine and the park. All units extend across the full depth of the building (15 m, or 17 m including the projecting balconies) and are extremely bright. The windows, framed in Oregon pine, overlook the Rhine in what is an optimal southern exposure and provide near-perfect noise protection.

Living areas overlooking the river

North-south section

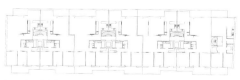

Second to sixth floor

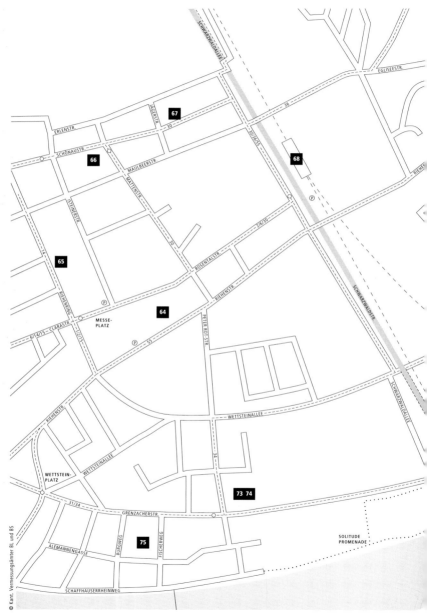

67

68

66

65

64

73 74

75

ERLENSTR.

SCHÖNAUSTR.

MAULBEERSTR.

MATTENSTR.

STEINENSTR.

JÄGERSTR.

ROSENTALSTR.

RIEHENSTR.

PETER ROT-STR.

RIEHENRING

6/14/15 – CLARASTR.

MESSE-PLATZ

WETTSTEINALLEE

RIEHENSTR.

WETTSTEINALLEE

WETTSTEIN-PLATZ

GRENZACHERSTR.

ALEMANNENGASSE

BURGWEG

FISCHERWEG

SCHAFFHAUSERRHEINWEG

SCHWARZWALDALLEE

EGLISEESTR.

RIEHEN

SCHWARZWALDSTR.

SCHWARZWALDALLEE

SOLITUDE PROMENADE

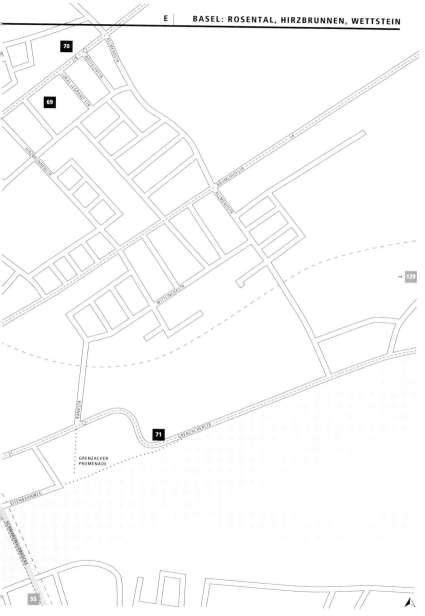

70

69

216

ROTFELBSTR

ALLMENDSTR

LUKAS LEGRAND STR

HIRZBRUNNENSTR

BÄUMLIHOFSTR

ALLMENDSTR

3A

WITTLINGERSTR

→ 129

RANKSTR

31

71

GRENZACHERSTR

GRENZACHER PROMENADE

EISENBAHNWEG

SCHWARZWALDBRÜCKE

55

Architect:	Morger Degelo Marques, Basel / Luzern
	Now: Morger & Dettli, Basel; www.morger-dettli.ch and
	Degelo Architekten, Basel; www.degelo.net
	with Marques AG, Lucerne; www.marques.ch
	Project management: Erich Offermann
	Execution: Manfred Kunz
Client:	Swiss Prime Site AG, represented by Credit Suisse Asset Management
Dates:	competition 1998, project planning 1999–2000, construction 2000–2003

HIGH-RISE FOR BASEL FAIR

Messeplatz, 4021 Basel | Tram 2 6 14 15: Messeplatz | Bus 31 34: Claraplatz

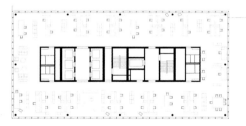

Floor plan

The 105-metre-high building was completed in 2003 and for seven years was Switzerland's tallest building (since 2010, this title has been held by the Prime Tower in Zurich, which measures 126 metres). The architects Morger, Degelo and Marques have housed the thirty-one upper storeys in an unembellished steel-and-glass cube, projecting the third and fourth floors elegantly into the street space to the east. The new tower is connected to Hans Hofmann's cylindrical courtyard building (1953/54) by a 60-metre-long reflecting pool. The wooded Rosental area to the east and the rigorously designed town square of the fair grounds to the south are improved by the glass tower, transformed into a green and urbane site. The high-rise continues the tradition of modern towers, begun by Ludwig Mies van der Rohe (860 Lake Shore Drive Apartments in Chicago, 1948–51 / Seagram Building in New York, together with Philip Johnson, 1954–58).

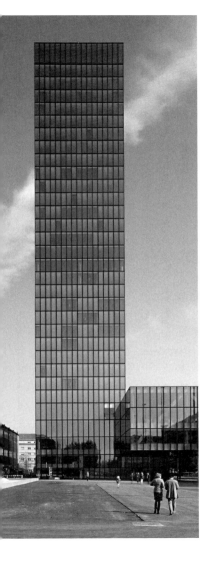

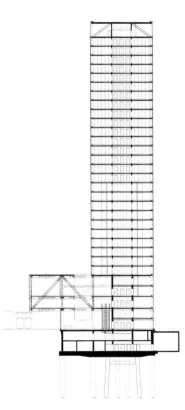

East-west section

Elevation as seen from the Messeplatz

Architect:	theo hotz partner, Zurich; www.theohotz.ch
Client:	Basel Fair, Basel
Dates:	competition 1996, construction 1998–1999

NEW FAIR HALL

Messeplatz 1 / Riehenring / Isteinerstrasse, 4058 Basel | Tram 2 6 14 15: Messeplatz |
Bus 30: Gewerbeschule

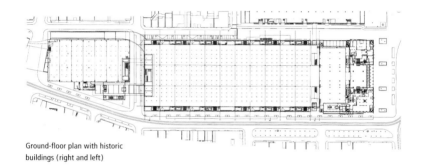

Ground-floor plan with historic
buildings (right and left)

Facade on Riehenring

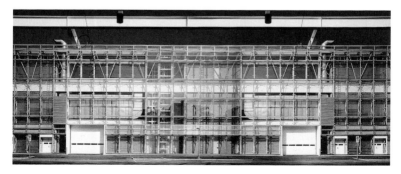

Ground floor of the large hall

Theo Hotz's new Fair Hall is proof that industrial architecture on a large scale (90 m wide, 210 m long, and some 20 m high) can indeed be elegant. The structure may be described as two halls, one on top of the other, creating grand room heights (10 m and 8 m, respectively) and monumental interiors. The architect added a glass and steel structure to the original building (1923–1927, demolished 2010). The new design has been as much a surprise to the exhibitors as it has to the fair visitors. The original building had a closed facade of dark clinker bricks. With its fully glazed end walls, the new building resembles a giant shop window. Since Basel's fairground is located in a residential and commercial district, this architecture – clearly visionary both from a technical and an aesthetic perspective – sets new standards.

Architect:	Diener & Diener Architekten, Basel; www.dienerdiener.ch
	Landscape design: August Künzel
Client:	Baukonsortium Stücki, Basel
Dates:	construction 2000–2002

STUDIO HOMES, APARTMENT BUILDING AND HOTEL

Atelierhäuser Isteinerstrasse 90–96, Dorinth Hotel Schönaustrasse 10 and 31–35, 4058 Basel ∣
Tram 14: Riehenring ∣ Bus 30: Mattenstrasse

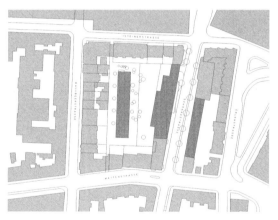

Site plan with the Isteinerstrasse (top)
and the Mattenstrasse (bottom)

For the 11 studio homes on the Isteinerstrasse, Diener & Diener employed the motif of the monumental staircase (here across two storeys) in housing construction (see projects 2, 124). In proximity to the fair, the single-family homes, a five-storey apartment building and a hotel represent new developments arranged with great precision on lots that were formerly dedicated to industrial uses. Linear access and plans, large to oversized fenestration and spatial arrangements set an urban milestone at this location. Together with the two large housing structures to the south (projects 60, 61), the architects have defined the culture of building in this district for thirty years.

The studio homes seen from the east

The continuous staircase in the
studio homes

Architect:	Proplaning Architekten, Basel; www.proplaning.ch
Client:	Basel civic servants pension fund, Basel
Dates:	planning and construction 1997–1999

HOUSING DEVELOPMENT

Schönaustrasse / Erlenstrasse, 4058 Basel | Bus 30: Mattenstrasse |
Tram 2 6, Bus 55: Badischer Bahnhof | Bus 36: Erlenmatt

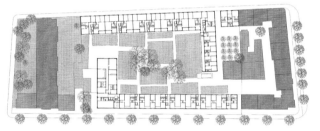

Ground floor

The two L-shaped buildings arranged by Proplaning to frame a 3000-square-metre courtyard have a total facade of 500 metres. The imposing volume is pushed by the two projections into an adjoining courtyard, which is surrounded by late-nineteenth-century buildings. The six-storey blocks contain 163 apartments ranging from 2.5 to 4.5 rooms in size, three workshops, a kindergarten, and a café / restaurant, thereby creating a neighbourhood within the neighbourhood. Fifty percent of the apartments have loggias. The floors are finished in oak or cast stone, and there is the added luxury of floor heating in these units.

Facade overlooking courtyard

Architect:	Fierz Architekten, Basel; www.fierzarchitekten.ch
Client:	Deutsche Bahn AG, Station & Service
Dates:	planning and construction 2001–2008

CONVERSION AND RENOVATION OF THE BADISCHE BAHNHOF (RAILWAY STATION)

Schwarzwaldallee 200, 4058 Basel ┃ Tram 2 6 ┃ Bus 30 36 55: Badischer Bahnhof

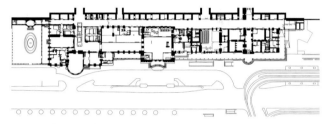

Ground plan of terminal building from 1913 with Schwarzwaldallee (bottom) and ticket hall (centre)

The Badische Bahnhof (railway station) was erected prior to the First World War by Robert Curjel and Karl Moser (1907–1913). The structure is 230 metres long and a treasure of modern architectural history. From 2001 to 2006 it has been renovated and converted in stages by Fierz Architekten. The ensemble composed of platforms, customs areas, waiting rooms, refreshment facilities and the formal "Fürstenbau" structure (erected for the Grand Duchy of Baden) was a permanent construction site throughout the 20th century. The demolition (in 1979/1980) of the 500-metre-long steel-and-glass roof (dating back to 1912), which spanned the tracks, was a stark loss for the substance of the ensemble. "Restoration" (of the dignity and form of the building), "optimization" (of public and administrative areas) and "opening" (restaurant, café, bistro and retail) are the keywords that describe the philosophy of the current intervention. Wherever possible, the original interiors with skylights and furnishings were re-created, damage to stone and wood surfaces was repaired and reconstructed. A glazed office cube was inserted into the middle section and the customs facility was redesigned with a slender and elegant infrastructure. In the 16-metre-high and nearly 700 square metres large ticket hall, the raw fair-faced concrete of the barrel vault was once again exposed.

The fair-faced concrete vaulted
ceiling in the ticket hall

A glazed office structure
as a "house-in-a-house" in
the customs ensemble

Architect:	Christian Dill, Basel; www.dill-architekt.ch
	Associates A. Dalla Favera and R. Brunner
Client:	Canton Basel-Stadt, Department of civil services and environment,
	Planning department, Basel
Dates:	competition 1991/1992, planning and construction 1992–1997

HOUSING AND THERAPY FACILITY

Riehenstrasse 300, 4058 Basel | Tram 2 6: Eglisee

The pavilion-style residential building

For a pilot project at the university's department of psychology, Christian Dill has designed a housing and therapy facility for mentally and physically handicapped adults. The complex consists of a two-storey residential building and a three-storey building for therapy and meetings. The buildings are almost completely faced in Douglas fir. The residential building follows the slight angle of the northern boundary on the park-like property. This elongated building is arranged around two courtyards, allowing for maximum light from all sides. The therapy and meeting building is located next to the high traffic road, and serves to shield the complex against noise and exhaust fumes. On this facade, the most public side of the complex, the architect arranged all the windows according to internal light requirements. The abstract character of the facade reminds one of a score for solo instrument.

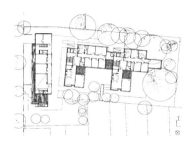

Second floor

Main building on Riehenstrasse

Architect:	Diener & Diener Architekten, Basel; www.dienerdiener.ch
Client:	Migros-Genossenschaft Basel, Basel
Dates:	construction 1996–1997

EGLISEE SUPERMARKET

Riehenstrasse 315, 4058 Basel | Tram 2 6: Eglisee

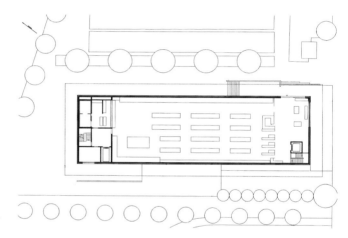

Ground floor

Diener & Diener built a supermarket on Riehenstrasse that breaks the mould in terms of typological design. The clean geometry of the rectangular shell is repeated in the interior, where the rhythm is echoed in the arrangement of shelves and aisles, introducing calm into a world overloaded with consumer goods. The large horizontal windows, reaching from the top of the shelves to just below the ceiling, are also part of this precise arrangement. With their material harmony, the poured concrete slabs of the facade create a new focal point in the heterogeneous architectural environment. Because of its use, the building signals openness and an urban character.

Entrance area on Riehenstrasse

Architect:	Michael Alder, Associate Roland Naegelin, Basel
	Now: Atelier Gemeinschaft (Hanspeter Müller, Roland Naegelin), Basel
Client:	Canton Basel-Stadt, Department of civil services and environment,
	Planning department, Basel
Dates:	project planning 1991/1992, construction 1993–1995

RANKHOF STADIUM

Grenzacherstrasse 351, 4058 Basel | Bus 31: Sportzentrum Rankhof

The column-free circulation area

The new Rankhof Stadium was created as part of the overall refurbishment of Basel's largest sports complex on the right bank of the Rhine. It is a functional building with a capacity of 15 000; the elegant grandstand has a total of 900 covered seats. In addition, the stadium houses twenty-four changing-rooms, club rooms, and a restaurant. Beneath the tiered grandstand is a column-free circulation area approximately 100 metres in length. On the other sides of the field, the seating is constructed of stacked 18-tonne prefabricated components, with seven steps between each landing. Concrete is the predominant material in the sports complex. The galvanized metal railings match the range of greys in the plastic-coated seats of the grandstand. The rear wall consists of a glass skin with black metal frames.

The grandstand

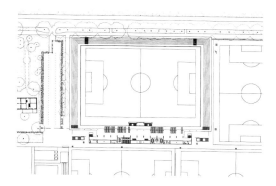

Plan

Architect:	Mario Botta Architteto, Lugano; www.botta.ch
	Project management and site supervision Georg Steiner
	in collaboration with Baucontrol AG, Basel
Client:	F. Hoffmann-La Roche AG, Basel
Dates:	project planning 1993, construction 1994–1996

JEAN TINGUELY MUSEUM

Grenzacherstrasse 210, 4058 Basel | Bus 31 36: Tinguely Museum

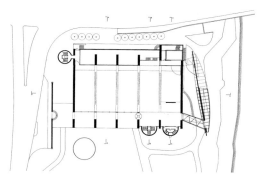

Ground floor

A small park called Solitude and Mario Botta's museum dedicated to the artist Jean Tinguely are located between a highway and office buildings designed for Hoffmann-La Roche. The architect used a windowless rear wall to shield the museum against noise and the park against exhaust fumes. The museum overlooks the Rhine on the south side and the park on the west side. Botta is an architect who loves the grand gesture: here, he has created a generously proportioned building around an 1800-square-metre central hall. All the circulation routes and visual axes are linear. An adjoining older building houses the museum's administration. The architect placed an enclosed footbridge along the Rhine in front of the museum, laying the river at the visitor's feet.

Footbridge and Rhine facade

Architekt:	Herzog & de Meuron, Basel; www.herzogdemeuron.com
	project management: Jacques Herzog, Pierre de Meurron, Robert Hösl (Partner in Charge)
Client:	F. Hoffmann–La Roche AG, Basel
Dates:	planning 2006–2008 (demolition of old building 2008), construction 2009–2011

ROCHE BUILDING 97

Wettsteinallee, 4058 Basel | Bus 30: Hoffmann-La Roche, Peter Rot-Strasse, Wettsteinallee |
Bus 31/38: Hoffmann-La Roche | Bus 34: Peter Rot-Strasse, Wettsteinallee

Roche Building 97 on Wettsteinallee.

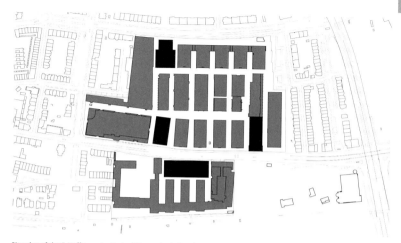

Site plan of the F. Hoffmann-La Roche AG complex in Basel.
Buildings by Herzog & de Meuron (in black): Building 92 (2000/middle right), Building 95 (2007/middle left),
Building 97 (2011/top) and Building 1 (2011-completion 2015/bottom).

When the pharmaceutical firm F. Hoffmann-La Roche AG was founded in 1896, its head office was located between Grenzacherstrasse and Rheinpromenade. Here the concern grew (its main administrative building was designed by Otto Rudolf Salvisberg, 1935–1937) on a 33 450 m² plot. From 1940 onwards, when the first production building was erected on Grenzacherstrasse in the north of the area, the built area spread to Wettsteinallee, covering an area of 85 800 m². Following Salvisberg's death in 1940, Roland Rohn took over as the firm's architect (until 1971, see project 129). And since 1991 (Building 92, 1991–2000) Herzog & de Meuron have been the architects for the firm's Basel location (Building 95, 2007; Building 1, under construction since 2011, planned completion autumn 2015). In 2011 their Building 97 for research (drugs for clinical studies) and galenical development (innovative forms of medication) was completed, following the demolition of a building by Roland Rohn (part of a laboratory ensemble on Wettsteinallee, 1967–1978). The new building is used for production facilities (small volumes), laboratories, and offices. It has eight upper levels of varying heights and – on the extended ground plan of the old building facing Wettsteinallee – almost double the use volume of the former building. On the southern side the building is 40 metres high and has 22 300 m² of floor space. It is composed of a four-storey cube (20.3 metres long, 29.55 metres wide, and 60.6 metres long) and a 19.7-metre-high block, which sits flush with the facade inside the area. This block is cantilevered to the west (from the fourth storey upwards, 35.7 metres) and to the east (from the sixth storey upwards, 41.3 metres). The edge of the roof is almost square (circa 35.7×38.9 metres). The load-bearing structure consists of steel girders embedded in concrete. The projecting sections are suspended from a framework in the top storey. All the levels of the cube containing work spaces feature continuous metal-framed window bands slightly set back from the covered and minimalistic facade exterior. The new building opens up the additive pattern of the Rohn buildings and creates new visual axes from the street onto the Roche complex, which will be given a new face along Wettsteinallee if the entire ensemble is rebuilt.

Ground plan of upper levels 4 to 6.

Ground plan of upper levels 1 and 2 (left)
and west-east section (right).

Visualization of the 175-metre-high Roche Building 1 on Grenzacherstrasse (begun 2011/completion 2015).
The Roche tower block designed by Roland Rohn and completed in 1961 (foreground) is 63 metres high.

Architect:	Diener & Diener Architekten, Basel; www.dienerdiener.ch
Client:	Warteck Invest AG, Basel
Dates:	construction 1994–1996

WARTECKHOF DEVELOPMENT

Grenzacherstrasse 62/64/Fischerweg 6–10/Alemannengasse 33–37, 4058 Basel |
Bus 31 34: Rosengartenweg | Tram 2 15: Wettsteinplatz

Floor plans of the two historic
buildings (left) and the new buildings
(right)

Two historic buildings were preserved on the property of the former Warteck Brewery.
Diener & Diener added a residential building (eighty-one units of up to five rooms per
unit and live-in studios) and an office and retail block. For the housing block and its
brickwork facade the architects entered into a dialogue with the original industrial
building; the other new building is located on a traffic artery through the eastern part
of the city and takes a definite contemporary stance with a facade composed of green
concrete slabs. The historic buildings were complemented with new buildings in such a
manner as to create a shifting landscape of open spaces, passages, and sightlines – thus
achieving correspondences and rhythm. The redeveloped area comes across as more
compact and thus, by definition, more urban.

View from fifth floor to the west

The former mashhouse (right) with
new buildings

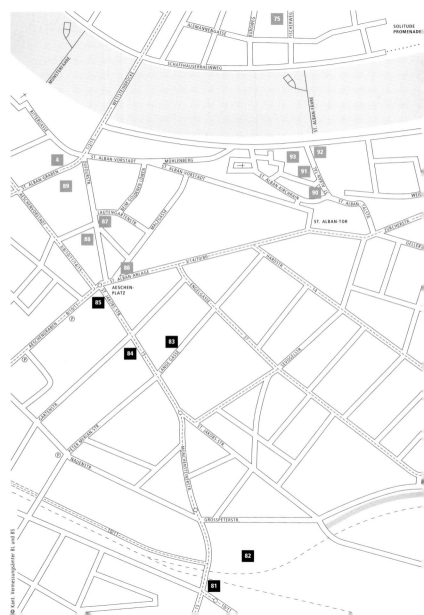

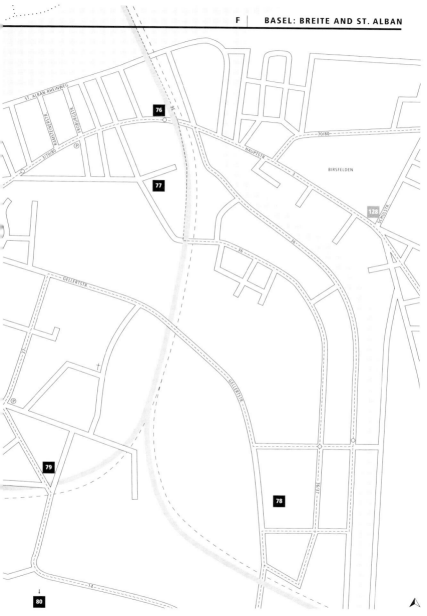

Architect:	sabarchitekten (Salathé, Reuter), Basel; www.sabarchitekten.ch
	Kägi Schnabel Architekten, Basel; www.kaegischnabel.com
	Interior work Hotel Breite: Larghi & Stula Architekten, Basel
	Interior work Centre for the Visually Impaired: Jecker Blanckarts Architekten, Basel
Client:	Breitezentrum Consortium, Basel
Dates:	competition 2000, planning 2000–2003, construction 2003–2005

BREITEZENTRUM BASEL

Zürcherstrasse 149, 4052 Basel | Tram 3, Bus 36 70 80: Breite

The winding staircase in the library

Located directly on the highway from Frankfurt am Main to Milan, the "Breite" district has been improved by a new structure. Some forty years ago, the highway cut a harsh and unflattering swath through this urban area. The "repair" began in 1993 in the form of a building by Bürgin Nissen Wentzlaff on the same side, followed – in 1997 – by the Jean Tinguely Museum (project 72) on the other side of the Rhine. This building axis, interrupted by the river, has been completed by sabarchitekten with their slender, U-shaped "Breitezentrum." Towards the south (Zürcherstrasse), the facade is opened up by means of a recessed courtyard. To the west and overlooking the small park on the north side, the building was designed with floor to ceiling glass sections. The "Breitezentrum" consists of a meeting place for local residents, a 36-room hotel, a library, a kindergarten as well as rooms for social services and space for commercial uses. Roughly 8000 square metres of floor area are spread across four floors. The square window ribbons and olive colouring of the facade invest this building with a distinctive identity. Inside the two-storey library, the winding staircase is an elegant three-dimensional sculpture.

The Breitezentrum with highway (right) and the Jean Tinguely museum (top, in the middle to the left)

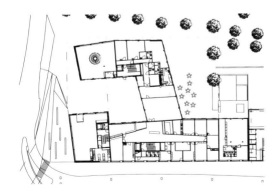

Ground floor plan

Architect:	Koechlin Schmidt Architekten, Basel; www.koechlinschmidt.ch
Client:	GGG Breite AG
Dates:	project 2008, construction 2009–2011

"WILDENSTEINEREGG" RESIDENTIAL DEVELOPMENT

Wildensteinerstrasse 10+12 / Baldeggerstrasse 30 / Bechburgerstrasse 9, 4052 Basel
Tram 3, Bus 36: Breite

View of courtyard.

The residential quality of the Breite neighbourhood, which was significantly compromised
by autobahn construction forty-five years ago, has been improved by the construction
of the "Wildensteineregg" residential development by Koechlin Schmidt Architekten. The
ensemble on Wildensteinerstrasse and Baldeggerstrasse (L-shaped volume) and on
Bechburgerstrasse (extension of a block fragment) encloses a large, planted interior courtyard. The five-storey buildings with a floor area of 6692 m² contain forty-eight residential
units comprising eighteen 2.5-room (between 52 and 86 m² of living space), sixteen
3.5-room (95–115 m²), ten 4.5-room (107–111 m²) and four 5.5-room (116–133 m²) apartments. The basement floors, which are on the same level as the courtyard, contain four
workshops, bicycle cellars, and laundries. In the L-shaped building, all the apartments
feature terraces or wide balconies opening onto the courtyard to the south-west. Open
kitchens are located in the middle of the living spaces, which extend over the entire
depth of the building. The building on Bechburgerstrasse offers living spaces 2.8 metres
high that recall the quality of Art Nouveau interiors. Each entrance area leads into a
living area featuring balconies on both sides (to the street and the courtyard). The quality
of the interiors is enhanced by floor-length glazing, oak parquet in the living areas, and
porcelain stoneware in the wet rooms.

Facade on Wildensteinerstrasse

Ground plan of ground floor on
Wildensteiner- (top), Baldegg- (right)
and Bechburgerstrasse (bottom).

Architect:	Miller & Maranta, Basel; www.millermaranta.ch
	Project management Peter Baumberger
Client:	Central office for public real estate transactions, Basel
Dates:	competition 2001, construction 2002–2004

SCHWARZPARK APARTMENT BUILDING

Gellertstrasse 135/137, 4052 Basel | Bus 36 37: Redingstrasse

Facade from northwest

Directional changes in the facade
create situations conducive
to communication.

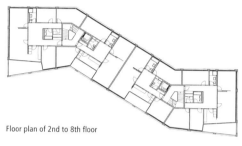

Floor plan of 2nd to 8th floor

Together with the engineer Jürg Conzett, Miller & Maranta architects erected an eight-storey building with 31 apartments (3.5 to 6.5 rooms per apartment, ranging from 72 to 142 square metres in floor area) on the 58 591 square-metre lot of the Schwarzpark. The total building volume of 20 000 cubic metres is broken up through shifts in the orientation. At sixty meters in width, the facade consists of seventy percent glass: with a gentle outward tilt from the raised basement level upward, it invests the structure with a dance-like lightness. In plan, the building is composed of two trapezoids and a parallelogram. At the intersections of these geometrical figures lie two glazed entrance halls (accessible on all sides) with windowless stairwell and elevator towers. This approach to providing access to the high-rise opens up the floor plans. Nearly all windows provide natural light exclusively for living areas. The apartments on the end sides feature residential atria as central plan elements leading to communal rooms (bathroom, kitchen, living room) or individual bedrooms or studies. Spacious axes provide generous views of the verdant and – nearly – downtown location of this lot.

Architect:	Zwimpfer Partner Architekten, Basel / Zurich; www.zwimpferpartner.ch
Client:	Volksbank AG, Basel
Dates:	planning 2007–2008, construction 2008–2009

THE OFFICE BUILDING AS RESIDENTIAL BUILDING

Adlerstrasse 35, 4052 Basel | Tram 14: Karl Barth-Platz / Zeughaus

Facade on Adlerstrasse

Penthouse terrace

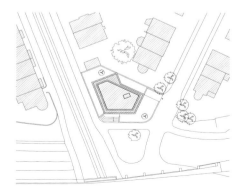

Situation of the hexagonal
ground plan in relation to Adlerstrasse (left)
and Speiserstrasse (right).

In the "Gellert" quarter of the St. Alban district, on a corner plot (615 m²) facing Adlerstrasse and Spieserstrasse, Zwimpfer Partner erected an office building with 1360 m² of floor space and an underground garage (with six parking spaces). The building complements the free-standing and terraced middle-class houses and town villas characteristic of the neighbourhood. The building lies on a lowered motorway route and marks the south-eastern entrance to the inner city. It represents an abstract expression of the design principle characterizing the quarter (built around and after 1900). The Wittmunder clinker bricks on the outside walls are supplemented by a stepped entrance area and a wall around the plot made of the same material. The three-storey building has a hexagonal ground plan and a penthouse with a large terrace (88 m²). The structure is supported by elements in the facade, which together with the stairway core (a 12.5-metre-high atrium), allow for flexibility in the floor plans. Twelve 2-metre-high wood-and-metal windows vary between 3.9 and 6.5 metres in width and are slightly offset such that the facade becomes a minimalistic arrangement framing the illuminated space in the interior. On the ground level the floors are made of Jura limestone and the doors of oak, while the office levels are carpeted.

The 12.5-meter-high atrium housing the stairs.

Engineer:	Schnetzer Puskas Ingenieure, Basel; www.schnetzerpuskas.com
Architect:	Steinmann & Schmid Architekten, Basel; www.steinmann-schmid.ch
	executive partner Herbert Schmid, project management Andreas Amrein
Client:	SBB (Federal Swiss Railroad), infrastructure division, Olten
	Canton Basel-Stadt, building department, construction, Basel
Dates:	project and planning 2003–2004, construction 2005–2006

URBAN RAIL TRANSIT STATION BASEL-DREISPITZ

Walkeweg / Walkewegbrücke, 4053 Basel | Tram 10 11, Bus 36 37: Dreispitz | Urban rail transit 3: Basel-Dreispitz

The elevator towers at the Walkeweg bridge

From 1901 onwards, the Dreispitz area was set up as a depot site. Hans Bernoulli erected the 92-metre-long Dreispitz streetcar depot on the eastern edge in 1915/16. Now Schnetzer Puskas have built the Basel-Dreispitz subway station next to it in collaboration with Steinmann & Schmid. With a length of 500 metres and a width of up to 50 metres, the structure infuses a sense of order and calm into the patchwork of this commercial area. The two Z-shaped roofs – each of which stretches across platforms (the tracks level), the stairs as well as the bicycle and moped stands (the bridge level) – are almost mirror images of one another. Four covered, single-span pedestrian perrons, arranged in the manner of loggias and with a rear wall painted in an invigorating neon green, bridge the height difference of roughly 8 metres. Expertly executed fair-faced concrete, beautifully designed lamps ("Channel" by Felice Dittli), public seating and waste bins illustrate the new spirit of departure that characterizes this district as does the elegant steel-and-glass construction of the user-friendly elevators. The Exhibition Warehouse of the Laurenz Foundation by Herzog & de Meuron (project 111) lies nearby.

Site plan of the 220-m-long
structure with Walkeweg
bridge (centre)

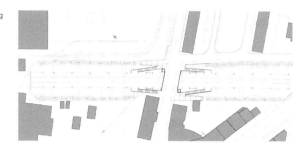

Platform with cascading stairs
and elevator tower

Architect:	Herzog & de Meuron, Basel; www.herzogdemeuron.com
	Project management Philippe Fürstenberger
Client:	Federal Swiss Railroad, Lucerne
Dates:	project planning 1995/1996, construction 1998–1999

CENTRAL SWITCH-YARD

Münchensteinerstrasse 115, 4052 Basel | Tram 10 11: Münchensteinerstrasse | Tram 15: Grosspeterstrasse

Site plan

In 1994 architects Herzog & de Meuron built a switch-yard for the Federal Swiss Railroad with a copper ribbon facade. It lies hidden to the east of the city. In 1999, another switch-yard was created for the same client on the edge of the city's downtown in a very exposed location. It features the same facade and, at 26 metres, rises to a height of approximately ten storeys. Set on the tracks, the ground plan is an uneven trapeze that mutates into a rectangle by the time it reaches the roof contour. These geometric forms merge rhythmically into one another across the full height of the building and the structure twists elegantly upward in a slightly convex movement. The architecture is both expressive and minimalist. Moreover, it has the presence of an outdoor sculpture.

Building as seen from the tracks (top) and from Münchensteiner bridge

Architect:	Bürgin & Nissen in association with Zwimpfer Partner
	Now: Nissen Wentzlaff Architekten, Basel; www.nwarch.ch
	Zwimpfer Partner, Basel; www.zwimpferpartner.ch
Client:	PTT General Management, Bern
Dates:	project planning and construction 1984–1989

SWISSCOM

Grosspeterstrasse 18, 4052 Basel | Tram 15: Grosspeterstrasse

Facade on Grosspeterstrasse

Swisscom (foreground) with high-
rises in the background

The telecommunications centre on Grosspeterstrasse is surrounded by a constant flow
of automobile and rail traffic. The calm volumes of this building, in some sections with
elegant ribbons of windows, reflect the subtlety and care with which Bürgin & Nissen
(chief architects) and Zwimpfer Partner approached the planning for this project. The
architects divided the spatial requirements into two separate volumes which follow
the slope in two steps to the large railway-yard of the train station. Upon completion,
the new building and the Lonza high-rise (1960–1962) were the only structures to occupy
this site on the edge of the city. Since then, other important architectural markers have
been added, especially the new switch-yard on the other side of the tracks (project 81).

Architect:	Burckhardt + Partner, Basel; www.burckhardtpartner.ch
Client:	Winterthur Life Insurance Group, Winterthur
Dates:	project planning 1997, construction 1998–2000

OFFICE BUILDING

Lange Gasse 15, 4052 Basel | Tram 3 8 10 11 14, Bus 37 70 80 : Aeschenplatz | Tram 15: Denkmal

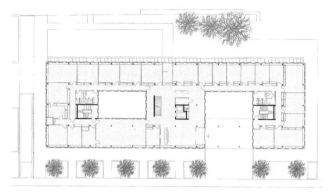

Ground floor

Architects Burckhardt + Partner designed an office building for Gellert, a residential neighbourhood. At 22 by 65 metres and four storeys, the fabric encloses a massive volume that is nevertheless cleverly integrated into its environment by being slightly set back from the frontage line and by the ground floor sunken. A supporting framework of 5.4 by 5.4 metres is the central structural element that allows for great flexibility of use and also gives the entire shape an air of tranquillity and clarity. The interior is characterized by two open light wells. The interior courtyard to the north leads to a generous entrance and lobby area; together, the courtyards provide natural light for almost all utility areas, while the offices, situated exclusively along the peripheral facade, benefit from optimal daylight through the abundant glazing. The facade is composed of wood and aluminium elements that break the surface into smaller units, creating a rhythm like a musical score.

View into one of the light wells

Elevation on Lange Gasse

Architect:	Herzog & de Meuron, Basel; www.herzogdemeuron.com
	Project management Kurt Lazzarini
Client:	Swiss Accident Insurance (SUVA), Lucerne
Dates:	project planning 1988, construction 1991–1993

SUVA HOUSE

St. Jakobs-Strasse 24 / Gartenstrasse 53 / 55, 4052 Basel | Tram 3 8 10 11 14 15,
Bus 37 70 80: Aeschenplatz

Facade on St. Jakobs-Strasse

On the edge of downtown, Herzog & de Meuron have converted and enlarged an office
building in Basel and added a residential section: the SUVA House has become one of
Basel's most elegant and striking architectural features. To integrate the original 1950
building with the new addition, both structures were encased in a glass skin on the
street facades. The opening of the office windows is now computer-regulated. On the
courtyard side, the stone facade of the old building meets the wood facade of the new
addition. A new café has been named after the Icarus bas-relief above the original 1950
main entrance. To generate a photographic wallpaper, the architects used an archival
Icarus image from the sixteenth century (by Pieter Brueghel the Elder).

Glass skin for historic building (left) and adjoining new residential building

Architect:	Mario Botta Architetto, Lugano; www.botta.ch
	Project management and building supervision in partnership with
	Burckhardt + Partner, Basel; www.burckhardtpartner.ch
Client:	Swiss Bank Association, Basel
Dates:	competition 1986, construction 1990–1995

BIS ADMINISTRATION BUILDING

Aeschenplatz 1, 4052 Basel | Tram 3 8 10 11 14 15, Bus 37 70 80: Aeschenplatz

Facade on Aeschenplatz

On Aeschenplatz, Mario Botta created a bank building whose 28-metre height and imposing volume surpass his cathedral in Paris Evry. The rotunda building is the architect's largest building north of the Alps. Among the many international architects who have designed buildings in Basel during the last decades, Botta has been the most controversial. And yet the powerful half-circle design is an architectural archetype common to the Mediterranean landscape. At the edge of the city's downtown, the building sets a strong urban accent and the boulevard, inspired in part by Botta's structure, has already expanded in the direction of the train station. The most characteristic element of the building is an enclosed light well that rises from the ground floor to the roof. Into this open space artist Felice Varini's suspended circles are extremely precise and equally sensuous.

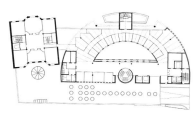

Ground floor

Enclosed atrium

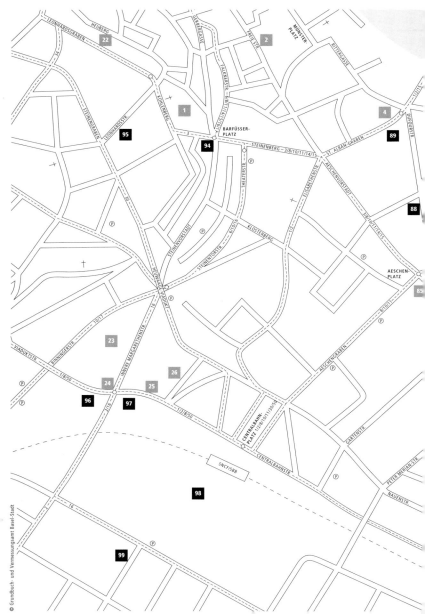

LEONHARDSGRABEN
HEUBERG
22
GERBERGASSE
THIERSTR
2
MÜNSTER-PLATZ
RITTERGASSE

LEONHARDSGRABEN
STEINENGRABEN
KOHLENBERG
1
BARFÜSSER-PLATZ
95
94
STEINENBERG – 3/8/10/11/14/15
ST. ALBAN GRABEN
4
89
DUFOURSTR

THEATERSTR
AESCHENVORSTADT
ELISABETHENSTR
88

STEINENVORSTADT
STEINENTORSTR
KLOSTERBERG

HEUWAAGE-VIADUKT
AESCHEN-PLATZ
85

VIADUKTSTR
BINNINGERSTR
INNERE MARGARETHENSTR
23
26
AESCHENGRABEN

24
25
96
97
CENTRALBAHN-PLATZ
GARTENSTR

1/2/8/30
CENTRALBAHNSTR
PETER MERIAN STR

SNCF/SBB
98
NAUENSTR

99

© Grundbuch- und Vermessungsamt Basel-Stadt

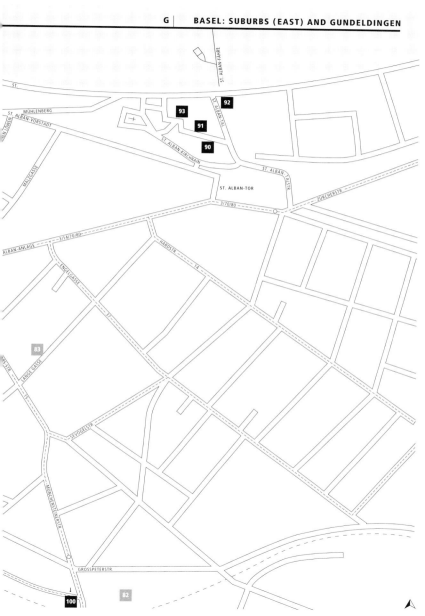

Architect:	Bürgin Nissen Wentzlaff, Basel
	Now: Nissen Wentzlaff Architekten, Basel; www.nwarch.ch
Client:	Pax Life Insurance Group, Basel
Dates:	competition 1988/1989, construction 1992–1994 and 1995–1997

PAX INSURANCE ADMINISTRATION BUILDING

Aeschenplatz 13, 4052 Basel | Tram 3 8 10 11 14 15, Bus 37 70 80: Aeschenplatz

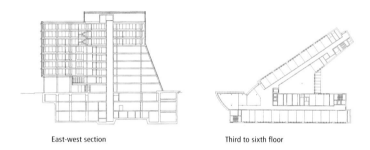

East-west section   Third to sixth floor

A new administration building for the Pax Insurance Group has been erected on Aeschenplatz. The building by Bürgin Nissen Wentzlaff includes a striking glass tower that is a complementary counterpoint to Mario Botta's rotunda building in the same square (project 85). Glass, steel, and the brickwork in the facade are the dominant materials. The tiered facade of the V-shaped design responds to the historic neighbourhood. On the boulevard side, nine storeys rise in an austere form. On the north-west side, where a neighbourhood of small lots leads to the historic downtown, the height has been reduced to three storeys in harmonious correspondence to the surroundings. The predominant materials are stone and wood, that is, granite and beech. Lamps and handrails are prototypes designed by the architects.

Entrance hall

Facade on Aeschenplatz

Architect:	Diener & Diener Architekten, Basel; www.dienerdiener.ch
Client:	Life Insurance Group of Basel, Basel
Dates:	competition 1987, construction 1990–1994

PICASSOPLATZ BUSINESSCENTER

Lautengartenstrasse 6 / Dufourstrasse, 4052 Basel | Tram 3 8 10 11 14 15, Bus 37 70 80: Aeschenplatz |
Tram 2 15: Kunstmuseum

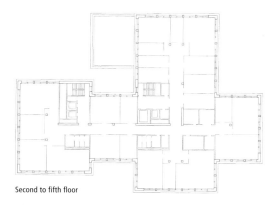

Second to fifth floor

On the far side of Picassoplatz, Diener & Diener erected an administration building for the Life Insurance Group of Basel. The complex in three sections (five, six, and eight storeys) occupies a trapezoidal lot. The building creates a new urban anchor for this prominent central location. One of the three sections is almost a perfect cube: an ideal geometry. The facade is polished green granite. Granite – albeit, in white and black – is also the material used in Luciano Fabro's large sculpture installation which surrounds the entire complex. The new building stands in a neighbourhood with an important architectural history, including Otto Rudolf Salvisberg's First Church of Christ, Scientist (1935/1936) and the art museum designed by Rudolf Christ, Paul Büchi, and Paul Bonatz (1929–1936).

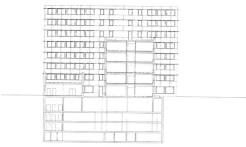

South section through connecting wing

Facade on Dufourstrasse

Architect:	Märkli Architekt, Zurich; www.maerkliarchitekt.ch
	Project management Jakob Frischknecht, Nathalie Spahn
Client:	Picassoplatz AG. A UBS (CH) Property Fund enterprise – Swiss Commercial
	«Swissreal», Basel
Dates:	competition 2002, construction 2003–2008

PICASSO HOUSE

Brunngässlein 12, 4052 Basel | Tram 3 8 10 11 14 15, Bus 37 70 80: Aeschenplatz |
Tram 2 15: Kunstmuseum

View of Picassoplatz
from the 7th floor

The floors in the stairwell are covered in brown-grey slate, complemented by doors in light olive wood.

Site plan with Picassoplatz (centre)

Picassoplatz is now home to the Picasso House by Peter Märkli. The entrance to the eight-storey structure lies on Brunngässlein. The upper floors are collapsed inward in the shape of a trapezoid, opening the narrow streetscape into a square. Thin steel sheeting profiles serve as facade cladding of the building with 4800 square metres of office space. In combination with the pilasters of the concrete structure, upright rectangles (panes and windows) transform this cladding into a glass-and-metal mosaic that is monochrome in appearance. Seven storeys have homogeneous room heights (2.6 to 2.9 metres). The loft like top floor (4.3 to 4.9 metres) adds visual height to the building. The elevator and stairwell tower has a metal-rod balustrade with an olive wood handrail. Entrance and floors of the "Piranesi" stairwell (with soaring ceiling height of 38.5 metres from the 4th underground floor to the 8th floor) are covered in brown-grey slate from Brazil. All interior walls abut the facade with floor-to-ceiling glass panes. This optimizes the ingress of light and gives the building a showcase-like character at night. A bronze relief by Hans Josephsohn graces the lobby wall.

Architect:	Gigon/Guyer Architekten, Zürich; www.gigon-guyer.ch
	Project management Christian Maggioni, supervision Thomas Hochstrasser,
	associate Florian Isler, furniture design in collaboration with Hannes Wettstein
Client:	Canton Basel-Stadt, building authorities, construction and
	planning department, Basel
Dates:	competition 2001, planning/construction 2003–2007 (in 3 stages)

CONVERSION OF MUSEUM AND LAURENZ BUILDING

St. Alban-Graben 10 and 16, 4051 Basel | Tram 2 15: Kunstmuseum

The former reading room
was converted into an exhibition
area for the collection.

The Museum of Fine Arts by Rudolf Christ and Paul Bonatz (1936) was connected to the adjacent "Laurenz Building" (erected in 1926 by Suter & Burckhardt as a national bank building) and converted. Museum administration, a university faculty and the public art library were moved into the "Laurenz Building"; the first construction stages in this regard were realized by Berger + Toffol. The engravings exhibit was provided with new, larger spaces in the "historic structure", while the space that became available as a result was reassigned to new uses as 760 square metres of exhibition area, a bookstore and a restaurant/café. Gigon/Guyer's intervention is characterized by "opening," "clarity," "dialogue" and "structural conservation." The historic enfilade and sequence of interior spaces in the "Laurenz Building" has been preserved. The 300-square-metre hall on the ground floor has been converted into a reading hall and reference library. Four new galleries were added to the right entrance wing of the historic structure. The former library corridor was converted into a restaurant with square tables set in front of a 35-metre-long bench and with windows and doors opening onto the courtyard. Reception area, bookstore, reading room and restaurant were all furnished with prototypical pieces. The materials (greyish blue and pink limestone) have been restored in the museum vestibule.

Ground floor plan with art museum
(top) and the Laurenz building.
The rooms in the areas marked in
grey were converted.

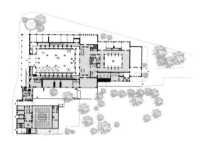

The new reading room in the teller
hall of the former national bank

Restaurant in the former library hallway

Architect:	Michael Alder, Associate Roland Naegelin, Basel
	Now: Atelier Gemeinschaft (Hanspeter Müller, Roland Naegelin), Basel
Client:	Residents' Cooperative St. Alban-Tal, Basel
Dates:	project planning 1984/1985, construction 1986

CONVERSION OF INDUSTRIAL ARCHITECTURE

St. Alban-Tal 42, 4052 Basel | Tram 3: St. Alban-Tor | Tram 2 15: Kunstmuseum

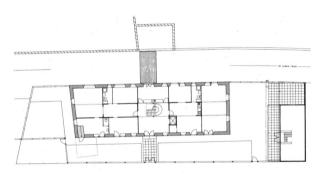

Ground-floor plan

Michael Alder has fully renovated and converted a nineteenth-century building whose historic use was to provide living quarters for paper mill workers, as well as drying rooms for the mill. In place of the original support structure of vertical elements along the central longitudinal axis, a new circulation zone has been inserted through the centre of the building. This creates the structural conditions required for the building's new and exclusively residential use while preserving the original girder structure. Externally, the conversion has also maintained a visual link to the original architecture through rows of equidistant window axes and a wooden envelope of Douglas fir facade strips. This building is a prime example of a trend that was unthinkable only a few years ago: the will to invest such care into existing buildings that are in poor repair.

The building after being stripped
to the shell (top)

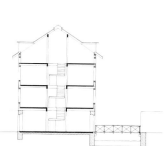

Plan after refurbishment (left) and
new facade

Architect:	Urs Gramelsbacher Architekt, Basel; www.gramelsbacher.ch
Client:	National Insurance Group, Basel
Dates:	construction 1997–1999

RESIDENTIAL BUILDING

St. Alban-Tal 38a, 4052 Basel | Tram 3: St. Alban-Tor | Tram 2 15: Kunstmuseum

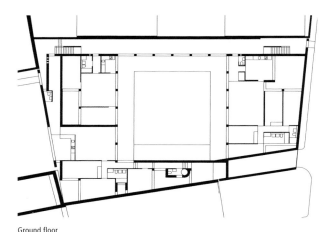

Ground floor

On the last free parcel of land remaining in the St. Alban valley-neighbourhood on the Rhine between Romanesque monastery architecture and the late medieval city wall, Urs Gramelsbacher constructed a new residential building with three- and five-room apartments. The two-storey-high structure is oriented towards a central courtyard (17 × 17 m). Exposed concrete is the dominant material. The courtyard fountain creates a veil of water flowing through a slit (10 m × 4 cm) in the concrete. The water collects in a glass-bottomed basin, which is in fact the ceiling of an underground car park designed to provide parking for all neighbouring houses. Wall openings integrate the new building with its environment.

Street facade

Courtyard

Architect:	Diener & Diener Architekten, Basel; www.dienerdiener.ch
Client:	Christoph Merian Foundation, Basel
Dates:	competition 1982, construction 1984–1986

RESIDENTIAL BUILDING WITH CRAFT STUDIOS

St. Alban-Rheinweg 94/96, 4052 Basel | Tram 3: St. Alban-Tor | Tram 2 15: Kunstmuseum

Facade overlooking the Rhine with
medieval city wall (left)

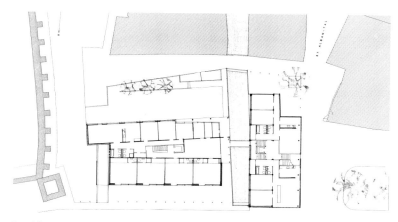

Ground floor

In the historic St. Alban valley (see project 93) Diener & Diener have built an exposed building on an undeveloped stretch along the Rhine. With its clean design, serial window arrangement, and the sculptural effect of the facade, the building is deliberately contemporary in tone. It is especially remarkable from the perspective of urban planning as the architecture interacts so harmoniously with its historic surroundings. The adjoining city wall along the riverbank dates from the late Middle Ages. And the buildings – used as paper mills from 1453 and 1478 onwards – bear witness to the city's early industrial development. The historic dialogue, present in several areas of the city, is at its best in this location (see projects 90 and 91).

Architect:	Wilfrid and Katharina Steib, Basel
Client:	Museum of Contemporary Art, the Emanuel Hoffmann Foundation, Basel,
	and the Public Art Collection in St. Alban-Tal, Basel
Dates:	construction 1977–1980

MUSEUM OF CONTEMPORARY ART

St. Alban-Rheinweg 60, 4052 Basel | Tram 3: St. Alban-Tor | Tram 2 15: Kunstmuseum

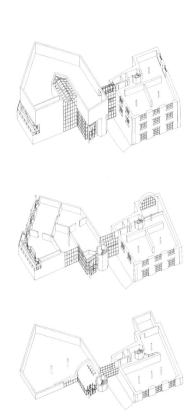

Axonometric of museum (top),
of second floor (middle),
and of ground floor

Facade with main entrance

In 1980 Basel became home to a new Museum of Contemporary Art with an exhibition space of 2800 square metres. In the same year, twenty-seven museums were under construction or projected for construction in Germany. The theatrical impulse of many of these architects is barely felt in Basel. For this museum, a former paper mill was partially demolished and the remaining volume nearly doubled through the addition of a new building. The architects designed the connecting structure and the entrance area in steel and glass – in keeping with the factory windows, which were preserved. The ground floor of the new building is partially below ground, such that the building heights vary only slightly. The large windows provide excellent light conditions, and the top floor of the new building is conceived as an open space with a full-ceiling skylight.

Architect:	Diener & Diener Architekten, Basel; www.dienerdiener.ch
Client:	M. Diener, Basel
Dates:	construction 1994–1995

RESIDENTIAL BUILDING WITH OFFICE AND RETAIL SPACE

Steinenvorstadt 2 / Kohlenberg 1, 4051 Basel | Tram 3 6 8 11 14 15 16: Barfüsserplatz |
Tram 10: Theater

The corner building on
Barfüsserplatz

Ground-floor plan (top),
standard floor plan, fourth to
sixth floor

Section from Kohlenberg perspective

On Barfüsserplatz, Diener & Diener designed a multi-use retail, office, and residential building. The colours and neon signage of the neighbouring buildings are a nondescript patchwork within which the unadorned six-storey building stands out as a calm and solitary component. The facade is composed of sand-coloured reinforced concrete slabs, the same material and similar hue used by the architects for a museum addition in Biel and an embassy wing in Berlin. The changing rhythm in the window axes is a subtle gesture borrowed from conceptual art: it acts as a stimulating visual irritant in this central urban location. Two floors of retail shops are topped by offices and finally by a penthouse apartment under the flat roof. Records show that buildings have existed on this site even prior to the earthquake of 1356.

Architect:	Burckhardt + Partner, Basel; www.burckhardtpartner.ch
Client:	Canton Basel-Stadt, Department of civil services and environment,
	Planning department, Basel
Dates:	construction 1995–1998

LEONHARD HIGH SCHOOL

Leonhardsstrasse 15, 4051 Basel | Tram 3: Musik-Akademie | Tram 6 8 11 14 15 16: Barfüsserplatz

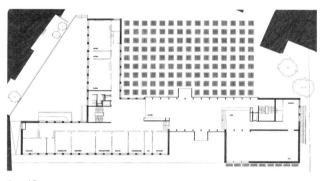

Ground floor

Architects Burckhardt + Partner have expanded a city high school on Leonhardsstrasse by an addition of 13 000 square metres of floor space. The school complex consists of buildings from various eras, the earliest being 1884, then 1904–1906, 1957–1959, and the new addition. Together, these buildings represent a wide range of styles, from classical revival to Art Nouveau, post-war modern architecture, and New Objectivity. On a winding lot, the spatial requirements have been accommodated in an S-shaped building to which a long element was added. The complex has five upper storeys. A gym was installed underground, beneath the schoolyard. The previously dreary setting has been considerably improved with the new red-brown facade, the generously glazed, wind-sheltered entrance area off the piazza, and the planting of well-established trees.

View from entrance hall to
schoolyard

Facade on schoolyard side with
the "windows" of the underground gym

Architect:	Diener & Diener Architekten, Basel; www.dienerdiener.ch
Client:	Swiss Bank Association, Basel
Dates:	construction 1990–1994

TRAINING AND CONFERENCE CENTRE

Viaduktstrasse 33, 4052 Basel | Tram 1 2 8 16: Markthalle | Tram 6 10: Heuwaage

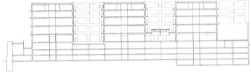

East-west section

Aerial view of complex from the east

The three-wing complex on
Viaduktstrasse

The training and conference centre, designed by Diener & Diener, together with the new building by Richard Meier (project 24, on the opposite side of the street), accentuates the west wing of the Swiss and French railway station in Basel. The architects composed the large complex (56 000 m²) out of long blocks in an orthogonal arrangement along a curve. Thanks to windows facing east, south, and west, the offices and lecture halls receive maximum natural light, while the facade on the busy main street is almost windowless. An underground car park is easily accessible at ground level behind a massive wall set into the hillside. In the near future, a new track for the Basel-Paris line will run parallel to the curved rear wall of the conference centre.

Architect:	Herzog & de Meuron, Basel; www.herzogdemeuron.com
	Project architect Philippe Fürstenberger,
	Associate General contractor: ARGE, Herzog & de Meuron and Proplaning AG;
	www.proplaning.ch
Client:	TK3 Basel (preconstruction phase) and TU Batigroup, Switzerland
	(joint ownership association SUVA and Publica, Switzerland)
Dates:	project 2000, construction 2002–2005

OFFICE AND RETAIL BUILDING "ELSÄSSERTOR II"

Centralbahnstrasse 4, 4065 Basel | Tram 1 2 8 16: Markthalle

Site plan with elongated inner atria
and the dome of the former market
hall (above)

The "Elsässertor" by Herzog & de Meuron is a five-storey building, the plan of which is in the shape of an elongated, compressed and truncated pentagon from the second floor onward (145×36 m floor area). The ground floor is gently recessed on the street side and markedly set back towards the west. A small square has been created at the Margarethen bridge. The four parallel glass ribbons of the facade are tinted red on the east side and blue on the west side. In combination with the clear "white" glass on the south and north sides, the result is a three-dimensional "tricolore": a homage to France (trains to Paris pass behind the building). Since the facade panels are mounted in a wide range of angles, the surroundings are mirrored in fractured prisms. The building has a total floor area of 17 870 square metres, underground parking (174 parking spots) and is arranged around three atria. At the track level, the site was raised creating a boulevard lined with birch trees and robinia (by Vogt Landschaftsarchitekten) along the street. Distinctive structures (projects 24, 25, 26, 96, 98) are located within sight on this western flank of the Swiss and French train station.

Boulevard with birch trees
and robinias (false acacias) and
the facade on Viaduktstrasse

Building seen from the west with
French railway station (right)

Reflections in an atrium

Architect:	Cruz y Ortiz Arquitectos, Seville; www.cruzyortis.com
	with Giraudi Wettstein Architetti, Lugano; www.giraudiwettstein.ch
Client:	Schweizerische Bundesbahnen AG, Bern
	Canton Basel-Stadt, Department of civil services and environment,
	Planning department, Basel
Dates:	competition 1996, project planning 1996–2001, construction 2001–2003

PEDESTRIAN OVERPASS AT SBB TRAIN STATION

Centralbahnplatz / Güterstrasse, 4002 Basel | Tram 1 2 8 10 11, Bus 30 50: Basel SBB | Tram 16: Bahnhofeingang Gundeldingen

With a length of 184 metres, a width of 30 metres and a height of 15 metres, the pedestrian overpass of the SBB train station has been created as a free-spanning space, the airiness and brightness of which are unequalled in the city. The steel and glass structure is raised on a 8000 tonne foundation slab, which is covered in Norwegian quartzite slabs. Thirty-three escalators, a moving sidewalk and countless elevators guide the daily stream of users from this level into the station concourse. The architects from Seville (Cruz y Ortiz) and Lugano (Giraudi Wettstein) have created a subtle division of the main terminal in the historic building by Faesch and la Roche (1904–07) and harmonized the rhythm of the new roof with the barrel vaults of the historic neighbouring structure. On the south side, the new structure projects dynamically into the Gundeldinger district. The project also created a new shopping promenade with 25 retail stores. A look at the Santa Justa train station in Seville (by Cruz y Ortiz 1988–91) reveals that the building masters from Spain and the Ticino have created a Mediterranean symbol.

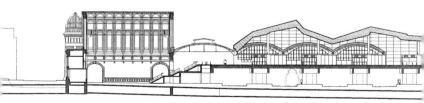

North-south section

The 184-metre-long overpass

View from west

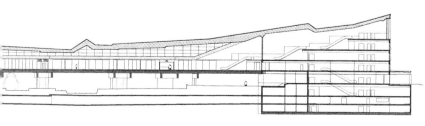

Architect:	Silvia Gmür Reto Gmür Architekten, Basel; www.gmuerarch.ch
	Associate F. Früh, supervision Peter Stocker
Client:	I. Müller, Basel
Dates:	planning and construction 2005–2006

APARTMENT AND STUDIO BUILDING

Frobenstrasse 4, 4053 Basel I Tram 16: Bahnhofeingang Gundeldingen I Bus 36 37: Frobenstrasse

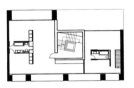 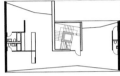 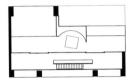

Floor plan of 2nd, 3rd and 5th floor
(left to right)

The new house on Frobenstrasse has two two-storey frames (from street level and from roof edge) with a completely column-free storey in the middle. This allows for generous and open living areas with light axes and flexible floor plans. The spatial program of this five-storey building is indeed unusual: a studio (72 m²), a bachelor apartment (36 m²), a 3.5-room apartment (87 m²) and two maisonette units (2nd and 3rd floor 89 m²; 4th and 5th floor 140 m²). All apartments have balconies and patios on the courtyard side where the L-shaped lot becomes narrow and includes a gravel area as a courtyard garden. The stairwell tower shaft, the core of which (elevator and stairs) is slightly rotated away from the axis, can be illuminated across four floors with a window. The floors are rendered in polished concrete. The frames on the street facade have a depth of 113 cm. The middle storey, which is inserted with a creased window hinge, appears like the horizon in a three-dimensional landscape painting. Cubic columns set into the facade frames diminish in size towards the top like column shafts, an abstract, twenty-first century interpretation of an antique architectonic motif.

Living room with recessed windows
overlooking the street

Facade on Frobenstrasse

Architect:	Burckhardt + Partner, Basel; www.burckhardtpartner.ch
Client:	Winterthur Leben, Winterthur
Dates:	competition 1999, construction 2001–2003

OFFICE AND HOUSING COMPLEX, THIERSTEINERALLEE

Thiersteinerallee 14–30, Tellstrasse 48–52, 60–66 | Tram 15 16: Heiliggeistkirche |
Tram 10 11: Münchensteinerstrasse | Bus 36: Thiersteinerschule

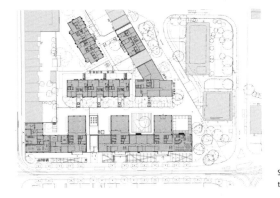

Site plan. In the foreground:
the Thiersteinerallee

On a lot of barely 14 000 square metres, Burckhardt + Partner have erected a large office complex for a commercial enterprise and 69 apartments spread across five structures. A 130-metre-long, five-storey volume has been raised diagonally across from the new central switch-yard (project 81). Four large and nearly square glazed sections of 220 square metres each subdivide the monumental facade and redefine one of the most important street axis in the Gundeldinger district. The comb-like projection of the principal structure into a rear courtyard allows for optimal natural lighting and made it possible to reduce the overall building height. The resulting structure establishes correspondences to the neighbouring buildings from the late nineteenth and early twentieth century. The landscape architects Fahrni and Breitenfeld designed a verdant, publicly accessible garden.

Facade overlooking the München-
steinerbrücke

The building slabs in the courtyard

Facade seen from the Heiliggeistkirche

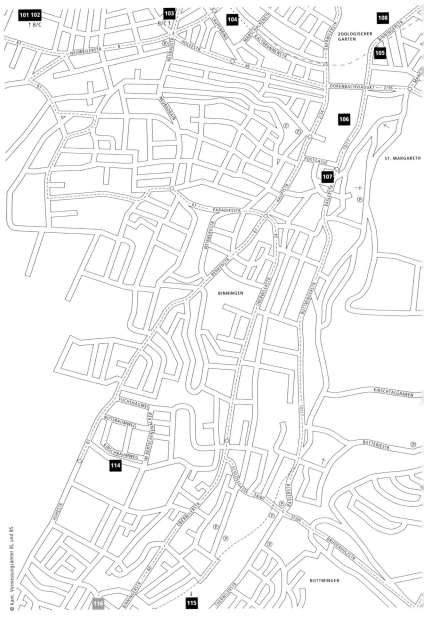

Architect:	Herzog & de Meuron, Basel; www.herzogdemeuron.com
	Project management: Jacques Herzog, Pierre de Meuron,
	Stefan Marbach (Partner in charge)
	General planner: ARGE GP Headquarters Actelion, Basel, Herzog de Meuron, Basel
	Proplaning AG, Basel; www.proplaning.ch
	Garden design and landscape planning: Tita Giese, Düsseldorf; www.tita-giese.com
Client:	Actelion Pharmaceuticals Ltd., Allschwil
Dates:	planning 2005–2006, construction 2007–2010

ACTELION BUSINESS CENTRE

Hegenheimermattweg 95, 4123 Allschwil | Bus 31 38 48 64: Im Brühl / Hagmattstrasse

The "facade" formed by the modules stacked and suspended on six spatial levels.

Steel structure in the interior space.

The Actelion Business Centre was built by Herzog & de Meuron in Allschwil on a plot measuring 7610 m² between Hegenheimermattweg and the border to France. This unique piece of architecture is composed of a series of layered and stacked white and clear-glass volumes supported by angled girders. The labyrinthine construction comprises two underground and six above-ground levels over 27 469 m² and contains 350 office-work spaces, a car park, an auditorium, a restaurant with a cafe-lounge, and a multifunctional entrance area. Synthesizing influences that range from ancient Yemeni cliff-face settlements and Native American terrace settlements to Italian Futurist (Antonio Sant'Elia) and Russian Revolutionary architectural drawings (El Lissitzky), the building combines a cloverleaf-like cross on the ground level with five frame-like spatial levels. The basic design module is an elongated, flat-roofed volume that is continuously glazed (without interruption by posts) from floor to ceiling on both sides. The floor plan of this module comprises a series of work and recreation zones (offices, meeting rooms, cafe kitchens, etc.) and a linear corridor. This access corridor is separated from the work zone by a glass wall that visually echoes the facade. The longest module (96 metres) is on the fourth upper level, the shortest (32 metres) on the third. Within the 21-metre-high steel structure, an open atrium is spanned by futuristic bridges, used as roof terraces on upper levels 3 (143 m²) and 5 (218 m²). The interior walls are composed of light-weight panelling. Four of the levels are arranged in a rectangle, and one in a heptagon. Lifts and stairways form four access towers at the points where the floors meet. On all levels the volumes audaciously extend beyond these interfaces out into the surrounding space. The glazed external facade has a surface area of 15 020 m². Within the urban space, the architecture creates a floating, ephemeral, airy, and light impression. In the interior, the pristine white work and communication spaces are flooded with light and exude a casual elegance and a sensory luxuriance. The plants and forms included in the garden design and landscape architecture extend this character over 4500 m² on the ground floor (between the building and the pathways made of poured asphalt and Eifel quartz) and across the flat roof surfaces.

Structure in the open inner courtyard.

Ground plans of three levels.
Level 1 (middle) lies on the cross
on the ground floor (bottom).
Level 5 (top) features a bridge over
the inner courtyard.

Architect:	Burckhardt + Partner AG, Basel; www.burckhardtpartner.ch,
	in collaboration with Tamara Brügger, Marco Husmann, Daniel Keller
	Landschaftsarchitekt Schönholzer + Stauffer Landschaftsarchitekten BSLA;
	www.schoenholzerstauffer.ch
Client:	AG für Planung und Überbauung, Basel and EBM Elektra Birseck, Münchenstein
Dates:	planning 2006, construction 2008–2012

ELCO-PARK HOUSING DEVELOPMENT

Baslerstrasse 270, 272, 274 / Merkurstrasse / Spitzwaldstrasse, 4123 Allschwil | Tram 6: Merkurstrasse

The free-standing dwellings have 4 or 5 storeys
and lie in a landscaped garden.

Plan with long building (Baslerstrasse/right),
free-standing dwellings (Spitzwaldstrasse/left)
and row houses (Merkurstrasse/top).

Staircase in free-standing dwelling.

The Elco-Park housing development erected by Burckhardt + Partner in Allschwil is located on the former site of a paper factory (15 964 m², main building 1923 and 1928/1948; demolished 2007). The ensemble between Baslerstrasse, Spitzwaldstrasse, and Merkurstrasse consists of a long building on the western side of the plot (five storeys, 80.5 metres long and 13.8 metres wide), seven multi-dwelling units to the north-west with identical ground plans (24.5 metres long, 15.7 metres wide) and four or five storeys (12.2 and 15 metres high), and seven row houses (three storeys each) along a 42.6-metre strip on the south-western edge. The complex contains eighty-seven owner-occupied apartments and seven single-family dwellings with loggias and/or terraces. The 80-metre-long cube on Baslerstrasse features the same closed morphology as the former industrial administrative buildings and the structure of an apartment house, containing units with 3.5, 4.5, and 5.5 rooms (104–150 m²). The free-standing multi-unit dwellings offer three types of apartment (3.5, 4.5, 5.5 rooms, 114–152 m²) for family living. Each of the buildings also includes an attic apartment (156 m²) with a roof terrace (130 m²). The row houses have 5.5 rooms, 179 m² of living area, and elegant features such as floors made of Jura limestone, oak parquet, ceramic slabs, and larch on the outside terraces.

Architect:	Wymann & Selva, Basel
	Now: Wymann Architektur, Basel; www.wymann.org and
	Luca Selva Architekten, Basel; www.selva-arch.ch,
	in collaboration with Hans Gritsch, Stefan Segessenmann
Client:	Canton Basel-Stadt, Department of civil services and environment,
	Planning department, Basel
Dates:	competition 1993/1994, construction 1995–1996

KALTBRUNNEN SCHOOLHOUSE

Kaltbrunnen-Promenade 95, 4054 Basel | Tram 8: Laupenring | Bus 36: Holee

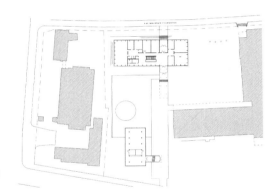

Site plan: to the left, Herman Baur's
All Saints Church

Next to the original Neubad Schoolhouse – a late 1940s complex designed by Giovanni Panozzo – Wymann & Selva have created the new Kaltbrunnen Schoolhouse, thereby more than doubling the size of the school complex. The new structure has a historic neighbour in Hermann Baur's All Saints Church (1948–1950). The architects consciously sought to avoid a stylistic clash; instead, they structured the open space, created differentiated building heights, and preserved the mature trees on the site. Located above a low-lying track of the Basel-France line, the exposed site allowed for fully glazed facades on all sides of the new four-storey main building. The concrete floors which project through the facades create an elegant visual rhythm. Christoph Rösch's "Sound Cylinder" could be described as a land-art object for this complex.

The light cube of the auditorium

Facade on low-lying railway track

Architect:	Luca Selva Architekten, Basel; www.selva-arch.ch
	Associates David Gschwind, Véronique Caviezel, Gian-Andrea Serena, Petra Waldburger
Client:	C. und Hj. Reinau-Krayer, Binningen
Dates:	Project planning 2010, construction 2011–2013

PIRANESIESQUE GENERATIONAL BUILDING

Höhenweg 53, 4102 Binningen | Tram 8, Bus 36: Neubad | Tram 2, Bus 34: Hohle Gasse

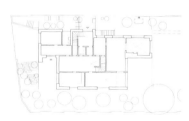

Ground-floor plan

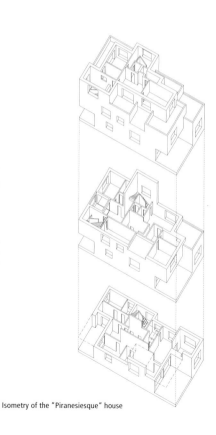

Isometry of the "Piranesiesque" house

Facade to Höhenweg

In Binningen Luca Selva architects constructed a home for two generations. It has two entrances and 431 m² of usable and living areas distributed over a basement level, ground floor, and two upper floors. The main apartment (for the parents) stretches over three floors and is accessed from Höhenweg. The annex apartment (for the grown-up children), stretches over the same three floors, is accessed from the eastern facade (entrance area with staircase) and offers living areas with attached bathrooms on the two upper levels. An eat-in kitchen and a large living room with stairs (5.5 metres high, upper levels 1 and 2) are shared spaces. This large living room is located against the facade facing north, opposite the access staircase on the ground floor. The normal room height of 2.6 metres is deviated from on the ground floor of the main apartment by a large living room (5.5 metres), a dining room (4.9 metres) and a cheminée room (4.1 metres). There is a correspondence between the floors (Istrian limestone set in sand and oak parquet) and the windows made of architectural bronze and set in the upper part of the wall in the high rooms abutting the facade. The apartments are connected by a three-sided lift (reaching all floors), a corridor, doors, and a rooftop terrace. The Piranesiesque arrangement of spaces was built using a steel bearing structure and poured concrete.

Architect:	Hanspeter Müller (Ateliergemeinschaft with Roland Naegelin), Basel
Client:	Binningen community association, Binningen
Dates:	project planning 1994, construction 1995

YOUTH CENTRE

In den Schutzmatten 10, 4102 Binningen | Tram 2, Bus 34: Hohle Gasse | Tram 10 17: Binningen Oberdorf

Facade overlooking the Birsig River

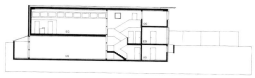

East-west section

Ground-floor plan

Hanspeter Müller designed a new youth centre in Binningen. The structure on Baslerstrasse is located next to a small tributary of the Rhine (the Birsig), in a green yet urban location with excellent access to public transportation. Large communal rooms (café, disco) and an equally spacious patio provide a well-considered physical environment for the varied and largely self-directed leisure activities of young people. The beautiful location is complemented by an architecture that appreciates the surrounding elements: this applies both to the sensitive choice of building materials and to the generous design of the interior and exterior spaces.

Architect:	TrinklerStulaPartner Architekten, Basel; www.trinklerstulapartner.ch
	collaborators Salvatore Achille, Bruno Trinkler
Client:	Rosenmund Immobilien AG, Basel
Dates:	project planning 2008, construction 2009–2010

RESIDENTIAL BUILDING

Schlüsselgasse 4, 4102 Binningen | Tram 10 17: Binningen Oberdorf

Ground plan of upper level 2

Ground plan of attic level

TrinklerStulaPartner architects erected a residential building on 1142 m² in Binningen on the corner of the noisy Baslerstrasse (which is used by trams) and Schlüsselgasse. Five storeys and a recessed attic level contain a total of nine owner-occupied apartments with a living area of 1265 m² and a garage, which is located on the underground level (covered ramp to Schlüsselgasse, wheelchair-accessible lift to all six levels). The facade is 31 metres wide and 16.3 metres high. It is clad in ochre-coloured clinker bricks that are punctuated by the tonally similar concrete ceilings of the different floors, creating a serial effect: windows on the street, northern and southern facades are single-unit, upright floor-to-ceiling (2.5 metres) rectangles. This minimalistic facade design protects the interior space from noise (the facade facing the garden features floor-to-ceiling glazing) and urbanizes the street space south of the zoo and in the direction of Leimen (F). Above the apartments on the ground and basement levels (each 144 m²), the first two upper levels contain two apartments each (132 m²). The third upper level and the attic level contain maisonettes (152 and 147 m² respectively). Balconies, seating areas, and terraces occupy an area of 258 m². The elegant staircase above the foyer is made of unfinished reinforced concrete and features balustrades made of black MDF panels.

Facade to Baslerstrasse with glazed entrance hall.

Room-high glazing on garden side.

Planted light well in the underground car park.

Architect:	Peter Stiner Architekt, Basel
Landscape design:	August + Margrith Künzel Landschaftsarchitekten, Basel;
	www.august-kuenzel.ch
	Execution: Martin Rauch, Schlins, Austria
Client:	Zoological Gardens, Basel
	Project management: Thomas Schönbächler
Dates:	construction 1998–2003

ETOSCHA HOUSE IN THE ZOOLOGICAL GARDENS

Binningerstrasse 40, 4054 Basel | Tram 10: Zoo | Tram 2, Bus 34 36: Zoo Dorenbach | Tram 6 16: Heuwaage

South elevation

Etoscha is a strip of land with a national park in Namibia. The pavilion for predators in the Zoological Gardens, which were opened in 1874, was named after this region. The architecture follows a philosophy that aims for a spatial continuum for grown nature (garden) and built nature (architecture). In this setting, buildings cannot enter the scene as confident gestures; instead they serve as subordinate elements in the overall form. The winding path through the polygon (roughly 1120 m²) combines experiential space with an environment that is compatible for the featured fauna and flora. The slanted, fan-shaped position of the windows renders them invisible, suggesting a feeling of being under the open skies. A panorama window at the entrance offers a link between the climate requirements of this region (air temperature / humidity, flora) and the recreated landscape of the outdoor enclosure. The rammed-earth walls are a reference to the aesthetics of building styles and materials in South-western Africa.

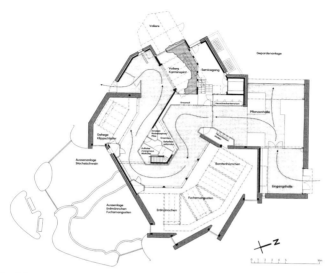

Ground plan

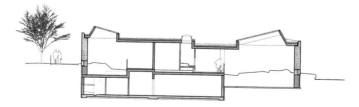

West-east section

Architect:	Silvia Gmür, Basel
	Now: Silvia Gmür Reto Gmür Architekten, Basel; www.gmuerarch.ch
Client:	F. Steiner, Basel
Dates:	construction 1990

ONE-ROOM HOUSE

Sonnenbergstrasse 92, 4059 Basel | Tram 15: Wolfschlucht | Tram 16: Hauensteinstrasse

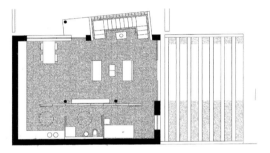

Ground floor

The Bruderholz neighbourhood was developed in the twentieth century and has few interesting architectural features. Some individual houses and row houses were co-operative projects. Many villas were constructed on large lots, and it is to this circumstance that Silvia Gmür's new building owes its existence: it occupies the space previously used for garages. The narrow structure on a concrete base, a single storey in steel and wood construction, is topped by a shallow gable roof. A kind of portico is set at a slight angle to the entrance facade. Two-thirds of the portico wall is glass brick, with the unfenestrated remainder providing a monumental frame around the front door. The glass-brick wall has the character of a very large minimalist picture that is transformed into a light sculpture when lit at night.

The portico on Sonnenbergstrasse

Interior with view of the garden

Architect:	Dolenc Scheiwiller Parli Architekten, Zurich; www.dsp-arch.ch
Client:	Martin Solèr, Basel
Dates:	design and planning 2008–2010, construction 2010–2011

VILLA AND APARTMENT HOUSE

Predigerhofstrasse 77+79, 4059 Basel | Bus 37 47: Bedrettostrasse

The terraced complex from the southeast.

Not far from the water tower, on the southern edge of the "Bruderholz" hill, Dolenc Scheiwiller Parli Architekten built a two-storey villa and an apartment house with four floors and three apartments with a shared vestibule. A shared car garage with room for eight cars is located between the buildings. Two lifts lead from here into all the apartments. The apartment house has two 4.5-room apartments (each with a guest bathroom) and, above them, an attic maisonette with 6.5 rooms and two bathrooms. The heights of the rooms range between 2.6 metres on the ground floor and 2.8 metres on the upper and attic levels. The plot measures 1790 m² and lies on the slope of a valley-like depression on the plateau between Binningen and Bottmingen (in the west) and Münchenstein and Reinach (in the east). The flat-roofed, clearly geometrically defined cubes are terraced into the slope. On the valley-side ground floor (2.6 metres high) and upper level (3 metres high) of the villa, a floor-to-ceiling sliding-sash "frameless" glass wall (only a 66 mm vertical profile is visible) stretching the entire width of the building opens onto the landscape. The floors are made of oak and large limestone plates. On all the levels and the roof of the apartment house, covered and open terraces (with a total area of 288 m²) provide a view of the hilly landscape of the northern Jura.

Ground plan of ground floor

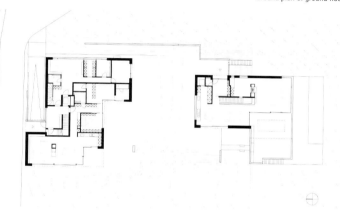

North-south section

Architect:	Herzog & de Meuron, Basel; www.herzogdemeuron.com
Client:	Laurenz-Stiftung, Münchenstein / Basel
Dates:	project planning 1998–1999, construction 2000–2003

SCHAULAGER OF THE LAURENZ FOUNDATION

Ruchfeldstrasse 19, 4141 Münchenstein | Tram 11, Bus 60: Schaulager | Bus 36: Dreispitz

West facade with a composite
of excavation pebble and concrete

With an area of 16 500 square metres on five floors, the exhibition warehouse of the Laurenz Foundation in the industrial district of Münchenstein is a building that presents a hermetically closed exterior and reveals its qualities in the interior. The exhibition areas (basement and ground floor, 3350 m²) and the storage areas (floors 2 to 4, 7500 m²) house the roughly 650 works of art of the Emanuel Hoffmann Foundation and are arranged around a 28-metre-high atrium. Virtual windows in the form of LED screens are incorporated into the entrance facade, wich is compressed into a trapezoid shape. Works from the collection are displayed in large-scale and monumental formats on these screens. The untreated oak floor in the basement and on the ground floor invests the building with the ambience of a luxury loft. The auditorium with 144 purple arm chairs, walls and ceiling covered in carefully worked metal screens and a picture window set into the face wall has the feeling of a sanctuary. The exhibition warehouse is only open to the public from May to September.

The 28-metre-high atrium

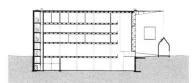

West-east section

Floor plan of 2nd to 4th floor

Architect:	Berrel Architekten, Basel, with Zwimpfer Partner Krarup Furrer, Basel
	Now: Berrel Berrel Kräutler, Basel; www.bbk-architekten.ch with
	Zwimpfer Partner, Basel; www.zwimpferpartner.ch
Client:	Genossenschaft Regionale Eissporthalle St. Jakob, Binningen
Dates:	project planning and construction 2001–2002

ST. JAKOBARENA

Brüglingen 33, 4142 Münchenstein | Tram 14, Bus 36 37: St. Jakob

Facade with main entrance

The facade is the dress for the new skating rink: the architects have stretched 30 textile squares, each roughly 80 square metres (8.9 by 9.7 metres), in front of the concrete oval foundation and their elegant steel-and-glass structure. The more than 100-metre-long and roughly 20-metre-high building, which can accommodate 6000 spectators, lies in the plain of St. Jakob like a monochromatic film strip. The site can look back on a long history of international sporting events. The arena features an innovative heating- and ventilation system, opening new doors in terms of ecological and economic operation. A filigree metal construction allows for a column-free 70-metre-wide interior. The zinc of the metal banisters and night-blue seats create an ambience of temporary and tranquil comfort. The usage programme is rounded out with facilities for intramurals and private sports clubs.

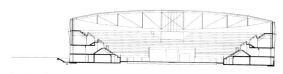

South-north section

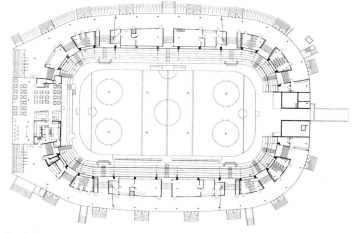

Ground plan

Architect:	Herzog & de Meuron, Basel; www.herzogdemeuron.com
	Project management Renée Levy
Client:	E. Brunner-Sulzer, Bottmingen
Dates:	project planning 1984, construction 1985

PLYWOOD HOUSE

Rappenbodenweg 6, 4103 Bottmingen | Bus 37 63: Bruderholzspital | Tram 15: Studio Basel

The bend in the facade,
designed to accommodate
the Paulownia imperialis

Rhythmic arrangement of windows
on the south side

Ground floor

The villa expansion came to be called the Plywood House because of the material used in the facade, while its shape was determined by the presence of a large tree on the site. To accommodate the tree, a Paulownia imperialis, architects Herzog & de Meuron slightly angled one side of the rectangular plan, creating an inward fold along one facade. The gently sloped gable roof extends into a generous overhang on all sides. Elevated on low supports, the structure has a lightness reminiscent of Japanese pavilions. The facade is divided into a grid of equal squares. The forty-two squares on the angled south side allow for playful treatment of windows: a ribbon of windows on one side, a panoramic window stretching the full height in the centre, and clerestory windows above.

Architect:	Michael Alder, Associate Roland Naegelin, Basel
	Now: Atelier Gemeinschaft (Hanspeter Müller, Roland Naegelin), Basel
Clients:	D. and M. Reicke, Bottmingen
Dates:	project planning 1987, construction 1988

SINGLE-FAMILY HOUSE

Kirschbaumweg 27, 4103 Bottmingen | Bus 61: Bertschenacker | Bus 34: Blauenstrasse

The facade overlooking the garden

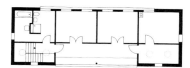

Second floor

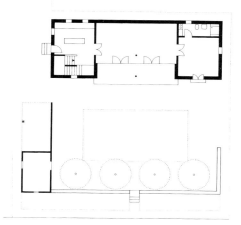

Ground floor and garden

It is rare for a single-family house to be designed around its central axes. Yet Michael Alder's layout for the house in Bottmingen is centred on both the longitudinal axis and the transverse axis. The entrance on the narrow west side leads straight into the living space. At the far wall of the adjoining room the corridor ends in a square window. The living room has a fully glazed wall looking onto the garden – a band of light that recurs on the upper floor in the hallway leading to the bedroom and library wing. The balanced harmony of the interior carries over to the exterior. With its fine wood siding, the facade exudes an air of contemplative stillness and confident containment.

Architect:	Ackermann & Friedli, Basel
	Now: Ackermann Architekt, Basel; www.ackermann-arch.ch
Client:	Community Living Foundation, Bottmingen
Dates:	competition 1994, project planning 1996/1997, construction 1998–1999

AM BIRSIG COMMUNITY CENTRE AND HOUSING

Löchlimattstrasse 6, 4103 Bottmingen | Tram 10 17: Stallen

Ground floor

On a quiet lot bordering the Birsig River and located slightly below a main artery road, Ackermann & Friedli have created a centre for community activities and community living. These separate uses are served by two individual structures whose main entrances face each other beneath a connecting roof. The residential unit has direct access to outdoor patios; the upper floor features operable skylights. These brick-faced buildings are animated by large windows, carefully selected wood and stone floors, and spacious entrance areas. Exterior views and interior perspectives are varied, creating a stimulating yet contemplative atmosphere.

Facade overlooking the Birsig River

Terrace on upper floor with wall
openings

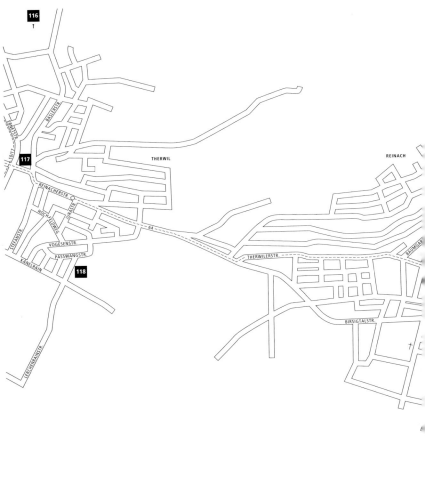

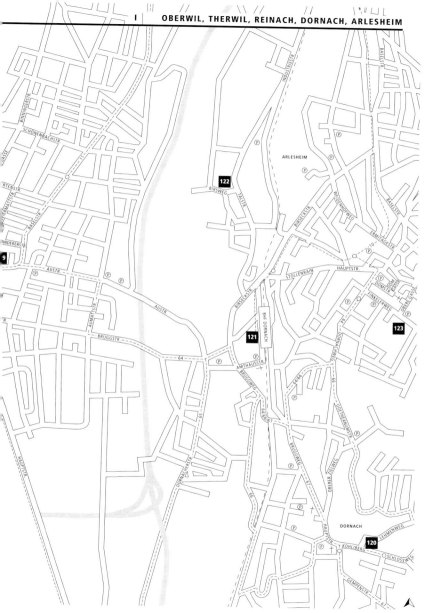

Architect:	Proplaning Architekten, Basel; www.proplaning.ch
Client:	BLT Baselland Transport AG, Oberwil
Dates:	competition 2001, project planning and construction 2004–2007

BUS AND STREETCAR DEPOT FOR BASELLAND TRANSPORT AG (BLT)

Grenzweg 1, 4104 Oberwil | Tram 10 17, Bus 61: Hüslimatt

Facade with aluminium panels on
west (top) and east elevations

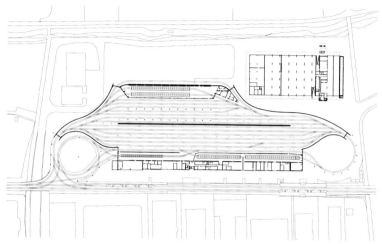

The entire streetcar and bus
depot ensemble covering nearly
22 000 square metres

Thirty years ago, the southern boundary of the trinational city was still located on the edge of Bottmingen. From this suburb, the road coming from downtown continued on to Oberwil (within eyesight) and further to Therwil. Today, this area is covered in a heterogeneous patchwork of commercial and industrial buildings. In these surroundings characterized by urban sprawl, the architects have converted and expanded a bus and streetcar depot, thus creating a visual anchor for the area. The original 10 500-square-metre floor area of the two halls (streetcar and bus depot), including service, maintenance and attached administration building, was doubled to nearly 22 000 square metres. The separate utility buildings for "road" and "rail," morphologically separated as a rectangular (bus depot) and a curved (streetcar depot) structure, are visually linked by glazed folding gates (nearly 5 metres in height). The almost hermetically closed facade – 430 metres long, 7 metres high and faced in pearl-blue aluminium panels – is the core feature of the ensemble. The building has the appearance of an outdoor sculpture.

Architect:	Nissen & Wentzlaff Architekten; www.nwarch.ch
	collaborators Daniel Wentzlaff, Ute Fromm, Hermann Raetzo, Anna Karg, Andreas Reus
Client:	Raiffeisenbank Therwil and TherMitte Wohngenossenschaft, Therwil
Dates:	competition 2004, planning and construction 2006–2009

THERWIL: BAHNHOFSTRASSE SÜD

Bahnhofstrasse 28, 4106 Therwil | Tram 10: Therwil Bahnhof

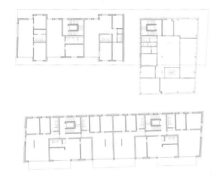

Ground plan of the three buildings
on Bahnhofstrasse (upper edge).

Facade on Bahnhofstrasse with
pre-weathered larch slats and the
clear glass box (bottom left).

View from courtyard through the passage onto Bahnhofstrasse and the luminous red rubber granulate.

On a 4234 m² area along Bahnhofstrasse in Therwil, Nissen & Wentzlaff Architekten erected three buildings with a total floor area of 6760 m². The complex consists of a 49-metre-long, two-part cube at the street (thirteen apartments with 2.5, 3.5, and 4.5 rooms). The structure projects to the east, where a glass box was built into it at ground level (containing a single floor four metres high). This clear glass box has been occupied by one of the client's branches. Parallel to this building and separated from it by a courtyard (an underground garage offers fifty-one parking spaces) is a three-storey residential building containing ten units (2.5, 3.5, and 4.5 rooms). Both buildings have shops or practices on their ground floors and two access zones (stairs, lifts). The building on the street features a facade made of pre-weathered larch slats that have been mounted to create an arrhythmic texture (see facade structure project 27). The ground around the buildings has been covered from the edge of the street over an area of 800 m² with luminous red rubber granulate, the same material used for the St. Gallen city lounge by Pipilotti Rist in 2005 (marking the headquarters of the client, Raffeisenbank). Strip lighting laid parallel to the street in the ground covering provides illumination at night.

Architect:	Herzog & de Meuron, Basel; www.herzogdemeuron.com
	Project management Annette Gigon
Clients:	H. and M. Vögtlin-König, Therwil
Dates:	project planning 1985, construction 1986

HOUSE FOR AN ART COLLECTOR

Lerchenrainstrasse 5, 4106 Therwil | Tram 10 17: Känelmatt | Bus 64: Jurastrasse

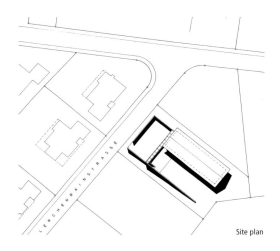

Site plan

The house for an art collector in Therwil is a single-family home with an exhibition space. The general orientation is similar to the Courtyard Residential Building (see project 8). The hermetic character of the building was perceived as provocative for some time in this rural town environment south of the city, perhaps owing to its uncompromising use of exposed concrete. With its introverted air and gravelled courtyard, the building makes clear reference to Tadao Ando's Japanese residential designs. The structure is oriented along the length of the deep lot. The lot extends slightly at the south-west end, making it hexagonal, which provides some rhythm in the design without disturbing its confident air of equanimity.

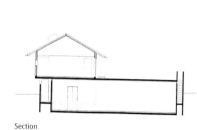

Section

Enclosed environment

The gravelled courtyard

Architect:	Morger & Degelo, Basel
	Now: Morger & Dettli, Basel; www.morger-dettli.ch and
	Degelo Architekten, Basel; www.degelo.net
Client:	Community of Reinach, Reinach
Dates:	competition 1997, project planning and construction 1998–2002

COMMUNITY CENTRE REINACH

Hauptstrasse 10, 4153 Reinach | Tram 11: Landererstrasse | Bus 64: Reinach Dorf

Facade on the main street

The goal was to achieve a presence with a building in Reinach comparable to that of similar public buildings in the old cities of northern Italy. This is precisely what Morger & Degelo succeeded in creating with a nearly square cube for the community administration. The four-storey glass block is the core of an ensemble that also contains apartment and commercial buildings. For the first time since 1964, the administration of the community is once again housed under one roof. In the interior of the "palazzo pubblico," an open gallery court directly behind the main entrance provides centralized access. The floor covering in Greek marble is both refined and hardwearing. Between the second and the fourth floor, where the corridors and window axes of the building rotate windmill-like by 90 degrees each, windows stretching across the entire height and width of the rooms offer twelve different picture postcard views. The space in front of the main street elevation has been gently terraced and has become a piazza for Reinach.

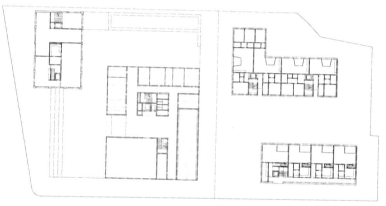

The four buildings of the ensemble
with the main street (left)

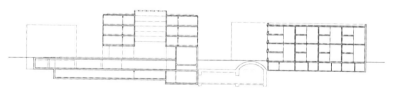

South-north section

Architect:	Morger & Degelo, Basel
	Associate Nadja Keller
	Now: Morger & Dettli, Basel; www.morger-dettli.ch and
	Degelo Architekten, Basel; www.degelo.net
Clients:	A. and Ch. Nadolny, Dornach
Dates:	project planning and construction 1995–1996

SINGLE-FAMILY HOUSE

Lehmenweg 2 / Schlossweg, 4143 Dornach | Bus 66: Quidum | Bus 67: Museumsplatz

South facade

Second floor

Ground floor

Architects Morger & Degelo built a single-family house in Dornach on the southern edge of metropolitan Basel, within walking distance of Rudolf Steiner's famous Goetheanum. The severe design – the unbroken cedar facade to the north gives the house a box-like appearance – echoes the traditional wooden farmhouses of the area, some of which are preserved in the village of Dornach. The two floors contain a total of 200 square metres of living space. Generously proportioned windows to the south, east, and west open the sophisticated wood structure to landscape and light. The public area (living room, etc.) and the private area (bedrooms, etc.) are set apart by the use of different materials: slate for the ground floor and parquet flooring upstairs. Two right angles are joined to form a slightly trapezoidal ground plan.

Architect:	Otto + Partner Architektur, Liestal; www.ottopartner.ch
	Associates Andreas Rüegg, Mario Cerri, Bruno Gräf, Christoph Stauffer,
	René Grellinger
Client:	Tiefbauamt, Kanton Basel-Landschaft, Liestal
Dates:	project 2006, planning and construction 2008–2009

BUS TERMINUS AT DORNACH-ARLESHEIM
RAILWAY STATION

Bahnhofstrasse, 4144 Arlesheim | Tram 10, S 3 : Bahnhof Dornach-Arlesheim

Section of the different wave movements of the three roofs.

The bus terminus was built by Otto + Partner architects on the border between the cantons of Basel-Landschaft (Arlesheim) and Solothurn (Dornach). Supported by 14 steel pillars with horizontal cross girders, the architects constructed a wooden roof 0.4 metres thick in the form of irregular waves (total area 1146 m²). The waves emulate the view of rolling hills provided by the surrounding Jura landscape, creating an impression of sound waves of different frequencies (first wave: 56 metres long, second: 54.5 metres, third: 42 metres). The lens-shaped spaces of varying dimensions (between 6.2 × 1.4 m and 3 × 0.4 m) between the waves have been covered with glass to create windows. These provide side lighting onto the expressively undulating ceiling. Although the structure is open on all sides, the impression created is comparable to that of a low (between 4.5 and 7.3 metres high) sacral building. The parallel roof of the Swiss Rail train platform is overlapped by the undulating structure, providing travellers with protection from rain when moving between trains and buses. The terminus is equipped with three boarding islands catering to six bus lines serving the villages of the northern Jura and the southern entrance to the actual city.

The structure in front of
the Dornach-Arlesheim station
platform roof.

The bus station by night.

Architect:	Proplaning Architekten, Basel; www.proplaning.ch
Client:	Baselland civic servants pension fund, Liestal;
	Basel civic servants pension fund, Basel
Dates:	construction 1997–1999

OBERE WIDEN RESIDENTIAL DEVELOPMENT

Birseckstrasse/Talstrasse, 4144 Arlesheim | Tram 10: Stollenrain | Zug, Bus 64 65 66 67: Dornach Bahnhof

One of five long buildings with
clinker-brick facades

The row houses in wood construction

Site plan: the clinker-faced buildings
frame the wooden row houses in
the centre.

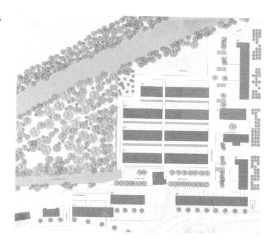

Proplaning designed a new residential complex in the town of Arlesheim on a 4.2-hectare
lot that includes an 8000-square-metre nature preserve along the Birs, a tributary of the
Rhine. Five powerful clinker-brick buildings, up to 100 metres long, line the site of a
former textile factory. The architects placed forty wooden row houses into the factory
court in four parallel rows that follow the lines of the former factory shed roofs. The
houses are structured in the fashion of maisonette apartments, with attic rooms on the
roof with large dormer windows. In the horizontal extension, the windows emulate the
window ribbons of early industrial architecture. The 180 apartments, with up to five
rooms per unit, set an urban accent in this area of suburban sprawl to the south-east
of Basel.

Architect:	Klaus Schuldt, Basel with Andreas Scheiwiller, Basel
	Now: Dorenbach Architekten, Basel; www.dorenbach.com and
	Dolenc Scheiwiller Parli, Zurich; www.dolenc-scheiwiller.ch
	Associates Carmen Müller, Thomas Grasser
Client:	Dorenbach AG, Basel; P. and S. Dudler, H.P. von Hahn, N. and L. Hosch,
	J. C. Müller, K. and G. Schuldt, Arlesheim
Dates:	project planning 1996, construction 1997–2000

ZUM WISSE SEGEL, VILLAS

Zum wisse Segel 5, 7, 10, 11, 12, 4144 Arlesheim I Bus 64: Obesunne I Tram 10: Arlesheim Dorf

Site plan with ground-floor plans

Architects Klaus Schuldt and Andreas Scheiwiller designed five two-storey detached homes ranging from 240 to 300 square metres in ground plan for a barely 5400-square-metre lot in Arlesheim. Despite the rural environment, the homes have an urban character by virtue of their precise arrangement and their proximity to the cathedral square. The Baroque ensemble and the cathedral itself, together with four massive residential and administration buildings, were the first major architecture outside the southern boundary of Basel. In the new development, the architects have structured the houses with floor-to-ceiling glass fronts, opening them to light and to the gardens. The designs deliberately reflect typologies developed by Mies van der Rohe in the 1920s (Wolf House in Guben, 1925–1926 and Lang House in Krefeld, 1928).

Northwest elevation of House 10
and House 12

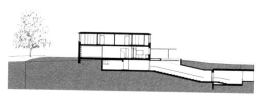

Longitudinal section of House 11

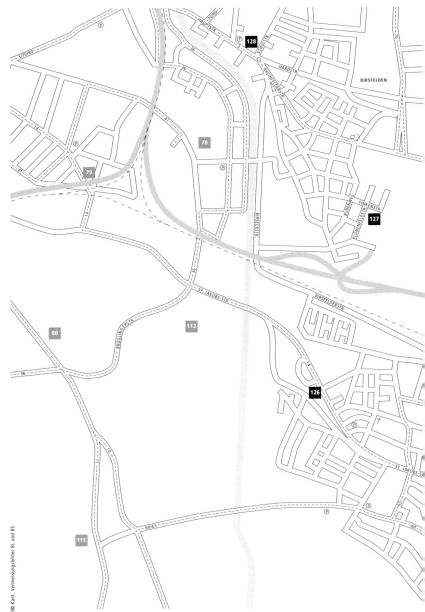

BASLERSTR

MARKGRAFENSTR

SCHEFFELSTR

EMIL BARELL STR

RHEINALLEE

129

RHEINALLEE

RHEINFELDERSTR

70/80

GRENZACHERSTR

BHF MUTTENZ

HOFACKERSTR

GRENZACHERSTR

MUTTENZ

63

60/70/80

60

HARDSTR

60

ST. JAKOBS-STR

NEUE BAHNHOFSTR

BAHNHOFSTR

FREIBURGERSTR

TRAMSTR

125

PRATTELERSTR

14

124

60

Architect:	Bürgin Nissen Wentzlaff, Basel
	Now: Nissen Wentzlaff Architekten, Basel; www.nwarch.ch
Client:	Coop Basel Liestal Fricktal, Basel
Dates:	project planning 1995, construction 1996–1998

HOTEL, SUPERMARKET, APARTMENTS

St. Jakobs-Strasse 1 / Ecke Hauptstrasse, 4132 Muttenz | Train: Muttenz Bahnhof |
Tram 14, Bus 60: Muttenz Dorf

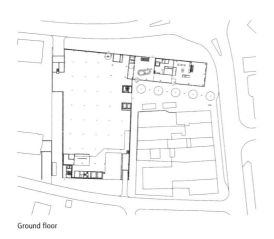

Ground floor

Architects Bürgin Nissen Wentzlaff designed a supermarket with 2500 square metres of
floor space, a 200-bed hotel, and apartments in the town of Muttenz for their client, the
Swiss grocery chain Coop. The fully glazed base was placed onto the L-shaped lot, and
two tall structures rise from this base. The one-flight staircase, accessing the five floors
and the hotel, is the most noticeable design element of the complex. On the south side
of the supermarket, five maisonette apartments were built, which can be reached by a
covered walkway. The facade with vertical glazed rectangles and perforated white aluminium shutters is a showcase feature.

The single-flight staircase across five floors

Architect:	Rosenmund + Rieder Architekten, Liestal; www.rosenmund-rieder.ch
Client:	J. and L. Tschudin-Manzoni, Muttenz
Dates:	planning 2005–2006, construction 2006–2007

APARTMENT BUILDING LANGMATTSTRASSE

Langmattstrasse 6, 4132 Muttenz | Tram 14, Bus 60: Muttenz Dorf | Urban rail transit 1 9:
Muttenz Bahnhof

Facades on St. Jakobs-Strasse (left)
and on Langmattstrasse

Near the Muttenz town centre (project 124) Rosenmund + Rieder have erected a four-storey building in fair-faced concrete with eight 3.5- and 4.5-room apartments ranging in size from 113 to 165 square metres. The floors are in wood (oak) and stone. The plan of the slender structure has the geometrical shape of a decahedron composed of a double pentagon. On the top floors, this plan changes into that of a creased hexagon as a result of balconies / patios. This rhythmic interplay of exterior and interior plan creates lively visual axes into and from the living spaces and an animated exterior form, especially noticeable on the facade overlooking the gardens on the southeast side (see also project 138). On the side facing the busy St. Jakobs-Strasse, the park-like garden and the building are lowered and sheltered behind a masonry wall. On Langmattstrasse, the facade is evenly divided by long, parallel window ribbons. The access to the underground garage is located on Gartenstrasse, which runs parallel to this street. In this sprawling suburb, the building serves as a symbol of urbanity.

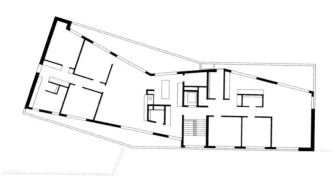

Floor plan of upper floors

Living room and kitchen with patio

Architect:	Rosenmund + Rieder Architekten, Liestal; www.rosenmund-rieder.ch
Client:	Freidorf housing cooperative, Muttenz
Dates:	competition 2000, planning 2004–2005, construction 2005–2006

EXPANSION OF "FREIDORF" HOUSING ESTATE WITH AN APARTMENT BUILDING

St. Jakobs-Strasse 143, 145, 147, 149, 151, 153, 4132 Muttenz | Tram 14: Freidorf

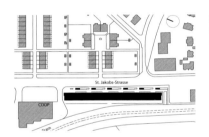

Site plan with new structure
(dark) and the historic "Freidorf"
(top left)

Building seen from the south-west

Floor plan module of upper floors in
all six building units

Stairwell landings and entrances
to apartments

As a contribution to urban, estate and housing construction, the "Freidorf" estate
(1919–1921), designed by the later Bauhaus director Hannes Meyer, is undeniable part
of architectural history. Eighty-five years later, Rosenmund + Rieder erected a four-storey
complementary building on the opposite side of St. Jakobs-Strasse. The previously
monotonous streetscape has thus been transformed into a framed space. At the same
time, forty-five 3- and 4-room apartments (70 to 92 m²), one 5-room apartment (108 m²)
and four bachelor apartments (32 m²) have expanded the use of Hannes Meyer's row
housing settlement. The spatial program resulted in a slender slab, 138 metres long and
12.5 metres wide, consisting of six identical units. Axes and landscaping on the street
elevation (privet hedge) tie in with the historic neighbour. The new, minimalistic structure, with slightly projecting floor slabs, is clad in varnished wood-metal windows and
panels. The apartments on the upper floors have large loggias which can be closed off
overlooking the tram tracks to the rear. A communal spirit is palpable in the circulation-
and communication-friendly stairwells.

Architect:	Frank O. Gehry + Associates, Santa Monica (CA)
	Now: Gehry Partners, Los Angeles; www.foga.com
	Project management, planning and site management Günter Pfeifer
	in partnership with Roland Mayer
	Now: Günther Pfeifer Architektur, Freiburg / Brsg.; www.pfeifer-kuhn.com;
	mayer bährle, Lörrach; www.mayer-baehrle.com
Client:	Vitrashop AG, Birsfelden
Dates:	construction 1992–1994

VITRA-CENTER

Klünenfeldstrasse 22, 4127 Birsfelden | Tram 3: Birsfelden Hard

The deconstructivist architecture
of the Villa

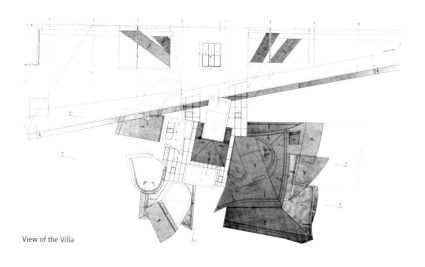

View of the Villa

Frank O. Gehry's first building in Switzerland – and Vitra's second home – was opened in Birsfelden in 1994 (see also project 153, Gehry's first building in Europe). The office wing responds to the existing Vitra building from 1957, whose facade is similarly structured. For the "Villa", which houses the reception rooms and serves as the main entrance to the company's head office, Gehry has delved into the treasure chest of his imagination for a playful combination of spherical, convex, concave, and other geometric shapes. These expressive forms are covered in titanium cladding; large lighting fixtures are prototypes; individual rooms are painted in pop colours. Some sections of the 6000-square-metre structure seem like a designer's adventure playground.

Architect:	Bürgin Nissen Wentzlaff, Basel
	Now: Nissen Wentzlaff Architekten, Basel; www.nwarch.ch
Client:	main building: Cantonal Bank of Baselland, Liestal;
	annex building: P. Leuenberger, Birsfelden
Dates:	project planning 1993, construction 1994–1996

BANK AND OFFICE BUILDING

Hauptstrasse 75/77, 4127 Birsfelden ⏐ Tram 3: Schulstrasse

The austere south facade

In Birsfelden the Cantonal Bank of Baselland commissioned a new office building complete with retail shops and office areas for its subsidiary. Architects Bürgin Nissen Wentzlaff were faced with a challenging site and designed a building that presents two very different faces. Its concept is both classically modern and anarchic. Two facades meet at a ninety-degree angle in a clash of contrasting materials (white stone, blue glass) and different design philosophies. The vertical windows on two sides are asynchronously arranged and the horizontal window ribbon makes one think of a jazz score. Nevertheless, this is a measured, "metric" architecture that follows an additive order. It creates a lyrical anchor for the "loud" urban site.

The melodic north facade

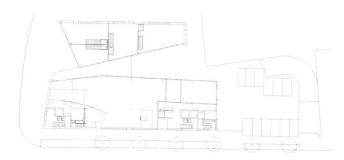

Ground floor

Architect:	Nissen Wentzlaff Architekten, Basel; www.nwarch.ch
	Daniel Wentzlaff, Michael Muellen, Stephan Schweizer
Client:	Roche Pharma AG, D-79639 Grenzach-Wyhlen
Dates:	competition 2005, planning and execution 2005–2007

OFFICE BUILDING FOR ROCHE PHARMA AG (BAU 200)

Emil-Barell-Strasse 1, D-79639 Grenzach-Wyhlen | Zug DB Grenzach-Bahnhof

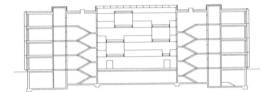

Cross-section of courtyard with
skylight (centre) and connecting
bridges

At the German Roche headquarters, Nissen Wentzlaff Architekten have erected a four-storey new building. The glazed structure (building 200) lies parallel to an administration building by Roland Rohn (building 44) from 1955. In the same year, Rohn also completed the expansion of the main administration headquarters in Basel designed by Otto Rudolf Salvisberg (1935/36). In Grenzach-Wyhlen Salvisberg's influence is visible in the elegant, fully glazed stairwell tower. At the sightline to the east, the new structure has been added facing south and measuring 54.6×22.6×16.2 metres (length/width/height). At the end sides, the building is linked to the original structure via a slim, single-storey office corridor and an open walkway. The addition also created an interior courtyard (30×42 metres) with a hilly grassy area and a level, green asphalt area (Dipol Landschaftsarchitekten). The facades of the new building are constructed of 450 frame modules, each 1.6×3.7 metres high (floor height). This gives the large volume (25 000 m³ with 3600 m² floor area) a surprising lightness. A covered atrium occupies the core of the building. In this space, inserted, glazed cubes are employed to create conference rooms, while bridges provide circulation links and relaxation zones (see also project 42).

Elevation of east facade in front
of historic structure with glazed
stairwell (right)

Facade overlooking courtyard with
open walkway

LANGE
ERLEN

139

136

138 137

134

135

133

134

132

131

130

INZLINGERSTR

ÜL 3

32

45

®

Architect:	Kunz und Mösch Architekten, Basel; www.kunzundmoesch.ch
Client:	Implenia Generalunternehmung AG, Geneva
Dates:	design 2007, planning and construction 2008–2009

FIVE UNITS IN A LONG HOUSE

Hörnliallee 1–9, 4125 Riehen | Bus 31 38: Hörnli Grenze

Ground plan of the 60-meter-
long and 6-meter-wide
building with 5 units.

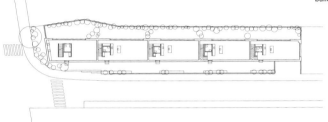

On a 940 m² plot (abutting Grenzacherstrasse and running for more than 60 metres along Hörnliallee), the architects Kunz und Mösch erected five residential units in an elongated cube (6 metres wide, 68 metres long, and 8 metres high). The narrow plot, its location on the busy Hörnliallee (to the east), and the area taken up by family gardens (to the west) have all played a role in shaping the overall design. On the side facing Hörnliallee, where the five entrances are located, the facade consists of a closed wall with windows in the upper storey. On the side facing the gardens (see project 71) the five, 13-metre-wide units are opened up on the ground floor by 9-metre-wide sliding windows in wooden frames, on the upper level by ribbon windows running almost the entire length of the facade, and in the cube forming the attic level (corresponding to the window on the street side) a panoramic window. The long house with its five units is constructed of concrete and painted with a grey-brown, monochrome glaze to create a visual unity. The units have from 3.5 to 5.5 rooms (140–160 m²), are accessed via alternating stairways against the external walls, and have floors made of sanded anhydrite and parquet. Each of them is equipped with an open terrace (35–38 m²) on the attic level and a sitting area (15–23 m²) on the ground floor.

The almost closed
facade to Hörnliallee.

Elevations of the street facade (top)
and garden facade (bottom).

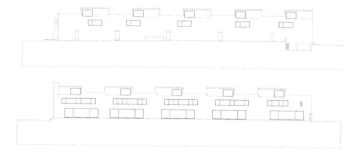

Architect:	Ueli Zbinden Architekt, Zurich; www.uelizbinden.ch
	Mitarbeit Stephan Corsten, Felix Frey, Mireya Heredero
Client:	Gemeinde Riehen; Kanton Basel-Stadt; Deutsche Bahn AG, Frankfurt/Main
Dates:	competition 2004, construction 2008

RIEHEN-NIEDERHOLZ S-BAHN STATION

Rauracherstrasse, 4125 Riehen | Tram 6: Niederholz | S-Bahn 6, DB 87869: Riehen-Niederholz

Presented with a cross-section of this design without any dimensions, one might well interpret the central volume as a drawing for a building around 18 metres wide and 65 metres high. However, the new Riehen-Niederholz railway station designed by Ueli Zbinden, which nestles sveltely and elegantly into the slope of a railway embankment, is in reality 3 metres wide and 10.7 metres high. The slender steel structure is completely clad in profiled glass. The pilasters in the vertical facade fields lend the glass wall a minimalistic structure where it slants towards Rauracherstrasse, which passes underneath the railway. In the interior a lift and a cascaded staircase lead up to the platform loggia (35 metres long, 4.5 metres wide, 3.75 metres high), which traverses the street like a bridge. The loggia features a roof projecting towards the tracks, a glass waiting room (3 metres wide, 6.5 metres long) and seating made of synthetic resin densified wood. The name of the station, Niederholz, is vertically mounted in red acrylic lettering stretching the entire height of the building behind the Profilit glazing. The stairs and lift also lead down to the underground level, which provides space for a car park planned with a shopping centre in the competition phase (2004).

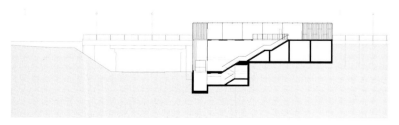

Axial section through the 35-meter-long structure.

The S-Bahn station with its profiled
glass cladding and lift (left).

The platform loggia.

Architect:	Rolf Brüderlin, Riehen
	Now: Brüderlin Merkle Architekten, Riehen; www.bmar.ch
	Associates Alex Callierotti, Giuseppe Pontillo
Client:	Canton Basel-Stadt, Department of civil services and environment,
	Planning department, Basel
Dates:	construction 1993–1994

HEBEL SCHOOL EXPANSION

Langenlängeweg 14, 4125 Riehen | Bus 31 34 35 45: Bahnhof Niederholz | Tram 6: Niederholz

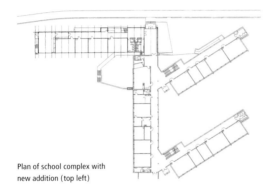

Plan of school complex with
new addition (top left)

Rolf Brüderlin added a long block onto an existing school complex designed by Tibère
Vadi (completed in 1951) in Riehen. Since the site was previously occupied by a kindergarten in wood construction designed by Hans Bernoulli (1945) – a structure much liked
by students, teachers, and local residents – the architect decided to employ the same
skin on the street facade. The reddish brown louvred facade functions as an element of
visual archaeology. The south and garden facades are kept a delicate yellow. Brüderlin
has established a link to the original building by means of a mirror image: the glass
stairwell. Vadi made the stairs visible from the outside through a two-storey glass rectangle. A few metres farther along, there now exists an almost exact duplicate.

The stairs at the two-storey-high windows

Architect:	Metron, Brugg; www.metron.ch
	Markus Gasser, Urs Deppeler, Heini Glauser
	Supervision Brogli + Müller, Basel
Client:	Wohnstadt Bau- und Verwaltungs-Genossenschaft Basel
Dates:	project planning 1990/1991, construction 1992–1994

IM NIEDERHOLZBODEN HOUSING DEVELOPMENT

Im Niederholzboden/Arnikastrasse 12–26, 4125 Riehen | Tram 6: Niederholz

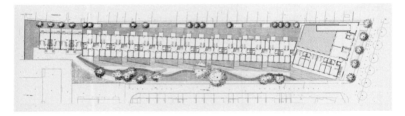

Plan of housing development

With a length of 200 metres, the Niederholzboden housing development lies like an anchor in heavily parcelled south Riehen. A main building with twelve apartments and two communal rooms is followed by another two-storey block that accommodates thirty apartments and four row houses. Metron Architekten were able to generate considerable energy savings for heating and ventilation, making this an energy-efficient development. Large balconies and a facade of yellow and red-brown wood panels define the look of the flat-roofed buildings, which enjoy a considerable depth of 14 metres. In den Habermatten (1924–1926) – a development that was equally trend-setting for its time – lies nearby.

Aerial view of the compact scheme

Main building with common rooms

Architect:	Rolf Furrer and François Fasnacht, Basel
	Now: Rolf Furrer Architekt, Basel
	and Fasnacht Architekten, Basel; www.fasnacht-architekten.ch
Client:	Basel Transport Services, Basel;
	Community of Riehen, Riehen
Dates:	project planning and construction 1992 and 1994–1995

RIEHEN DORF TRAM SHELTER

Baselstrasse | Tram 6: Riehen Dorf

LACHENWEG BUS SHELTER

Lachenweg / Grenzacherweg | Bus 34 35 45: Lachenweg

A competition in 1985 helped to create a new look for Basel's 230 tram and bus shelters. Two standard types for tram and bus shelters were established. The first has a rectangular plan which can be adapted to local topography in depth and width; and the second is a round, rain-protected shelter with seating, intended mostly for residential neighbourhoods. The elliptical shape of the stop in the village of Riehen is a prototype. The elegant structure designed by Rolf Furrer and François Fasnacht creates a focal point for the Riehen streetscape. The small structure is characterized by glass walls in a stacked arrangement and a skylight. As of 2011, 82 shelters based on this design had been built at 70 stops. Rolf Furrer took over sole management of the project in 1996.

Section and plan of the tram shelter
Riehen-Dorf

The elliptical construction

The bus shelter Lachenweg:
front view, plan, and section

Architect:	Stump & Schibli Architekten, Basel; www.stumpschibliarch.ch
Client:	Canton Basel-Stadt, Department of civil services and environment,
	Planning department, Basel
Dates:	competition 1995, construction 2000–2005

"ZUR HOFFNUNG"– RESIDENTIAL SCHOOL FOR CHILDREN

Wenkenstrasse 33, 4125 Riehen | Tram 6: Bettingerstr. | Bus 32: Martinsrain | Bus 34 35 45:
Bahnübergang | S6: Riehen-Bahnhof

One of the facades overlooking
the Wenkenstrasse

On the eastern slope overlooking the old town core of Riehen, Stump & Schibli have
transformed the "Zur Hoffnung" school into a small residential and training centre for
children with disabilities. Two massive stone buildings (both circa 1900) have been
preserved from the historic site on the nearly 29 000-square-metre lot and expanded
into an ensemble through the creation of a new administration building, two residential
buildings, a schoolhouse, a therapy building (with indoor pool), a stable and a nursery.
Three residential- and communal buildings have been set into the slope in such a clever
manner as to appear like large private residences with their generous windows and clear
outlines. Concrete, brick coping, parquet flooring and a sensual as well as efficient
lighting scheme generate an atmosphere of warm and elegant objectivity. The visual links
between all of the volumes create a spatial cohesion within the park-like setting.

View from the pool in the physiotherapy building

Site plan

Architect:	Renzo Piano Building Workshop, Paris; www.rpbw.com
	Management Burckhardt + Partner, Basel; www.burckhardtpartner.ch
Client:	Beyeler Foundation, Riehen
Dates:	project planning 1992, construction 1994–1997, expansion 2000

BEYELER FOUNDATION MUSEUM

Baselstrasse 101, 4125 Riehen | Tram 6: Fondation Beyeler | Bus 16 ÜL3: Weilstrasse

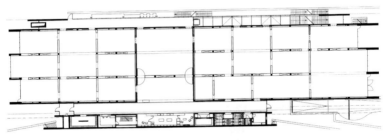

Ground floor

For the art collection of the Beyeler Foundation, Renzo Piano has created an elegant museum suffused with light. The approximately 3000-square-metre exhibition area is spread across two floors in a 125-metre-long building. Slightly lowered into the ground, the delicate structure is only visible in its entirety from a river plain behind the building. Since the administration and museum restaurant are located in a Baroque-style house, the architect was free to build a museum that represents an ideal within this typology. This work joins the ranks of famous museums worldwide, such as those designed by Henry van de Velde (Otterloo), Jørgen Bo and Vilhelm Wohlert (Zeeland), Frank Lloyd Wright (New York), Ludwig Mies van der Rohe (Berlin), and Louis I. Kahn (Fort Worth).

The museum and the park

Architect:	Wilfrid and Katharina Steib, Basel
Client:	Ecumenical Foundation, Wendelin House Nursing Home, Riehen
Dates:	competition 1985, construction 1986–1988

HAUS ZUM WENDELIN NURSING HOME

Inzlingerstrasse 50, 4125 Riehen | Bus 32 35 ÜL3: Hinter Gärten | Tram 6, Bus 16: Weilstrasse

Facades on garden side

Facade on Inzlingerstrasse

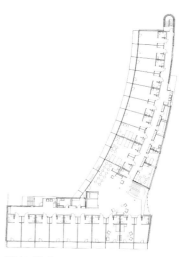

Third to fifth floor

The Wendelin House nursing home in Riehen follows the street in a gentle curve. The south facade on the garden side of the four-storey, L-shaped building describes a dynamic, outward-reaching curve. Wilfrid and Katharina Steib's design on this side is almost fully glazed, with balconies formed by covered walkways that run the length of each floor. The administration offices and communal rooms are on the ground floor. The entrance to this area lies on the fully glazed garden side, and these rooms are thus suffused with light. The predominant colours are pastel shades. Notable architectural projects (projects 136, 138 and 139) have been realized to the north, west and south almost in the same neighbourhood.

Architect:	Stump & Schibli Architekten, Basel; www.stumpschibliarch.ch
	Associates Dorothea Herbst, Jörg Grüner
Client:	Landpfrundhaus Riehen / Bettingen
Dates:	study commission 2004, planning 2004–2005, construction 2006–2007

RETIREMENT HOME IN THE OBERDORF

Inzlingerstrasse 46, 4125 Riehen | Tram 6: Weilstrasse | Bus 32 35 UL3: Hinter Gärten | Urban rail transit 6: Bahnhof-Riehen

The building on Spittlerwegli with the Wendelin House (bottom left)

A retirement home in Riehen with buildings on Oberdorfstrasse, Inzlingerstrasse and on Schützengasse was expanded in the park that occupies the central courtyard. Stump & Schibli erected a four-storey building with retirement units and a daycare facility. The enclosed fabric is raised on a plan in the form of a pentagon and accommodates twelve 3.5- and 4.5-room apartments (ranging from 90 to 110 m² in size) across three floors. Flexible lightweight walls make it possible to reconfigure rooms or apartments. The ground floor houses the daycare facilities (dining room, craft room, rest area and office), a small common room for the entire complex and a therapy space. The residential floors feature balconies on all sides with enclosed balustrades, expanding the plan of the pentagon into a creased octagon and investing the facade with a sculptural energy (see also project 94). The inner fabric is fully glazed and flooded with light; the apartments receive natural light from two sides through corner windows. Each landing of the stairwell includes a picture window and communal zone. Awnings transform the balconies into intimate loggias. The daycare on the ground floor is linked to the Wendelin House (project 137) via an underground, crescent-shaped corridor lit through a skylight.

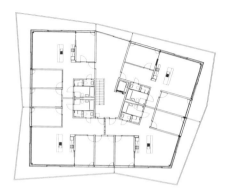

Floor plan of upper floors

The wrap-around patios on
the south side

The living rooms receive light from
two sides (corner windows).

Architect:	Michael Alder, Associate Roland Naegelin, Basel
	Now: Atelier Gemeinschaft (Hanspeter Müller, Roland Naegelin), Basel
Client:	HERA and Kettenacker housing cooperative, Riehen
Dates:	competition 1989, construction 1991–1992

VOGELBACH HOUSING DEVELOPMENT

Friedhofweg 30–80, 4125 Riehen | Tram 6, Bus 16 ÜL3: Weilstrasse

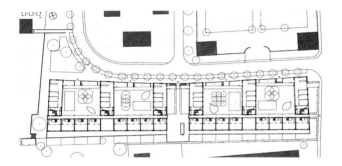

Plan of the 200-metre-long complex

Close to the German border, Michael Alder designed the Vogelbach housing co-op in Riehen. The complex contains forty single-level and duplex apartments, ranging from bachelor to five rooms. Since the 1920s, Riehen has been the site of many cooperative building projects. Paul Artaria, Hans Schmidt, and Hans Bernoulli, three pioneers of the New Architecture, have left their imprint in this district. Michael Alder continued the tradition: he grouped the differentiated cubical volumes around courtyards, arranging balconies, patios, and all exterior spaces along the south side for maximum sun exposure. Alder's design is deliberately urban by comparison to Hans Schmidt's more rural development from the post-war period.

Facade on Friedhofweg

One of five courtyards

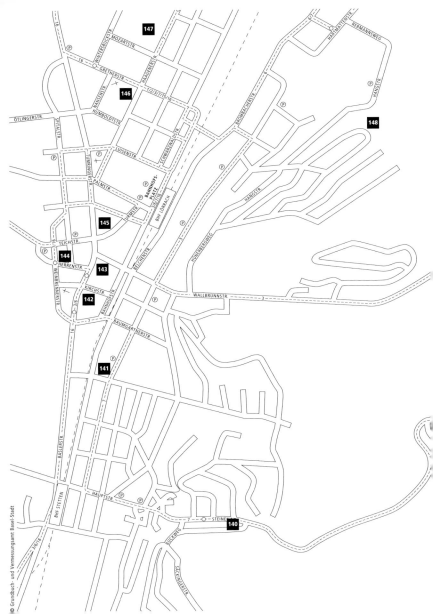

Architect:	Wilhelm and Hovenbitzer and Partner, Lörrach;
	www.wilhelm-hovenbitzer-partner.com
Client:	Hovenbitzer family, Lörrach
Dates:	original building 1956; renovation, planning, and construction
	of the extension 2009–2010

EXTENSION AND RENOVATION OF A SINGLE-FAMILY DWELLING

Steinenweg 22, D-79540 Lörrach ⎮ S-Bahn 6: Lörrach-Stetten ⎮ Bus (SWEG) 7: Steinenweg

The 3-meter-high living space on upper level 1.

In 1956, in Lörrach-Stetten near the border to Switzerland, the architect Walter Strasser constructed a good-quality residential building containing 126 m² of living space on a raised ground level with an upper level crowned by a deep gable roof (eaves height 3.7 metres / ridge height 8.15 metres). The ground plan of the house on Steinenweg is oriented north-south and lies on the street leading to the commuter town of Lörrach-Salzert (since 1963). The architects Wilhelm and Hovenbitzer and Partner extended this building with a two-storey poured-concrete, rectangular structure on the western side. The extension lies parallel to the sloping boundary of the property to the west, creating a trapezoid internal space towards the old building. The raised ground floor area (room height 2.4 metres) has been expanded with a hall-like room (height 3 metres). Pine floors now merge into oak parquet, and the old limestone staircase has been extended with slate stairs. By utilizing the slope of the property, the architects have transformed the raised ground floor of the old building into a new upper level and the basement into a new ground floor (with a second entrance). The living area has been increased from 126 m² to 198 m² and large, aluminium-and-oak panoramic windows have been installed.

The ensemble on Steinenweg.

Dialog across 50 years: the new facade (2010) with the old building (1956).

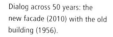

HANG-
GESCHOSS

Ground plan of ground floor of new building (left) with basement of old building.

ANSICHT WEST

Architect:	Thoma.Lay.Buchler.Architekten, Todtnau; www.tlb-architekten.de
	Project management Edgar Thoma, Udo Lay; construction management Dieter Dudssus
	Landscape architects: w + p Landschaften, Berlin; www.wp-landschaften.de
Client:	Städtische Wohnbaugesellschaft Lörrach mbH, Lörrach
Dates:	competition 2008, planning and construction 2010–2013

NIEDERFELDPLATZ NEIGHBOURHOOD

Brühlstrasse 18–26 / Kreuzstrasse 50–56, D-79540 Lörrach | S-Bahn S5 S6: Museum Burghof

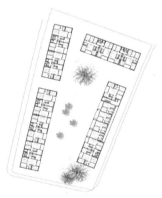

Ground plan of upper levels 1 to 3
(left: Brühlstrasse).

Facade over one hundred meters
long on Brühlstrasse.

Living space with
expansive windows.

In 2008 the architects Thoma.Lay.Buchler won a competition run by Wohnbau Lörrach (which owns 3000 and manages 800 dwellings) to construct a rental-apartment complex. The result was eighty-eight units in four buildings on the over-ground rail line (S-Bahn). Two of these buildings (41.5 and 62 metres long, respectively) are located on the eastern edge of Brühlstrasse and constitute the visible face of the quarter. The addition of the third (65.7 metres long) and fourth buildings (43 metres long) created an interior courtyard with a clear geometry. At the southern end of a new "wetland" (above an underground garage with eighty-eight parking spaces), the 8700 m² plot is bordered by a concrete wall. The 12.4-metre-high buildings are accessed via nine expansively glazed entrance towers containing stairs and lifts (the corner avant-corps on Brühlstrasse is 18.6 metres high). The complex contains four 1-room, twenty 2-room, twenty-six 3-room, twenty-five 4-room (each with two bathrooms) and twelve 5-room apartments, with areas ranging from 57 m² to 137 m². The quality of the complex is evident in its parquet floors, recessed loggias and terraces, and its spacious windows in the living areas framed with Black Forest silver fir.

Architect:	Günter Pfeifer in partnership with Roland Mayer
	Now: Günter Pfeifer Architektur, Freiburg / Brsg.; www.pfeifer-kuhn.com
	mayer bährle, Lörrach; www.mayer-baehrle.com
Client:	City of Lörrach, Stadtbauamt, Lörrach
Dates:	construction 1992–1993

DEPARTMENT STORE CONVERSION INTO LIBRARY

Baslerstrasse 128, D-79539 Lörrach I Bus ÜL3 3 6 7 8 16: Museum I Train: Lörrach Bahnhof

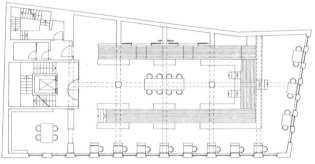

Third floor

A department store from circa 1900 was converted by Günter Pfeifer into Lörrach's public library. The four-storey structure with windows on two sides now includes an open-plan library, well-lit study areas, and a play area in the children's and youth section. The auditorium in the basement is reserved for lectures and other events. The architect has surrounded two load-bearing columns in the entrance area with four symmetrically arranged round metal pieces in a matt finish, connecting them by means of an elliptical polished rail into a sculptural unit. This creates an acoustic and visual barrier between the lending and the reading areas, and also serves as an exhibition space for new library acquisitions.

View into reading area

Architect:	Schaudt Architekten, Konstanz; www.schaudt-architekten.de
Client:	Verlagshaus Oberbadisches Volksblatt with Sparkasse Lörrach and ÖVA Mannheim
Dates:	competition 1992, project planning and construction 1993–1996

ALT STAZIONE CINEMA CAFÉ

Baslerstrasse 164/166, D-79539 Lörrach | Bus ÜL3 3 6 7 16: Alter Markt | Train: Lörrach Bahnhof

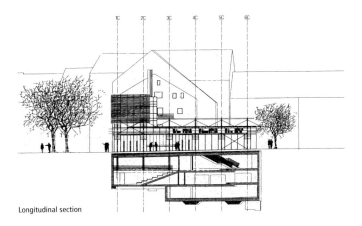

Longitudinal section

In the 1990s the Alter Markt neighbourhood was extensively refurbished and several new buildings were erected in the area. The most decisive intervention occurred with the construction of a slender steel and glass building designed by Schaudt Architekten. A mere 4 metres in width, more than 20 metres long, and approximately 10 metres high, it accommodates a café and three cinemas located underground. Miniature in its built environment, the structure nevertheless has an air of autonomy and urbanity because it doesn't seek to compete visually with any of the surrounding architecture. It is constructed on a modular grid and exudes the confident air of a free-standing building, even though it was simply added on to a four-storey office and residential building. The fire wall remains unchanged, with the exception of a new surface treatment.

Facade on Baslerstrasse

Architect:	Wilfrid and Katharina Steib, Basel
Client:	Stadt Lörrach, Stadtbauamt, Lörrach
Dates:	competition 1995, construction 1996–1998

AUF DEM BURGHOF THEATRE AND CONVENTION COMPLEX

Herrenstrasse 5, D-79539 Lörrach | Bus 3 6 7 8 16: Burghof | Train: Lörrach Bahnhof

The entrance portal

With the Burghof concert, theatre, convention, and exhibition complex Wilfrid and Katharina Steib have realized a multifunctional public building for the city of Lörrach. The 84-metre-long roof rises gently to the south where the theatre is located. The hall, with seating in a prototype design, has a maximum capacity of 900 visitors. Acoustics and ventilation are regulated by means of a specially designed wood floor and louvred mahogany panelling. Along the street front, the facade is nearly hermetically sealed, while a glass skin opens the building up on the courtyard side. The interiors in bold red and blue with shimmering ribbons of milk glass set into the flooring and the stairs create a tranquil and focused atmosphere. A large sculpture by Bruce Naumann stands next to the main entrance.

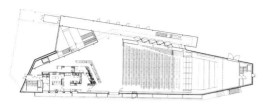

Ground floor

The large hall

Architect:	Würkert & Partner Architekten, Lörrach; www.wuerkert.eu
Client:	City of Lörrach and Regio Bau & Immobilien GmbH, Lörrach
Dates:	competition 2006, project 2006–2008, construction; 2008–2010

PEJA RESTAURANT, NEW BUILDING AND REMODELLING WITH A PASSAGEWAY TO CHESTERPLATZ

Chesterplatz 5, D-79539 Lörrach | BS-Bahn S5, S6: Lörrach

Peja Restaurant with glass wall to inner courtyard (back left).   Concrete wall on the passageway to Turmstrasse.

It was chance that led to the construction of a new building and a passageway in the old town of Lörrach. The town building department used a gap left by a demolition on Turmstrasse as an opportunity to initiate an urban planning project. The competition to select a design for a new passageway connecting Turmstrasse and Chesterplatz was won by Würkert & Partner. The overall project included a new 220 m² restaurant building (plus an interior courtyard above a cellar), which had to be implanted within an urban framework dating back to the nineteenth century. The result is the Peja Restaurant, whose 27.5-metre poured concrete wall forms the passageway facade. The wall runs flush with a concrete slab that abuts Turmstrasse (a counterpart is situated on the opposite corner) and accentuates the restaurant entrance with a glass section 5.6 metres high and 8.7 metres wide under a projecting roof. The path into the interior is laid along a single axis and leads first into a two-storey saloon with a gallery (120 m² and 40 m², respectively) and then into a 100 m² room in the earlier building (which was for the most part demolished). The height of the glass wall at the entrance matches that of the ceiling in the saloon and the window wall looking onto the interior courtyard. The parquet floors and window frames are made of oak. A shop has been built onto the passageway.

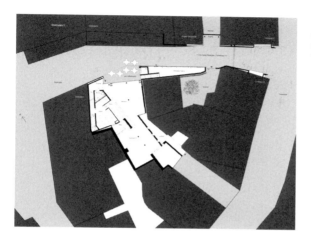

Site plan with the ground plan of the restaurant, Chesterplatz (top) and Turmstrasse (right).

The 5.6-meter-high glass entrance on Chesterplatz.

Architect:	Detlef Würkert and Hans Ueli Felchlin, Lörrach
	Now: Würkert & Partner Architekten, Lörrach; www.wuerkert.eu
	Felchlin & Partner, Frenkendorf
Client:	Städtische Wohnbaugesellschaft Lörrach, Lörrach
Dates:	project planning and construction 1994–1997

NANSENPARK HOUSING DEVELOPMENT

Nansenstrasse 5/7 / Gretherstrasse / Haagenerstrasse, D-79539 Lörrach |
Bus 1 2 3 7 15 16: Gewerbeschule

Facade on Nansenstrasse

Entrance hall

North of the downtown, Detlef Würkert and Hans Ueli Felchlin have created two build-ings with twenty-one residential units and four office or clinic spaces as well as a car park. The envelopes are in tune with the built environment of this former villa neigh-bourhood. The three-storey-high residential buildings extend into L-shapes created by two-storey office and clinic wings along the street front. Two fully glazed lobbies provide access to twenty-one apartments – three four-room units, twelve three-room units, and six two-room units – with large balconies above covered walkways. Two monumental wintergardens are the focal point of the structure.

Architect:	Wilhelm + Partner, Lörrach
	Now: Wilhelm and Hovenbitzer and Partner, Lörrach; www.wilhelm-partner.com
Client:	Städtische Wohnbaugesellschaft Lörrach, Lörrach
Dates:	construction 1990–1994

STADION HOUSING DEVELOPMENT

Haagener Strasse/Wintersbuckstrasse, D-79539 Lörrach | Bus 7: Heithemstrasse

Linear access and large balconies

The oval of a former sports arena is the site of a housing development by architects Wilhelm + Partner in Lörrach. The four-storey complex consists of fourteen buildings with a total of 220 residential units. Access is provided by a network of roads and paths intersecting at right angles. Archway buildings are located at the mid-point on each side while driveways provide access at the curved sections of the oval. The units in the buildings located at the two semi-circles have continuous front-to-back floor plans; in combination with the balconies to both courtyard and street front, this layout results in units that are flooded with light. The floor plans diminish into rounded triangles. The development is surrounded by rows of low-rise residential buildings, single and multi-family homes; from a planning perspective, the area seems rather rural. The new development has increased the density and thus the urban character of the area.

Aerial view of housing development

Architect:	Lederer Ragnarsdóttir Oei, Stuttgart; www.archlro.de
	Project management Arno Lederer, Jorunn Ragnarsdóttir, Marc Oei
Client:	Ministry of Science, Research and the Arts, Stuttgart, represented by the
	Baden-Württemberg State Agency for Property and Construction,
	Freiburg office, Freiburg/Brsg.
Dates:	competition 2003, project 2004, construction 2006–2008

BADEN-WÜRTTEMBERG COOPERATIVE STATE UNIVERSITY (DHBW) / NEW BUILDING FOR THE LÖRRACH VOCATIONAL ACADEMY

Hangstrasse 46–50, D-79539 Lörrach | S-Bahn 6: Lörrach-Zell

The university seen from the south.

In 2009 Lederer Ragnarsdóttir Oei remodelled and extended a building in Lörrach for the Baden-Württemberg Cooperative State University (DHBW). Built in 1963 to house the Eichendorff elementary school, it was converted into a teaching training college in 1966, and in 1981, into the Lörrach Vocational Academy, now part of the DHBW. The new ground plan on the axes of the existing facility lies parallel to the contour lines of the Hünerberg. A three-storey building 147 metres long was constructed parallel to Hangstrasse along with a pavilion ensemble on the downhill slope and a connecting terrace. The main entrance to the campus (42 000 m²) is through the courtyard on Hangstrasse (featuring a 10.5-metre-tall tower). The floor space offered by the old building (3935 m²) was more than doubled (8820 m²). To this was added the library, which resulted from an independent remodelling of the former gymnasium. The main building has a linear north-south access system (three lifts) leading to the administrative areas on the eastern side and the workshops and laboratories on the western side. Three interconnected pavilions on the slope each contain seminar rooms and two small lecture auditoriums. These are supplemented on the southern side of the complex by a round building housing a large auditorium. The buildings are fronted by a sand-lime brick plinth and a natural slate facade.

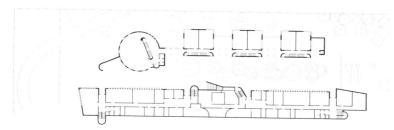

Ground plan of the 147-meter-long main
building, the round auditorium building
and the 3 pavilions.

The tower at the main entrance
seen from the terrace.

Stairway lamps embedded in the
cast concrete.

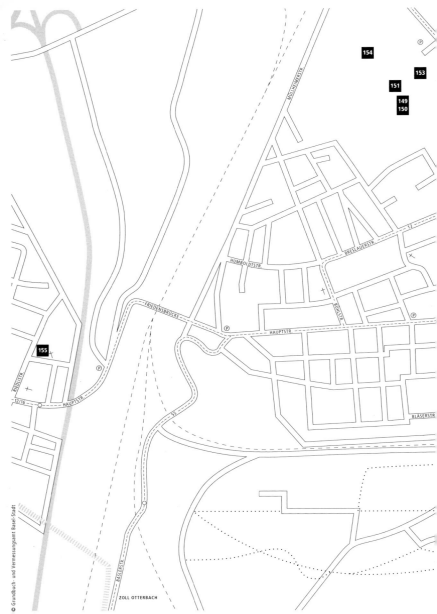

Architect:	SANAA (Kazuyo) Sejima And (Ryue) Nishizawa And Associates, Tokyo;
	www.sanaa.co.jp
	Project management Takayuki Hasegawa, Nicole Kerstin Berganski,
	Marieke Kums, Andreas Krawczyk
Construction:	Mayer Bährle Freie Architekten, Lörrach; www.mayer-baehrle.com
Client:	Vitra Verwaltungs GmbH, Weil am Rhein
Dates:	design and project planning 2006, construction 2007–2008 (first phase),
	2009–2012 (second phase)

PRODUCTION BUILDING MARKING 30 YEARS OF VITRA CAMPUS

Charles Eames-Strasse 2, D-79576 Weil am Rhein | Bus 12 55: Vitra

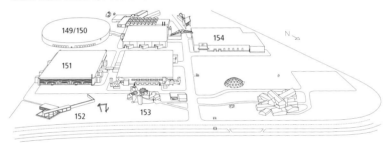

Isometric drawing of the Vitra Campus with Charles Eames-Strasse (middle) and Römerstrasse (bottom).

On the southern edge of the Vitra site in Weil am Rhein, the architects Kazuyo Sejima and Ryue Nishizawa erected a production building on a 50 000 m² plot for the shop fitting company Vitrashop. Located next to the first Vitra building by Nicholas Grimshaw (1981, project 151), the "round" structure designed by the Tokyo architects marks the end of a 30-year timeline on the Vitra Campus. The last free plot available on the campus's historic Römerstrasse is located on the site's northern edge between the production building by Álvaro Siza da Vieira (project 154) and the VitraHaus (2008–2010) by Herzog & de Meuron. This area is being temporarily occupied by Richard Buckminster Fuller's Dome. The new building by SANAA replaces the last Vitra building (12 000 m²) to remain in use following the large fire on the firm's site in 1981. The new building, which covers a total area of 20 455 m², was erected in two stages: the first part was completed in 2008 and the second, following the demolition of the old building, in 2012. The compressed and flattened circular form of the new building (diameter: north-south 159 metres, east-west 156 metres / volume: 206 600 m³), whose roof is supported by axial, floor-to-ceiling concrete elements and slender steel columns (in a grid based on units of 17.5×22.8 metres) houses a high-rack storage area for semi-finished products provided by suppliers, an assembly zone, and a second high-rack storage area for finished products prior to shipping. The homogeneous design of the building technology installations (electronics, ventilation, roof drainage, sprinklers, specially designed screws for the high-rack storage systems, etc.) makes the completely transparent and naturally lit interior appear astoundingly light and, for a piece of industrial architecture, almost

Elegantly roofed path from the new production building to a building by Nicholas Grimshaw (1986).

The round building
with loading bays.

Facade elevation with varying
1.8-meter-wide acrylic glass panels.

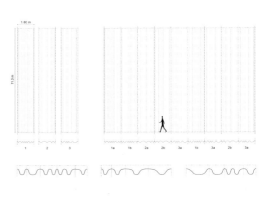

1.80 m

11.3 m

| 1 | 2 | 3 | | 1a | 1b | 2a | 2b | 3a | 1b | 3a | 2b | 3a |

The hall from inside.

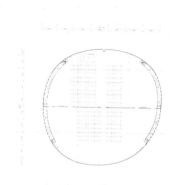

Ground plan of the hall with its compressed and flattened circular form.

elegant. Offices and loading bays are positioned along the facade, which is made of
1.8-metre-wide acrylic glass panels (area: 5740 m²). The outer layer is completely transparent, while the inner layer is an opaque white colour. The acrylic glass sheets were
heated to 60°C and vacuum-moulded to create a varying wave structure (resembling
the display on a cardiac monitor). As a result of the partly reversed assembly of the
panels (whereby the outside becomes the inside and vice versa) the 11.3-metre-high
acrylic channels form six distinct wave elements around the building. From even a short
distance away the facade creates the effect of a textile curtain and the overall impression of an artistic sculpture disconnected from function. The circular form of the new
building is slightly distorted, suggesting the Japanese notion of imperfection as aesthetic consummation. The building in Weil thus represents a singular interpretation of
the typology of the "factory building". It is also equipped with an underground car park
(240 parking spaces on 10 565 m²).

Architect:	Nicholas Grimshaw and Partners, London
	Now: Grimshaw, New York; www.grimshaw-architects.com
Client:	Vitra GmbH, Weil am Rhein
Dates:	project planning and construction 1981

VITRA FURNITURE FACTORY

Charles Eames-Strasse 2, D-79576 Weil am Rhein | Bus 12 55: Vitra

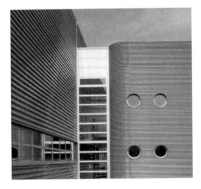

Detail of facade

When Nicholas Grimshaw rebuilt the burnt-down Vitra factory in just six months in 1981, the tight schedule was made possible by one particular circumstance: the building in Weil is one of many industrial buildings designed by the British architect. It resembles his design for a factory in Bath (1976) in many aspects: the cubature is almost identical, as are the access lanes and entrances, and the arrangements of the delivery and loading areas. The facades are clad in industrial materials and the corners rounded off. Grimshaw added six supply towers to the large structure (11 900 m²) at rhythmic intervals. A pre-fabricated concrete frame with a 25-metre span is the key structural element. In 1986, the architect added a second manufacturing hall.

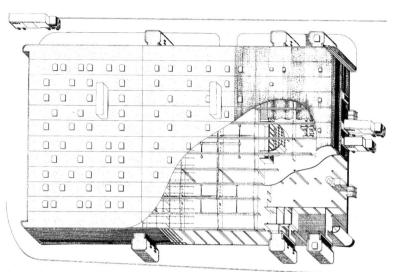

Axonometric

The north-east facade

Architect:	Tadao Ando, Osaka; www.andotadao.org
	Project management, planning and site management Günter Pfeifer in partnership
	with Roland Mayer
	Now: Günter Pfeifer Architektur, Freiburg / Brsg.; www.pfeifer-kuhn.com
	and mayer bährle, Lörrach; www.mayer-baehrle.com
Client:	Vitra GmbH, Weil am Rhein
Dates:	project 1989, construction 1992–1993

VITRA CONFERENCE PAVILION

Charles Eames-Strasse 1, D-79576 Weil am Rhein | Bus 12 55: Vitra

Stairs to courtyard

A conference pavilion for the Vitra company was Japanese architect Tadao Ando's first European building in 1993. He created 420 square metres of floor space on two levels. The building surrounds a sunken courtyard, which gives the complex a monastic atmosphere. The property itself – and its cherry trees – contribute to the intimate quality of the architecture. The master builder realized yet another project based on his classic theme: the dialogue between "built" and "grown" architecture. The complex features unfinished concrete walls and American red oak flooring. The scheme accommodates one conference and three seminar rooms, a guest room, a library, and space for the building installations. The house lies directly next to Frank O. Gehry's Vitra Design Museum (project 153).

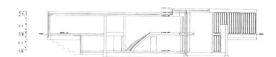

North-south section

The garden facade

Architect:	Frank O. Gehry + Associates, Santa Monica, CA
	Now: Gehry Partners, Los Angeles; www.foga.com
	Project management, planning and site management Günter Pfeifer in partnership
	with Roland Mayer
	Now: Günter Pfeifer Architektur, Freiburg / Brsg.; www.pfeifer-kuhn.com
	mayer bährle, Lörrach; www.mayer-baehrle.com
Client:	Vitra GmbH, Weil am Rhein
Dates:	project planning 1987, construction 1988–1989

VITRA DESIGN MUSEUM

Charles Eames-Strasse 1, D-79576 Weil am Rhein | Bus 12 55: Vitra

The building with rectangular roof
above entrance area (right)

In his first European building – the Vitra Design Museum – Frank O. Gehry has created
a floor space of 740 square metres. A cross-vault that seems to be inspired by the
Gothic style provides interior support for a ceiling made to look ethereal with two large
light wells. The upstairs is designed as a galleria and the walls merge in intersecting
perspectives. Here, the design makes no attempt to guide the eye by means of sightlines created by enfilades or vertical perspectives. The convex, foreshortened, and
curved shapes of the dynamic building are best appreciated when standing in front
of the entrance, where one also has an ideal view of the rectangular roof which seems
to float above the entrance. From its inception the building has been compared to Le
Corbusier's church at Ronchamp (1950–1954). Tadao Ando's conference pavilion is
located next door (project 152).

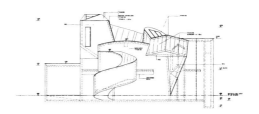

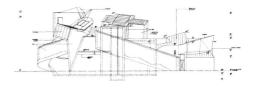

Elevations and sections of the
animated building fabric

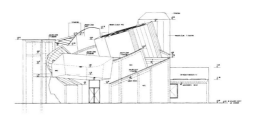

Architect:	Álvaro Siza da Vieira, Porto; www.alvarosizavieira.com
	Project management, planning and site management Günter
	Pfeifer in partnership with Roland Mayer
	Now: Günter Pfeifer Architektur, Freiburg / Brsg.; www.pfeifer-kuhn.com
	mayer bährle, Lörrach; www.mayer-baehrle.com
Client:	Vitra GmbH, Weil am Rhein
Dates:	project planning 1991, construction 1992–1993

VITRASHOP FACTORY HALL

Charles Eames-Strasse 2, D-79576 Weil am Rhein | Bus 12 55: Vitra

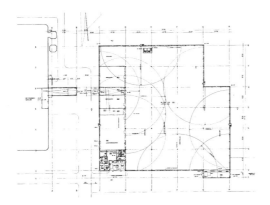

Ground floor

Álvaro Siza realized a single-storey factory hall for Vitra with a footprint of over 20 000 square metres. At 11 metres in height, the flat-roofed building is located next to the vast railway-yard of the Deutsche Bahn. With its clinker-brick facade, granite base, and rhythmically arranged 4-metre-high windows, the building resembles a minimalist sculpture. The vocabulary of this facade has much in common with the architectonic language of early industrial buildings. The gigantic hall has an interior ceiling height of 9 metres, where slender metal pylons create a simplicity and clarity of line usually associated with the naves of Romanesque churches. Tadao Ando's pavilion (project 152) and Siza's factory hall solidly anchor the company grounds and also provide a barrier to the north.

The factory seen from
Charles Eames-Strasse

The monolithic building next to
Zaha M. Hadid's fire station

Architect:	Herzog & de Meuron, Basel; www.herzogdemeuron.com
Client:	U. and R. Frei-Reimann, Fischingen
Dates:	project planning 1981, construction 1981–1982

FREI PHOTO STUDIO

Riedlistrasse 41, D-79576 Weil am Rhein | Bus 12 16: Riedlistrasse

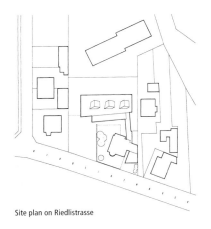

Site plan on Riedlistrasse

Herzog & de Meuron added a photo studio to a detached house in Weil. The new addition and a connecting corridor create a U-shaped complex on the 1900-square-metre property. The original building – a massive, two-storey stone house from the late nineteenth century with a square plan, a hipped roof, and an oriel – is now confronted by a trapezoid with a gently sloped shed roof and three cubed skylights that resemble great boulders. The facade clad in planks, plywood, and asphalt subscribes to an "aesthetic of poverty;" the cubed skylights, on the other hand, re-interpret the shed roof typology while adding a sculptural element.

Detail of facade in plywood

The studio with cubed skylights

Architect:	Zaha M. Hadid in collaboration with Patrick Schumacher, mayer bährle
	Zaha Hadid Architects, London; www.zaha-hadid.com
	mayer bährle, Lörrach; www.mayer-baehrle.com
Client:	Landesgartenschau Weil am Rhein 1999 GmbH, Weil am Rhein
Dates:	project planning and construction 1996–1999

TRINATIONAL ENVIRONMENTAL CENTRE

Mattrain 1, D-79576 Weil am Rhein | Bus 55: Grün 99 | Train: Weil-Gartenstadt

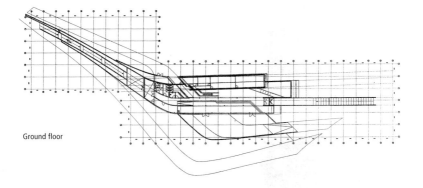

Ground floor

The pavilion designed by Zaha M. Hadid for the national garden show "Green 99" is a 140-metre-long building that gives an urban anchor in the rural space between south Weil and Basel. A ramp-like path bisects the entire building along the middle axis, creating an inviting gesture to take a stroll. Expansive glazed sections infuse the expressive building with light and energy. The building is exclusively constructed from poured concrete, and the individualistic geometric treatment gives it a sculptural presence. The ground plan reveals similarities to basilica plans, similarities that are less evident on the interior. The main entrance, for example, opens onto a raised central aisle with a view of the left side aisle, while the right aisle lies hidden behind a dividing wall. The central aisle is topped by a ribbon of windows much like the clerestories in a church.

The ramp-like path onto the roof

ILLUSTRATION INDEX OF PROJECTS AND MAPS

Actelion Pharmaceuticals Ltd. | 101/102↖→↙

Altenkirch, Dirk | 146↖↗

Arazebra, Helbing & Kupferschmid | 71↖↗

Archäologische Bodenforschung Basel-Stadt, Patrick Nagy / Simon Vogt | 37↗ (far right)

Archiv Blaser Architekten AG | 25↖

ARGE Stauffenegger+ Stutz_Rüdisühli+Ibach | 4↔→

Atelier Fontana | 76↔→

Barcelo Baumann Architekten | 56↖↘

Bensberg, Ralph | 65→

Biondo, Adriano | 35↗ | 104↗↘

Bisig, Tom | 6→↘ | 66→↘ | 68↘ | 125↔↙ | 126↔↙

Blaser, Werner | 137↔↗

Bräuning, Niggi | 93→ | 133↗↘ | 136→

Bryant, Richard | 127↔ | 152↔→

Clerc, HR+P | 20→

De Pietri, Paola | 45↖↗

Diener & Diener | 41↗

Disch Photograph | 75↗↘

Dolenc Scheiwiller Parli Architekten | 110↔

Ege, Hans | 65↔

Egger, Laura | 131↗↘

Fierz Architekten | 68↔

Fontana, Michael | 12↖↔→

Fotostudio M. Wolf | 83↗↘

Frei, Roger | 17↗↘

Gambino, Mario | 107↖↘↘

Giese, André | 15↔→

Grimshaw, Nicholas & Partners | 151↗

Halbe, Roland | 148↔↘↘

Helbling, A & Ineichen | 32↔ | 139↗↘

Helfenstein, Heinrich | 16↗↘ | 55↔→ | 89↔↗↘

Herzog & de Meuron | 31↔ | 97↔ | 111→

Hessmann, Karin | 153↔

Isler, Vera | 90↘

Jecklin, Cilla | 19↔→ | 106↗

Kehl, Lilli | 29↖↗

Lichtenberg, Christian | 5↗↘ | 7↗↘ | 54↗

Mair, Walter | 88↖↗

Marburg, Johannes | 44↗↘ | 49→ | 51↗

Markthalle Basel | 25→

Mayer, Thomas | 46↗↘

Meyer, Erich | 147→

Muelhaupt, André | 90↗

Musi, Pino | 72↗ | 85↔↘

Niedermann, Mark | 3↗↘

PlanetObserver.com / Satellite photo

Reid, Jo und Peck, John | 151↔↘

Richters, Christian | 156→ | 26↘ | 53↔↗

Richters, Christian for Novartis, © Novartis | 41↔→

Rosselli, Paolo | 43↔ | 47↘ | 48↔→ | 50↗↘

Rosselli, Paolo for Novartis, © Novartis | 43↗→

Roth, Lukas for Novartis, © Novartis | 38↔→ | 47↗

SANAA | 42↔

Schwarz, David for Novartis, © Novartis | 42↖

Schweizerischer Bankverein | 96↖

Scherrer, Theodor | 69↘ | 91↗↘

Schmidt, Erik | 68→

Schulthess, Kathrin | 77↔ | 122↔→

Spiluttini, Margherita | 8↗↘ | 10↔→ | 11↗↘ | 27↗↘ | 30→ | 31↗↘ | 81↗↘ | 97↗→↘ | 90↗↘ | 113↔↗ | 118↗↘ | 155↗↘

Stutz, Ruedi | 143→

SwissAir | 37→

Vitra AG | 149/150→↖↖

Voegelin, Andreas | 2↔ | 9↗↘ | 134↗↘

Vogt, Christian © 2014, Pro Litteris, Zurich | 39→ | 40↔

Von Bartha | 33↔→

Walti, Ruedi | 1→ | 7↗↘ | 18↔→ | 22↔→ | 28→ | 36↗ | 52↗↘ | 57↔→ | 58→ | 64↗ | 69↔ | 77→ | 78↖↗ | 84↗↖ | 98↔→ | 105→ | 111↗↗ | 112↔→ | 117↔→ | 119↔ | 120↔ | 124↖ | 128→ | 129↘ | 135↔↗ | 138↔→(far right) | 144↔→ | 154↗↘

Wilhem und Hovenbitzer und Partner | 140↔→

Windhöfel, Lutz | 30↗ | 63↔

Zerdoun, Yohan | 26↗

Zimmermann, Jürg | 113↗

Abbreviations: the arrows indicate the position of the photographs on each project double page.

top right: ↗   bottom right: ↘
bottom left: ↙   top left: ↖   right: →
left: ↔

Unless otherwise indicated, the photographs and maps were created by the architects themselves or commissioned by each firm. We have made every effort to locate and list the copyright for all illustrations. Where the copyright is not listed, it is either held by the architect or we have been unable to determine the copyright holder, in which case we would ask the copyright holder to contact the publisher.

INDEX OF ARCHITECTS AND COMPANIES

The names mentioned in the Introduction "The Star Is the City" are indicated with an "I" (Introduction) and the page number. The other numbers represent the project numbers. The listed companies and/or architects had architectural and entrepreneurial executive responsibility for all projects marked in **bold**.

Achille, Salvatore | 107

Ackermann & Friedli | **55** | **115**

Ackermann Architekt | 55 | 115

Ackermann, Heinrich | 12

Alder, Michael | **19** | **32** | **71** | **90** | **114** | **139**

Alioth Langlotz Stalder Buol | 21

Amrein, Andreas | 80

Andersson, Thorbjörn | 50

Ando, Tadao | **152** | 153 | 154

Arcoplan | 46

Artaria, Paul | **139**

Atelier-Gemeinschaft | **19** | 32 | 71 | 90 | 114 | 139

Baader Architekten | **15**

Barcelo Baumann Architekten | **56**

Baumann Architektur | **76**

Baumberger, Peter | 78

Baur, Hermann | **9** | **10** | **104**

Benevolo, Leonardo | I 19

Berchtold Lenzin Landschafts-architekten | **17**

Berganski, Nicole Kerstin | **42** | **149–150**

Berger + Toffol | 9 | 89

Bernoulli, Hans | 80 | 132 | 139

Berrel Architekten | **112**

Blaser Architekten | **25**

Blaser, Christian W. | **25**

Bo, Jørgen | 136

Bohm, Jens | 45

Bonatz, Paul | 87 | 89

Botta, Mario | **72** | **85** | 86

Braccini, Roger | 52

Bretterbauer, Gilbert | 47

Brodbeck & Bohny | 37–38

Brogli, Esther & Müller, Daniel | **20** | 133

Brüderlin, Rolf | **132**

Brügger, Tamara | 103

Brueghel, Pieter d. Ä. | 84

Brunner, R. | 69

Büchi, Paul | 87

Bürgin & Nissen | **82**

Bürgin Nissen Wentzlaff | 76 | 86 | **124** | **128**

Burckhardt + Partner | **83** | **85** | **95** | **100** | **103** | **136**

Buser, [Bruno] & Zaeslin, [Jakob] | **54**

Buser, Renate | 28

Butscher, Christoph | 5

Cabrita Reis, Pedro | 50

Cäsar, Julius | I 21f

Callierotti, Alex | 132

Camenzind, Melanie | 52

Caviezel, Véronique | 105

Cerri, Mario | 121

Chipperfield, David | **48**

Christ, Rudolf | 87 | 89

Conzett, Jürg | 78

Corsten, Stephan | 131

Cruz y Ortiz | **98**

Curjel, Robert | 68

Dalla Favera, A. | 69

Degelo Architekten | **1** | **57** | **58** | **59** | **64** | **119** | **120**

Delitz, Heike | I 17

Deppler, Urs | **133**

Diener & Diener Architekten | **14** | **21** | **26** | **34** | **41** | **42** | **53** | **60** | **61** | **66** | **70** | **75** | **87** | **92** | **94** | **96**

Dill, Christian | 69

Dipol Landschaftsarchitekten | **129**

Diserens, Eric | 30

Dittli, Felice | 80

Döblin, Alfred | I 30

Dolenc Scheiwiller Parli Architekten | **110** | 123

Dorenbach Architekten | 123

Dudssus, Dieter | 141

Eames, Charles and Ray | 43

Eigenheer, Samuel | 20

Egger, Martin | 25

Egli, Lukas | 57 | 58

englerarchitekten | 62

Engler, H.R. | 62

Erny, Gramelsbacher, Schneider | 34

Erny & Schneider | **34**

Fabro, Luciano | 87

Faesch, Emil | 98

Fahrni und Breitenfeld | 53 | **100**

Fasnacht, François | 134

Federle, Helmut | 41 | 42

Felchlin, Hans Ueli | **146**

Ferrara Architekten | 62

Ferrara, Giovanni | 62

Fierz Architekten | **6** | **15** | **68**

Fierz & Baader | **15**

Fischer, Michael | 101–102

Frank, Birgit | 47

Frey, Felix | 131

Frey, Mathias E. | **3**

Frischknecht, Jakob | 88

Fröhlich, Martin | 101–102

Fromm, Ute | 117

Früh, F. | 99

Fürstenberger, Philippe | 81 | 97

Fuller, Richard Buckminster | 149–150

Furrer & Fasnacht | **134**

Furrer, Rolf | **134**

Gasser, Markus | 133

Gehry, Frank O. | 39 | **46** | **127** | 152 | **153**

Giese, Tita | 101–102

Gigon, Annette | 27 | 118

Gigon / Guyer Architekten | **89**

INDEX OF ARCHITECTS AND COMPANIES

Giraudi & Wettstein Architetti | **98**

Gmür, Silvia | **2** | **5** | **9** | **10** | **99** | **109**

Glauser, Heini | **133**

Gmür, Silvia | Gmür, Reto | **2** | **5** | 9 | 10 | **99** | 109

Gmür [Silvia] | Vacchini [Livio] | **2** | **9** | **10**

Gräf, Bruno | **121**

Gramelsbacher, Urs | **18** | **34** | **35** | **91**

Grasser, Thomas | **123**

Grellinger, René | **121**

Grimshaw, Nicholas | **149–150** | **151**

Grüner, Jörg | **138**

Gschwind, David | 105

Hadid, Zaha M. | **156**

Häfeli, Moser, Steiger | 6

Haito [Bischof von Basel] | I 24

Haller, Bruno, and Fritz | 28

Hammans, Daniel | 13

Hänzi, Beni M. | **3**

Häussermann, Hartmut | I 17

Hardegger, August | 57

Hasegawa, Takayuki | 42 | 149–150

Herbst, Dorothea | 138

Heredero, Mireya | 131

Herter, Alex | 43

Herzog & de Meuron Architekten | **8** | **11** | **27** | **30** | **31** | **73–74** | 80 | **81** | **84** | **97** | **101–102** | **111** | **113** | **118** | 149–150 | **155**

Hochstrasser, Thomas | 89

Hofmann, Hans | 64

Holzer, Jenny | 43

Hotz, Theo | **65**

Huber, Dorothee | I 28

Husmann, Marco | 103

Isler, Florian | 89

Jecker Blanckarts Architekten | **76**

Johnson, Philip | 64

Josephsohn, Hans | 88

Kägi & Schnabel | **76**

Kahn, Louis I. | 136

Karg, Anna | 117

Karpf, Bernhard | 24

Kaufmann, Andreas | 16

Keller, Daniel | 103

Keller, Nadja | 120

Kempf, Marianne | 57

Koechlin & Schmidt | **77**

Kolb, Frank | I 16

Kostof, Spiro | I 19

Krawczyk, Andreas | 149–150

Krischanitz [Adolf], Architekt | **47**

Künzel, August | 31 | 45 | **52** | 66 | **108**

Künzel, Margrith | **52**

Kums, Marieke | 149–150

Kunz, Manfred | 64

Kunz und Mösch Architekten | **130**

Larghi & Stula Architekten | **76**

La Roche, Emanuel | 98

Lay, Udo | **141**

Lazzarini, Kurt | 84

Le Corbusier | 153

Lederer, Arno | **148**

Lederer Ragnarsdóttir Oei | **148**

Leisinger, K. | 57

Levy, Renée | 113

Lissitzky, El | 101–102

Llamera, Corina | 25

LOST Architekten | **12**

Lovegrove, Ross | 48

Märkli [Peter] | **43** | **88**

Maggioni, Christian | 89

Magnago Lampugnani, Vittorio | I 19f | **37–38** | **45**

Maki, Fumihiko | **49**

Mangler, Markus | 37–38

Marques [Daniele] | **64**

Martignoni, Silvio | **22**

Mayer, Roland | **127** | **152** | **153** | **154**

Mayer Bährle | 127 | **142** | 149–150 | 152 | 153 | 154 | **156**

Meier, Mario | 8

Meier, Richard | **24** | 96

Meier, Samuel | 25

Merian, Matthäus d. Ä. | E 27

Metron [Markus Gasser, Urs Deppeler, Heini Glauser] | **133**

Meyer, Hannes | 126

Mies van der Rohe, Ludwig | 64 | 123 | 136

Milgram, Stanley | I 17

Miller, Quintus & Maranta, Paola | **36** | **78**

Morger & Degelo | **1** | **57** | **58** | **64** | **119** | **120**

Morger & Dettli | 1 | 57 | 58 | 64 | 119 | 120

Moscatelli, Fleur | 37–38

Moser, Karl | 68

Muellen, Michael | 129

Müller, Carmen | 123

Müller, Daniel | **20**

Müller, Hanspeter | **19** | **32** | 71 | 90 | **106** | 114 | 139

Mumford, Lewis | I 13f | I 16 | I 19

Munatius Plancus, L. [ucius] | I 21f

Naef, Studer & Studer | **7**

Naegelin, Roland | **19** | **32** | 71 | 90 | **114** | **106** | **139**

Nauman, Bruce | 144

Nishiyama, Yuka | 42

Nissen & Wentzlaff Architekten | **46** | 82 | 86 | **117** | 124 | 128 | **129**

Nussbaumer, Kurt | **9**

Nussbaumer Trüssel | 13

Oei, Marc | 148

Oeri-Hoffmann, Vera | 22

Offermann, Erich | 64

Oswald, Caspar | 43

Otto + Partner Architektur | 121

Palkowitsch, Isabell | 25

Panozzo, Giovanni | 104

Pausa, Mauro | 25

Piano, Renzo | **136**
Piranesi, Giambattista | 16
Pfeifer, Günter | **127** | **142** |
152 | **153** | **154**
Polke, Sigmar | 47
Pontillo, Giuseppe | 132
Porsia, Francesco | 37–38
Proksch, Sonja | 25
Proplaning | **31** | **67** | **97** |
101–102 | **116** | **122**
Raetzo, Hermann | 117
Ragnarsdóttir, Jorunn | **148**
Rauch, Martin | 108
Reus, Andreas | 117
Rist, Pipilotti | 117
Rösch, Christoph | 104
Rohn, Roland | **6** | 73–74 | 129
Roost, Andrea | **16**
Rosenmund + Rieder
Architekten | **125** | **126**
Rossi, Aldo | I 19 | 30f
Rousseau, Jean-Jacques | I 13
Rüdisühli Ibach Architekten | **4**
Rüegg, Andreas | 121
Ruge, Lars | 39
Ruskin, John | I 13
sabarchitekten [Salathé,
Reuter] | **76**
Salvisberg, Otto Rudolf | 73–74 |
87 | 129
SANAA – Kazuyo Sejima +
Ryue Nishizawa | 41 | **42** | 43 |
149–150
Sant' Elia, Antonio | **101–102**
Sassen, Saskia | I 17
Savonarola, Girolamo | I 13
Schaudt Architekten | **143**
Scheiwiller, Andreas | **123**
Scherkamp, Fiona | 37–38
Schmid, Herbert | **80**
Schmidt, Hans | **139**
Schnetzer Puskas Ingenieure | **80**
Schönholzer + Stauffer | **103**
Schuldt, Klaus | **123**

Schumacher, Patrick | **156**
Schwarz, Alexander | 48
Schwarz, Rosmarie | 20
Schwarzburg, Jürg | 37–38
Schweizer, Stephan | 129
Segessenmann, Stefan | 104
Selva, Luca | **52** | 104 | **105**
Serena, Gian-Andrea | 52 | 105
Serra, Marco | 40
Shinohara, Isao | 42
Simmel, Georg | E 16ff
Siza da Vieira, Álvaro | 50 | **51** |
149–150 | **154**
Souto de Moura, Eduardo |
50 | 51
Spahn, Nathalie | 88
Spitzer, Serge | 48
Stauffenegger + Stutz | **4**
Stauffer, Christoph | 121
Steib, Wilfrid and Katharina |
23 | **54** | **63** | **93** | **137** | **144**
Steiner, Rudolf | 120
Steinmann & Schmid
Architekten | **80**
Stefani, Daniel & Wendling,
Bernard | 29
Stiner, Peter | **108**
Stocker, Peter | 99
Strasser, Patrik | 3
Strasser, Walter | 140
Stump & Schibli | **17** | **135** | **138**
Stutz, Lukas | **22**
Suter & Burckhardt | 2 | 89
Suter + Suter | 9
Taniguchi, Yoshio | **44**
Tannenberger, Heiri | 16
Thoma, Edgar | 141
Thoma.Lay.Buchler | 141
Tinguely, Jean | 72 | 76
Tinner, Mathis S. | 11
Toffol + Berger | 9
Trinkler, Bruno | **107**
TrinklerStulaPartner Architekt |
62 | **107**

Trinkler, B. + Engler,
H.R. Architekten | **62**
Trinkler Engler Ferrara | **62**
Vacchini, Livio | **2** | **9** | **10**
Vadi, Tibère | 132
Van de Velde, Henry | 136
Varini, Felice | 85
Vercingetorix | I 21
Vierzigmann, Sigrid | 52
Vischer Architekten + Planer |
5 | **22**
Vitruv [Marcus Vitruvius Pollio] |
I 14 | I 23 | 37–38
Voellmy Schmidlin Architektur |
33
Vogt Landschaftsarchitek-
ten | **39** | **41** | **53** | **97**
Von Fenis, Burkhard [Bischof von
Basel] | I 26
Waldburger, Petra | **105**
Walker, Peter; PWP Landscape
Architecture | 37–38
Weber, Adrian | 20
Weber, Max | I 15ff | I 31
Wentzlaff, Daniel | **117** | **129**
Wettstein, Hannes | **89**
Wiederin, Gerold | **41** | 42
Wilhelm and Hovenbitzer and
Partner | **140**
Wilhelm + Partner | **147**
Wohlert, Vilhelm | 136
w + p Landschaften | **141**
Wright, Frank Lloyd | 136
Würkert, Detlef | **145** | **146**
Wymann & Selva | **104**
Wymann, Jean-Pierre | 104
Zbinden, Ueli | **131**
Zinkernagel, Peter | **28**
Zwimpfer Partner | **79** | **82**
Zwimpfer Partner Krarup
Furrer | **112**

INDEX OF BUILDING TYPES AND USES

Buildings for children and youth | 29 | 34 | 53 | 58 | 62 | 67 | 76 | 106

Schools | 14 | 28 | 36 | 55 | 57 | 95 | 104 | 132 | 148

Training centers, meeting halls, and conference centres | 43 | 46 | 47 | 64 | 76 | 96 | 152 | 156

Research and university buildings | 5 | 6 | 7 | 11 | 15 | 16 | 44 | 47 | 48 | 49 | 50 | 51 | 73–74 | 89 | 148

Sports complexes | 30 | 71 | 112

Single-family houses | 35 | 66 | 105 | 109 | 110 | 113 | 114 | 118 | 120 | 122 | 123 | 130 | 140

Multi–family houses | 8 | 18 | 27 | 32 | 34 | 57 | 58 | 60 | 61 | 62 | 63 | 67 | 75 | 77 | 78 | 90 | 91 | 92 | 99 | 100 | 103 | 105 | 107 | 110 | 117 | 119 | 122 | 125 | 126 | 133 | 141 | 146 | 147

Residential buildings | 7 | 26 | 32 | 34 | 62 | 63 | 66 | 75 | 77 | 78 | 90 | 103 | 107 | 117 | 124 | 125 | 139 | 141

Apartments | 7 | 59 | 61 | 99 | 105 | 110 | 139

Studios and lofts | 12 | 56 | 60 | 61 | 62 | 67 | 92 | 94 | 99 | 109 | 155

Residential developments | 34 | 52 | 54 | 67 | 75 | 103 | 122 | 126 | 133 | 135 | 139 | 141 | 147

Residential and office buildings (mixed use) | 26 | 27 | 60 | 61 | 117

Retail stores and shopping centres | 2 | 25 | 53 | 68 | 70 | 75 | 98 | 119 | 124 | 128

Office and administration buildings | 12 | 23 | 24 | 41 | 42 | 43 | 45 | 46 | 64 | 73–74 | 78 | 83 | 84 | 85 | 86 | 87 | 88 | 96 | 100 | 101–102 | 119 | 127 | 128 | 129

Industrial buildings and fair halls | 25 | 64 | 65 | 82 | 149–150 | 151 | 154

Transportation buildings | 4 | 13 | 40 | 68 | 80 | 81 | 98 | 116 | 121 | 131 | 134

Parks and gardens | 17 | 21 | 37–38 | 39 | 52 | 53 | 62 | 108

Hotels | 53 | 64 | 66 | 76 | 124

Restaurants, cafés, bars | 6 | 9 | 12 | 17 | 31 | 64 | 68 | 72 | 89 | 96 | 98 | 143 | 145

Libraries | 5 | 7 | 22 | 76 | 89 | 142

Cinemas and theater | 143 | 144

Museum buildings | 1 | 3 | 33 | 72 | 89 | 93 | 111 | 136 | 153 | 156

Church buildings | 18

Hospital and care facilities | 9 | 10 | 11 | 17 | 19 | 21 | 31 | 59 | 69 | 115 | 135

Nursing homes and buildings for community living | 20 | 21 | 137 | 138

Conversion, renovation, heritage preservation | 3 | 5 | 6 | 9 | 12 | 25 | 68

The publisher and the author would like to thank for their generous support in making the Architectural Guide Basel possible:

Singenberg Stiftung, Basel
Freiwillige Akademische Gesellschaft, Basel
Claire Sturzenegger-Jeanfavre Stiftung, Basel

The fourth edition is also available in a German language edition (ISBN 978-3-03821-939-2)

Translation from German into English by Elizabeth Schwaiger, Toronto and Joseph O'Donnell, Berlin

Editorial deadline 30.06.2013

Design: Muriel Comby, Basel

Printed on acid-free paper produced from chlorine-free pulp. TCF

Printed in Germany

ISBN: 978-3-03821-397-0

www.birkhauser.ch
9 8 7 6 5 4 3 2 1